Aren't You Afraid?

AMERICAN DISCOVERY TRAIL FROM THE ATLANTIC OCEAN TO NEBRASKA

Mary E. Davison

Aren't You Afraid?

ISBN: 978-1-7354174-1-7

Published: 11 September, 2020 by Vandeleigh Publishing in the United States of America.

Davison, Mary E. **Aren't You Afraid?** Vandeleigh Publishing.

Cover art by Lindsay Heider Diamond; www.lindsayheider.com.

Cover photo courtesy of Rachel Goetze Black.

This photo is not from the American Discovery Trail, but from Tennessee on Little River Road in the Smokies. I love the capture of light coming in the gap in the distance giving the feel of something to anticipate up ahead, who knows what it will be. That is the feel of the ADT for me. The back cover is from a photo I took one night in Iowa on the ADT.

Maps in this book are from the *American Discovery Trail* website and have been printed here, with their permission.

DEDICATION

This book is dedicated to my family who have
gone on before me.

My parents, Dale and Elma,

my brother, Robert, and my sister, Ethel.

TABLE OF CONTENTS

PROLOGUE
AMERICAN DISCOVERY TRAIL

American Discovery Trail

The American Discovery Trail goes from Cape Henlopen State Park, Delaware to Pt. Reyes National Seashore, California. The Missouri River separates Iowa and Nebraska. This book is about

Mary E. Davison

my experiences from Cape Henlopen to Nebraska,
slightly less than half of a walk across America.

Aren't You Afraid?

Hesitantly, I approach the house and knock on the door. I wear a backpack, and I use hiking poles—a bit strange for this part of suburbia in the eastern half of the United States not near the Appalachian Trail. When the door opens, I step back slightly so as not to appear threatening, smile, and say:

"Hi. My name is Mary Davison, and I'm hiking on the American Discovery Trail—the ADT. It's a way-marked trail that goes across America from coast to coast. You probably have never heard of it, but it goes right in front of your house. I'm tired now, and I have to find a place to put my tent. May I put my tent in your yard?"

The incredulous response: "You're WHAT?"

I repeat my little opening spiel with what I hope is a winning smile. I'm not a large person. In fact, I'm an old lady, and I do need to find a place to be for the night.

The person at the door looks around me, their eyes searching to see if there is someone else with me, perhaps a group letting me do the talking. But there is no one within sight.

"Are you *alone*?" the person asks in amazement.

"Yes, I am hiking alone. I have hiked long trails alone before. Actually, quite a few hikers who hike long trails, hike solo," I explain.

The even more incredulous response:

"Aren't you afraid?"

This scenario—or something very like it—was repeated many nights on the American Discovery Trail between Cape Henlopen, Delaware and the Missouri River. The American Discovery Trail, more than any other long-distance trail, has given me the joy of meeting local people as I walk, because it was necessary for me to ask for a place to be. Hiking the ADT also gave me the opportunity to reflect on and talk with people about fear.

HIKER TURNED WRITER

I am a mother of two, a grandma of ten, a former physical therapist, a retired Lutheran pastor, and a long-distance hiker. All my life, I have loved the outdoors. Ever since I was a child, I have loved camping and hiking. The statement under my picture in the high-school yearbook (written by someone else) said: "Stuffy classrooms with ceilings and floors, were not for this girl who loved the outdoors." My birth family camped on trips, and I learned to hike in the Girls Scouts, with skills added as a young adult in the Mountaineers.

I am not a thru hiker. Thru hikers are the truly crazy folks who are gone from home three-to-six or even eight months at a time as they hike long trails end to end. Being only half crazy, I take two long-distance hikes a year, three-hundred to five-hundred miles each. I am seventy-nine years old, have white hair cut short, and I still love the outdoors and walking in it.

Although I have camped and hiked from my youth, I didn't begin long-distance hiking until 2001, the year I turned 60, when my daughter and I hiked the Wonderland Trail around Mt. Rainier in Washington State, along with friends who hiked parts of it with us. That led me into many years of long section hiking, completing long distance hiking's Triple Crown by the time I reached 76. The Triple Crown is composed of the Appalachian Trail (AT), the Pacific Crest Trail (PCT), and the Continental Divide Trail (CDT).

On my last hiking day on the Triple Crown, I decided to write a book about that journey: *Old Lady on the Trail*. I also thought about other trails I had walked or was still walking and wondered if I wanted to write other books. Many people loved my first book and encouraged me to continue writing.

What I write reflects myself, not the experience of others. I am not a generic hiker. No hiker is. Each hiker is unique; trails are too. Being mother, grandma, physical therapist and pastor influences what I write, as does my upbringing, my birth family, my friends, and my life experiences.

My initial goals in writing *Aren't you Afraid?* were primarily to share a trail not well known and my reflections on fear and leaving fear behind. As I re-read old journals and began to write, my experiences off and on the trail dictated that my faith also be shared. It is part of my identity, the way I walk, the thoughts I think, the way I see the world.

Other hikers and readers may have a different view than mine, but there are commonalities. I hope to pique your interest about a different way of hiking, challenge or confirm your thoughts on fear, and, perhaps, stir your understanding of *your* own faith, whether it be similar or quite different from mine.

So here is a journey on the American Discovery Trail from Cape Henlopen Delaware to Omaha, Nebraska, some experiences from my life, thoughts on leaving fear behind, and an interplay of faith that happens to be mine. If you are touched in any way by what I have written, my goals will be fulfilled, regardless of my writing talent or lack of it.

This book is not a novel. It's full of stories of many, many people I met on this trail. Real people. Called by real names—if I remembered them, and first names only. Hikers are called by *trail names*.

At first, when people started hiking long trails, their trail names tagged where they came from. But nowadays, trail names are handles. They're chosen because they somehow describe a person or event on a trail. Some hikers choose their own and some hikers have their names chosen by others.

Some names are unique and clever; some endlessly repeated such as the many hikers named Achilles because of blisters on their heels. Whether real given name or trail name, each one is a real person, and my descriptions are my impressions given with what we experienced together.

A Different Kind of Trail

In the winter of 2015, I was recovering from a shoulder replacement and contemplating where I should hike for my usual spring and fall hikes. I had completed the AT and the PCT. I would be hiking on the CDT in late summer and fall. But I had exhausted the opportunities for hiking on the CDT in the spring. The high country on the Continental Divide Trail which I still had left to complete required a later start than spring to avoid the snow which would not melt until much later. Yet I liked my practice of two hikes a year, one in spring and one in late summer or fall.

Where should I go?

The year before, I had hiked the Camino de Santiago in Spain in the spring and had loved it. That trail had hostels in which to stay at the end of a hiking day instead of a tent, and I liked that style of hiking as well as wilderness hiking with my tent. I wished there were hostels on trails in the United States but knew of none.

I wasn't excited about carrying a lot of water, as it's heavy. So, the Arizona Trail, an arid land requiring lots of water to be carried, which was popular with many long-distance hikers, didn't seem right for me. I just wanted to go for a long walk, and quite frankly, I didn't want to work too hard going up and down or carrying too much weight.

Sometime after 2009, Mary Barcik, a trail angel (a person who helps hikers on long trails) on the PCT had mentioned the American Discovery Trail. At the time, I had dismissed that idea with, "Who would ever want to walk on that?" Hiking flat country was not my desire. I loved alpine country, high mountain lakes and expansive views. Who would want to walk across the middle of America?

There is an enormous lot of mostly flat country in the middle of the United States. Although I had also hiked the AT, which has a great deal of up and down, as a Westerner, I admit to a bias for the West. Yet in 2015, a flat area attracted me, and I chose one of the flattest parts of the country I could find for my hike.

The American Discovery Trail was new to me. In fact, its website proclaims the ADT to be a new breed of national trail—part city, part small town, part forest, part mountains, part desert—all in one trail. Opened in the spring of 2000, it is 6,800+ miles of continuous, multiuse trail stretching from Cape Henlopen State Park, Delaware, to Pt Reyes National Seashore, California.

The ADT includes some wilderness, but obviously, much of the country from the Atlantic to the Rockies is not wilderness. The ADT is waymarked for GPS. A waymark is a dot of some kind that shows up on the map on a computer or on a hand-held global positioning device.

Waymarks are placed correlating to Turn-by-Turn

printed directions. The ADT is primarily for foot or bicycle, though horses can traverse some sections. It includes foot trails, country roads, and even highways.

Not many brave this trail as a thru hike since it is so very long. A hiker younger and more able than I must commit six-to-eight months to complete the ADT as a thru hike.

I am not young, and I like to hike long sections rather than an entire long trail at one go. It was, and is, doubtful, although not entirely impossible, that I could ever complete the ADT. But in 2015, I just wanted a long, relatively level place to walk a lot of miles. A section on the ADT seemed to fill the bill.

Used to America's long-distance scenic trails, I am comfortable in the wilderness. I can pick out a campsite, hike alone in the woods, and take care of myself in wild places. But this trail was not all wilderness. Different skills would be needed. Going from town to town, and even through cities, would certainly be different. Small towns and farm country sounded unique and interesting to me. But cities sounded a bit scarier. The ADT route rarely passes in walking distance of motels. I researched how hikers found a place to stay at night

I read some hiking journals and particularly enjoyed Boston and Cubby's journals of the National Scenic Trails, written on Trailjournals.com. (Boston and Cubby are trail names) Reading their ADT journal, and others, I learned about asking local people for places to put up tents. I never had to do that before. But, by gum, if others could do that, why couldn't I?

I ordered the Turn-by-Turn (pages of directions saying roughly, "go down this road x miles and turn on x road and proceed x miles"). On the ADT, hikers call it the T-by-T. In their trail journals I learned Boston and Cubby had used DeLorme Atlases to draw in the route on its pages of maps to see the bigger picture across states, orienting trail to towns and roads. I did the same.

I planned the hike in my usual fashion, by mileage I thought I could accomplish in a day, less than Boston and Cubby could do, but appropriate for me. I was, after all, seventy-four that year, and I had never been as strong as thru hikers.

I figured out stops and motels (usually the cheapest motel available, when I could find one) and five-to-six days' worth of food to carry. I planned to buy meals whenever possible. That would help me get more miles in before I needed a re-supply box (a box I would pack at home and send to myself where I thought I would need it).

The T-by-T helpfully had an M printed at any town that had meal possibilities and an L with any that had lodging possibilities. I had to sleuth out what those were myself online. So, I pored over maps, paper and digital, and researched motels. I asked friends who knew friends along the way who might help.

Mary E. Davison

Plan complete, I was ready, more or less, to go discover America, or at least the section from Milford, Ohio west through America's heartland to the Mississippi River.

JOURNAL ENTRY

One last preparation was to make initial entries on Trailjournals.com, the online site I had used to record my hiking journeys since 2007. The rules were to submit at least three journal entries on each year's hike before they could be published online for others to read. I had read a journal entry by another hiker about fear, and I decided something along those lines would be a good entry for me, too.

I did not know at the time that the topic of fear would repeatedly come up in my journey that year and in the years ahead—years I had not yet conceived of hiking on the ADT. My journal entry was a bit long and divided into parts:

March 6, 2015

FEAR, DANGER, ADVENTURE AND TRUST

Fear:

A truism in hiking circles is that we pack for our fears. When carrying all the gear you need to survive in the wilderness, it is easy to overload your pack to the point that you cannot carry it. If you have some piece of gear to meet every possible contingency, you will have too much to carry. On the other hand, there are some things one carries for a bit of insurance against possible disasters. Our level of fear is often the determining factor in what we carry.

Fear may or may not have any relation to reality. Last year, the anticipation of crossing a particular river in Wyoming completely psyched me out with fear. Yet, although it was challenging, with (my friend) RockStar's calm presence, it did not turn out to be worse than numerous others I'd forded.

Fear itself does not seem to be a particularly reliable guide in hiking or in life. And I have observed numerous people whose fears have crippled their lives in some way or another. Long ago I resolved not to have my life ruled by fear. Generally speaking, that has been a good decision and has helped ground me when I have been afraid.

Danger:

Well, that said, there are dangers in long-distance hiking. The weather can kill you. Hypothermia, snow and ice, floods can kill you. Tornados, and earthquakes can kill you. You can be killed by rockslide or an avalanche or a falling tree you happen to be under.

I have seen bears and a cougar and several very large moose, who eyed me askance. I have come to no harm from the four-legged critters in the wilderness. But I could, although it's not likely. I've seen rattlesnakes and other poisonous snakes, as well.

All these creatures and even the forces of nature are amazing, wonderful, and potentially dangerous. People often ask if long-distance hikers carry guns. The answer is usually no, it would add weight to the pack.

And the animals are protected in wilderness. Statistically, driving to a trailhead is far more dangerous than walking on a trail. And, in truth, one can slip and fall on a curb outside a motel or in a bathtub and be brain-damaged or die, and I have known those who have.

We are fairly fragile creatures in some ways. And living, even getting out of bed in the morning, involves some danger. Really, we just become accustomed to our more usual kinds of danger and pay them little heed.

It is only the dangers that seem out of the ordinary for the average walk of life that seem dangerous— even though we know that is not so.

Adventure:

Some people, long-distance hikers among them, like adventures, they like doing things out of the ordinary for a variety of reasons.

Lately I have talked to a few non-hikers who remember with joy and enthusiasm some adventure experienced in their past although their life journeys may be on calmer paths now. I can remember as a sick child I thought going to the hospital was an exciting adventure.

I must have had an amazing mother to have instilled that love of adventure in me around the age of six. Many folks who hike a long trail call it the adventure of a lifetime. I don't like that phrase simply because I have had no intention of having only one adventure in a lifetime. All of life is filled with adventure. So, I am soon to go off on another adventure.

There will be some dangers—some anticipated and some not yet known. I may be afraid at times. I will also know joy, see new sights, meet new people, experience new things. It is even possible I may not return from this or some other adventure.

After all, we do all die sometime, although I would rather not hurry the process. One does think about that the older one gets.

Trust:

So, do long-distance hikers just trust themselves? Or the trail, or the universe? Or do they think they are immortal (Twenty-year-olds generally think so.) Or do they just not think about it at all?

Well, there are lots of hikers and therefore lots of answers. In ultimate terms I choose to trust the God who holds me in life and in death. I will try to be mindful of that embrace through raindrops on leaves, sunrises, creepy crawly critters, relationships with two legged critters, roads and towns and cities, noisy traffic and the silence of night.

The context of this particular trail will be different than the wilderness I am more used to, but no less of an adventure. And life will be good.

I am not trying to be preachy. I do not wish to turn off those who walk much different paths spiritually. But for me, perhaps this hike and these entries will be more reflective than my usual. Or not. We will see where the trail and God and my reflections take me.

2015

American Discovery Trail

LEARNING CURVE IN OHIO

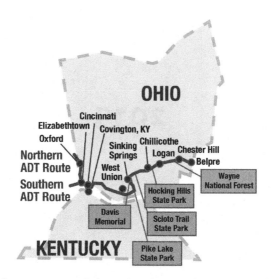

Ohio portion of the American Discovery Trail

On April 8, 2015, I was met at the Cincinnati airport by Don Burrell, the Ohio ADT Coordinator. He travels the ADT by bicycle though he picked me up at the airport in a car. (Remember, this trail is for foot or bicycle.) We dropped off my duffel and a heavy load of food at the B&B in Cincinnati to which I would walk the next day.

He then took me to get some Cincinnati Chili. I did not know Cincinnati was famous for chili. It was the strangest chili I ever tasted—heavy with cinnamon and chocolate and served over spaghetti—absolutely nothing like Mexican/Southwest chili. It was layered heavily with grated cheese, which saved it. It was not my favorite. But I was on the

American Discovery Trail and already had discovered a different part of America.

Don drove me out to Milford and dropped me off just as a thunderstorm hit. I hurriedly put up my tent on a square of concrete between three picnic tables under a small shelter roof right next to a big toy in the park. The picnic tables were metal mesh, so it was not too hard to get guy lines somewhat laid out and tied into the table mesh. The tent was certainly needed as Midwest rain comes sideways, blown by wind.

Any dampness or inconvenience of tenting on concrete was more than made up for by the fact that there were flush rest rooms fifteen-feet away. What luxury that was for a hiker used to wilderness camping. I had my first adventure in small-town camping without walking at all. After the storm passed, I listened to car tires on wet pavement a couple blocks away and the rumbling of thunder in the distance.

In the morning, I set off early for Cincinnati. Fifteen-and-a-half miles was a long way for someone not in tip-top shape for hiking (due to a nasty cold acquired a week before hiking.) But I had a goal, a B&B I had discovered that made a Cincinnati stop an easy decision. This dealt with my worry about where I could stay in the big city, and I had a light pack, having already dropped my food at the B&B.

Park in Cincinnati

The day was long, all on the paved surfaces of bike trails or sidewalks, just straightforward walking. (In this book, whenever I speak of bike or biker I mean bicyclist or bicycle, not a motorcycle. I do not hear bikers refer to themselves much as cyclists or call their trails cycle trails. Common terminology is simply bike.) Spring flowers and magnolias cheered me, and since there were plenty of places to buy food, I ate more than I should have so early in a long hike.

I was close to getting blisters on the bottom of my heels from repetitively hitting the hard surfaces, and I did get wet from passing rain showers, but I missed the hailstorm which hit after I reached the B&B at 5:00. Into my pack, I loaded the food Don and I had previously dropped there, and I packed my duffel bag—the same one I had used from the flight to Cincinnati—into a flat-rate box to send to Moline, Illinois. I'd use it on my flight home at the end of the hike.

The next day, I found the trail in Cincinnati to be a bit confusing and the T-by-T not entirely accurate, but I did find my way to the Roebling Bridge past construction problems and made my way into Kentucky.

The trail in Kentucky was brief, only 8.1 miles, before I crossed the Ohio River again, this time on the little eight-car Anderson Ferry. Cars had to pay $4.00, but I only had to pay $.50. It was a lovely day and fun to ride the ferry over the roiling brown, high water of the Ohio. The ferry had been open for just two days and muddy water still flooded over the banks among the trees lining the river, high with spring runoff.

Somewhere on Hillside Drive as I continued west, I knew I needed to find a place to put my tent. I knew that was how this trail had to be done. I knew I would have to knock on a door and ask for a tenting spot.

But as the time grew closer to the need to stop, I realized that was a lot easier to plan than to accomplish. I am not an extrovert. The gift of gab does not come naturally to me, so I carefully mentally rehearsed what I wanted to say.

The houses were all set back from the road with uphill driveways. People in the first two houses where I tried out my little speech turned me down. The occupants were renters and thought they might get in trouble with their landlord if they let me camp in their yards. OK, this was harder than those journals I had read suggested. I was getting worried I would not find anyone who would let me camp. Whatever would I do then?

At the third house, a nice older man pointed out a vacant lot across the road and said I could probably put my tent up there. I asked at the house beside the lot, and they thought it fine, also.

In great relief, I pitched my tent next to a fir tree. I had met the challenge of knocking on a door and finding a place to be for the night for the very first time.

The first big challenge on the ADT was finding a place to sleep. Of course, walking every day is an obvious test, but finding a place to be at the end of a day in a world of human habitation was very different from wilderness trails.

I had solved three nights' worth of lodging. My first night was solved by reading journals and knowing there were two or three small parks in Milford that other hikers had used without asking for permission.

My second night was solved by planning a B&B in a populated area that was very close to the trail. My third night was the real deal of asking for permission by knocking on a door. Those techniques, plus a few friends along the way, are how I traversed much of the ADT.

Some hikers just put their tents up wherever, without asking permission. I suppose I was leery of being in trouble for randomly tenting on private property, as well as feeling less bold as a solo hiker than those who went two by two. Even at parks, I usually asked permission of neighbors near the parks.

There is added safety in asking. If someone gives you permission, they *know* you are there, and they begin looking out for you. If you are on their property, they seem to sense a bit of responsibility for you. This usually is not spoken aloud, but it benefits a solo hiker.

A double-plus bonus first showed up on night five: Knocking on doors, I made friends and got to know local people along the trail. Being forced by the nature of this trail to talk to locals along the way became the charm of the ADT for me.

As I left in the morning after my first night of making the ask, I continued beside and above the Ohio on high banks with beautiful views. Some houses even had benches by the road on which to rest briefly to take in the sight of the Ohio River below the bluff. The Ohio River was the main transportation corridor west in the early days of our country. The river cut through thick, tall forests on either side. In the 1700s, Ohio was 90% thick forest. I imagined early pioneers on flat boats floating on the river, headed west.

Elizabethtown is the separation point on the ADT between the Southern Route (continuing along the Ohio River into Indiana and Illinois and then across Missouri and Kansas to Colorado) and the Northern Route (heading north over some of Ohio and then over to just below Chicago, crossing Indiana, Illinois, Iowa and Nebraska to Colorado).

Northern and Southern Routes meet in Denver for the trip further west to the Pacific Ocean. I chose the Northern Route simply because I liked Boston and Cubby's journal (previous thru hikers of the ADT) and that is the route they chose. I also did get the flatter land, which I wanted, as land near rivers is hillier than open farmland. (Water runs downhill and carves through land, making land near rivers generally hilly.) Another plus for me in my decision to take the Northern Route was the prospect of walking along canals in Illinois.

At Elizabethtown, Ohio, my westward trail headed north, while the Southern Route kept along the Ohio River.

In Elizabethtown, I needed another place to stay. I saw a church with a sign saying it was served by a woman pastor. That sounded like a good place to ask, but no one was there. A neighbor suggested I ask the church caretaker, but, while

I was walking toward their house, I saw them get in their car and drive away before I could ask. I ate my dinner sitting on a bench in the cemetery, and I wondered what house I should try next. I knocked at one of the houses near the edge of town. They had chickens in the yard; maybe they wouldn't mind a tent. So I asked.

"Sure," they said. "Pick any place you like."

I set up facing trees and bushes for semi-privacy. They gave me plenty of water to wash myself, my socks, and my undies, and I felt refreshed.

Heading north from the Ohio River the route became Ohio-farm flat, or mostly flat. While I walked on roads, many people waved as they drove by, giving me smiles and sometimes steering wheel salutes, lifting fingers off the steering wheel in greeting while still holding on. In one car at a stop sign by the freeway, a couple of very cute, older women gave me enthusiastic thumbs up and smiles from ear to ear. I grinned back. That was fun. I liked my cheering squad.

Miami Whitewater Forest in Hamilton County Park was filled with people out enjoying the beautiful weather on a Sunday afternoon. The Shaker Trace Trail had an eight-mile bicycle-and-walking path, half of which was my route. Numerous people I passed said *hello*, and some asked if I was getting ready for a hike. "Nope. I'm on one."

I have always liked walking. Even as a kid I liked to walk. As a teenager I liked walking as it always made me feel good—free and at peace, leaving teenage angst behind. I suppose some of that was due to endorphins, the body's own natural feel-good chemicals, but I think there was more to it than that.

Even this non-wilderness hike was enjoyable. Yes, the pavement hurt my feet, and I got tired and needed to rest. But something about the rhythm of the steps and the poles was hypnotic and drew me ever onward. The book *Born to Run* was popular a few years ago. Well, I can't run due to arthritic joints, but I could morph that title to *Born to Walk*. Our bodies were created to be active. Their proper use is *use*. Not using them in activity is not good for them. Lack of use, lack of activity makes our bodies unhealthy.

Oxford Road had very nice homes with acres of lawns. No chickens were in those yards. I wasn't sure how asking to camp there would be received. I tried one door, but there was no answer. I already had passed a house with a picnic table in their side yard, so I walked back to that one. Their front door was standing open.

Nate, a young man, maybe late teens or early twenties, answered my knock at the door. He said he would have to call his mom. I could not imagine that an absent mom would OK this request, but she did. I heard him telling her on the phone, "No, she is for real. She has a big pack and everything."

I pitched my tent next to the picnic table under the pine tree. And I met Nate's fiancé Olivia, his younger brother Max and his Dad Steve, when he got home from work. (Steve was a deputy Sherriff who worked in the Cincinnati jail.)

They were more than gracious, repeatedly asking if I needed anything. What I needed was a bathroom, but I was too embarrassed to ask. Steve then specifically asked if I needed to use the bathroom. When I shared that embarrassment had prevented me from asking, he asked me if I thought I was going to stop being human? All of us need to go to the bathroom. It is a human need. I have remembered his statement over the years whenever asking for that necessity.

They also asked if I would like a shower. Still being somewhat embarrassed about asking strangers for personal things, I turned them down for the shower, although I did use their bathroom sink to clean up, which surely beat a Ziploc bath (using the water in a Ziploc bag to wash myself, something I do when camping in the wilderness). I decided as I was washing myself that turning down the offer of a shower had been silly. After this learning experience, I never refused anyone else who offered me a shower.

They left their screen door open all night, so I would be able to freely come in and use their bathroom near the back door. What gracious people! This stop bolstered my confidence in knocking on doors and overwhelmed me with the generosity of people, which I would experience repeatedly on the ADT.

If the first huge challenge on the ADT is learning how to ask strangers for a place to be, the second huge test is trying to find appropriate places to take care of nature's needs. The ADT is not often in the wilderness. That means the wilderness skills of popping a squat wherever you need to or digging a hole in the ground for leave-no-trace deposits don't always work.

Urban areas and country roads do not present opportunities for privacy for personal acts. Walking from Milford to Oxford Road, I had found a park restroom, restaurants, fast-food places, gas stations, a senior center, construction porta potties, as well as some countryside useful for wilderness-style stops.

I concluded any business establishment probably has a bathroom, and if I looked pitiful enough and asked politely, use might be granted. Darkness of night gives some cover for watering the grass, but I did not want to make solid deposits in flower beds. Finding a place for nature's needs was indeed daunting.

Perhaps this is too much information for some, so

feel free to skip such portions. But as Steve said, we are all human animals, and we cannot stop having those needs, even when walking through inhabited areas. With no car to cover distances quickly to find a restroom, meeting nature's needs can be tricky.

We have also been taught not to talk about such things; they are private. Yet, every one of us must take care of that private need even when we do not have the privacy of a house or a car to quickly take us to a gas station with a restroom. Taking this hike has also made me realize the desperate straits of the homeless, not just for shelter but for a spot in privacy to do what we all must do.

In the morning, I met Dianne, the mom who had OKed my stay. She was busily cooking breakfast in shifts for all her family. She would have cooked for me, too, but I had my own food and didn't want to carry it; I needed to eat it to make my pack lighter.

The day was a country-road walk over rolling hills. I stopped for lunch at a lovely little shelter at an off-road campsite in a woodsy area with eastern wildflowers: spring beauties, Dutchman's breeches, and May apples. Before flowering, May apples poke up with leaves like furled umbrellas, which then open to hide a large white drooping flower. Any time hiking in the East, I have loved their umbrellas shading patches of forest floor.

Although the ADT is not a wilderness trail, there is beauty everywhere. On the Wonderland Trail, PCT or CDT, there are carpets of flowers in the desert, craggy peaks with snow, or mountain streams tumbling down rocky slopes. On wilderness trails the beauty is so intense it almost assaults the senses.

On this trail, I needed to look with a little more intent. But the bright green of pastures, purple weeds in unplowed fields, small patches of woods dotted with wildflowers, and the yellow-streaked sky of morning sunrise proclaimed beauty of a different sort.

I found a bit of adventure at the end of the day. The T-by-T said to go through a field. There *were* ADT signs stuck to a fence post, so I went through the field, although it was also clearly posted *no trespassing*.

I found the second ADT sign in the field on a small tree so entering the field was correct, but then there were no more signs. After a fence line, the pasture ended in a completely overgrown woods with no sign of a trail. There was a hole in the fence, and I could see a green gate beyond another field, in the general direction of the next waypoint. I walked in that direction, heaved my pack over the gate, and climbed over it, making my way to still another gate where I did the same, finally coming out at Garner Road. I was relieved no farmer came after me with a shotgun for my short trespass.

After I walked down the road, I found Bunker Hill Haven for Boys, which was listed on the T-by-T. However, the supposed shelter was back somewhere in the woods, and the boys said it was in bad shape.

The woman in charge said, according to her board of directors, it was against their rules to have anyone around their boys without a proper background check. Violating that rule sounded more serious than a short bit of trespassing, so I just asked for water. She directed me to a house and followed me with her car. Then she took pity on me, and suggested I stay in their gym, since thunderstorms were imminent. I would not be around their boys, since I promised to stay in the gym until I left the next morning.

On the ADT, most of the time, I never knew where I would end up sleeping. That night I slept in a gym. They turned on the water, including the *hot* water in the building, just for me, so I got a shower, too. I shook out my sleeping bag on the carpeted floor of the gymnasium and hung my daily wash on stored volleyball nets. I guess I could have shot some hoops for a while, too, but after two shots and one basket, just because I could, I crawled inside my sleeping bag and went to sleep while rain poured outside.

The next day was cooler, with gray cloudy skies all day. I liked it a lot. When the sun was shining, it was really hot, and the humidity was high, too. I was drenched with sweat the first few days and had too much sun. I'm from Washington State, and I liked the cool-and-cloudy weather, reminding me of home. In cool weather, I walked all day with long sleeves, light gloves, and headband and needed my coat when I stopped to eat and rest.

I enjoyed a rest stop along Indian Creek. There were woods with blood root blooming, another eastern flower. Even if you miss its bloom, its wonderfully scalloped leaves add interest to the trailside greenery. My presence on the trail disturbed a pair of Canada Geese. I took their picture and they took off, honking loudly.

In my various hiking adventures over the last seventeen years in the wilderness, I have been fortunate to see bear (both black and grizzly), cougar, elk, moose, many deer, beaver, martin, innumerable squirrels, and chipmunks, as well as many feathered friends.

Thus far in Ohio, I had seen beaver, raccoon, squirrels, rabbits, deer, turkey, turkey vultures, ducks, geese, many bright-red flashes of cardinals, red-winged blackbirds and other birds I could not identify. Wildlife were not absent in Ohio's farmland and the pockets of woods remaining between larger tracts of cultivated land.

Walking through the college town of Oxford, I stopped at a Subway for a footlong and to charge my phone, then traveled on to Pugh's Mill Covered Bridge. Covered bridges are not too uncommon in the Eastern part of the United States, but they are an interesting treat for those from the West. I finally stopped at a farmhouse halfway between Summerville and Butler Roads.

My tent was pitched just outside the fenced yard at the edge of a cornfield cut to stubble. The house dogs jumped over the fence to be petted. I was accepted by both the four-footed and two-footed critters in that place. Fortunately, they left my tent alone. One bounding dog on a tent would have been a disaster.

Tent in Ohio

I had been hoping for a little trail-walking in Hueston Woods, but even more, I had been hoping for cover to take care of nature's needs. Inside the woods, off the abandoned road past some low bushes under a canopy of leafless taller bushes, I found what seemed like a good place to use the *facilities*. There were no houses for at least a quarter mile; there was good cover, and I would not be on any trail. Leaving my pack on the abandoned road, I went into the woods and dug my hole and proceeded with the morning business.

"Hey, what are you doing?" A concerned park ranger had seen my pack left on the abandoned road and investigated.

"Duh! What do ya think?" An old lady with her drawers lowered squatting over a hole? I should never have left my pack on that old road. I pulled up my drawers and reassured him I was not doing anything nefarious, and he left. I thought he could have used a little more couth and trail etiquette.

The T-by-T said to go on named trails through Hueston Woods. But the south end had no trail signs. After searching around, I finally saw the pole with ADT stickers, although it was lying on the ground mostly under leaves and weeds. The trail went a little way and then was almost hidden by a trailer. After that, the trail wasn't very maintained. After crawling in the mud under the third downed log, I decided the trail in Hueston Woods wasn't worth it.

I walked out past the archery range to the loop

road and proceeded on pavement. I had chosen the ADT for a straightforward walking trail. I had gone over and under plenty of downed trees on wilderness trails. I didn't feel I needed to do that on the ADT with the road right nearby, and straighter from point to point than the trails that wandered east and west when my goal was northward. It was a nice enough woods, but I was more interested in moving on.

Walking the road for the rest of the day was nice. Beside Four Mile Creek, running clear and peacefully, I saw trout lilies and red trillium. I also saw two deer. I passed two more covered bridges and the Fairhaven meeting house from the early 1800s, a stop for pioneers and cattle drivers.

More importantly to me, the Community Church had cars, meaning it was open. As I was contemplating going in, the Pastor opened the door and asked if I wanted to use the rest room. Yes! Thank you very much!

A little farther on, a very cute beagle wanted to follow me. Not needing a dog following me to the Mississippi River, I stopped at the next farmhouse a quarter mile away and asked the woman there to hold him until I was around the corner and down the road. Hopefully, he then made his way back home.

That night I didn't have to knock on a door to find a place to be. The T-by-T told me Concord Church allowed hikers to camp in the churchyard. There was even an old outhouse behind the church, so

I did not have to worry about finding a bathroom. Tucked into my tent, a soft rain began, and I was lulled to sleep listening to the gentle patter of raindrops on my tent.

Along the trail in those first days, I was learning. Most importantly, I learned how to ask people for what I needed. And I learned that gracious people were everywhere.

I found water in commercial establishments, from houses I passed, and from the kind people who let me camp on their property. Except for the first two times I'd asked for a place to stay, everyone I asked for anything, said *yes*. Most had no idea there was a waymarked trail that went past their homes. They did not know me. And they knew nothing about walking trails, yet they graciously helped with my needs.

Interestingly, hikers who hike the long scenic trails in America advise newbies to stay away from roads and people as the safest option. Novices are advised how to deal with wild animals, and new hikers are usually reassured to know there is not a great deal to fear from four-legged critters.

Yes, one does need to know something about the wilderness, about dealing with wildlife, wilderness skills, and leave-no-trace behavior. But veteran hikers caution solo hikers, particularly women, about people. Many hikers say they are safer on a trail in the wilderness than walking in town. An undercurrent of fear and danger regarding people remains in most hikers' minds.

Yet, here I was on a trail that was more road than trail, going through towns and suburban areas, and depending on my reception from other people. I had to get past my own fear and worry to knock on doors, be polite, and smile.

I met generosity, friendly comments, hospitality, and interest. There was indeed a learning curve. (And I am still learning.) But door by door, meeting new people every day, fear changed to unfear. (Unfear is a word I have made up. It does not mean no fear or never having feared. But it does mean fear left behind.

GREENVILLE

The next day I crossed from Ohio to Indiana. Farms in Indiana looked a lot like farms in Ohio.

After reaching Indiana, I needed a rest. The trail entering Indiana wasn't far from Greenville, Ohio. My first husband grew up there. Over the years I had kept in touch with some of that clan. So Lianne, my husband's brother's first wife, picked me up just below Richmond, Indiana and took me to Greeneville for a rest day and a chance to catch up on the past years of our lives.

I laundered my clothes and picked up the food box I had sent ahead to Greenville. Lianne was a published poet, and she took me to the Greenville Poet's Group. What a fun evening, meeting Lianne's peeps and watching her happy dance to the live instrumental music.

Bob, another member of that clan, also came to visit me with Lianne, and we all had a lovely time. Bob was very interested in my long-distance hiking. He asked me what had been scary when I hiked. So I told him bear stories and river-crossing stories and about the two guys in an AT shelter in Georgia I'd thought were on the lam from the law.

Considering that I had hiked 6,000 miles or more

in the previous 13 years, there had been remarkably little that had been scary, although I did have a few good stories.

It is not uncommon for people to ask me, "What has been the most frightening thing?" or "Aren't you afraid?" Fear interests people. That I should have been afraid is expected. That there hasn't been much to fear is not expected.

Rest days are important to long-distance hikers. Important also was connecting with old friends. I was not young, and Lianne and Bob were older. Washington and Ohio are far apart. This hike across the country gave me an opportunity to connect with past relatives and old friends, another gift of the trail. And we were at the age where seeing each other again would not be a certainty.

Indiana—Old Friends and Good Old Boys

Indiana portion of the American Discovery Trail

When Lianne and Bob took me back to the trail, Bob said, "You look like a professional hiker."

I responded, "I sort of am."

Mary near Richmond, Indiana

Around the west side of Richmond, Indiana, I walked up a woodsy bike trail beside bright-yellow beds of marsh marigolds. There was a bit of urban-road walking, which gave me lunch at an Arby's, and then I was on the Cardinal Greenway, a paved bike trail that ran for many miles. It had regular porta potties for my needs as it coursed through woods, beside a river, or in open country.

It was a hot day, and I replenished my water twice—once from a farmhouse and once from a man walking his dogs near the Webster Trailhead.

As I rested and ate my dinner sitting on a nice bench, I saw a woman on a lawn mower start to mow the grass. I had met her husband on a bike a bit earlier. He had told me they were the maintainers of the Webster Trailhead and that I might

Mary E. Davison

see her mowing the grass. When she got to where I was sitting, she stopped the mower and asked if I was the woman to whom her husband had talked. Yes, I was. They wanted to invite me for dinner and to stay the night. I said I had already eaten, but I would not turn down a bed.

She directed me how to find their house, about three tenths mile off trail. So, Diane finished mowing while I walked to their house and met her husband, Cliff, outside. He invited me in and offered a shower. I had learned to accept offers, and the shower was wonderful after such a hot-and-sticky day.

When his wife returned, they ate dinner, and we talked into the night. They were very interested in long-distance hiking and asked me many questions, which I gladly answered at length. They were even ELCA Lutherans too and volunteered to take me to church the next day. I had a long day scheduled and regretfully said *no*.

They had been hikers in Colorado, and their son lived in Washington State, so we had a lot of connections. Sadly, I am unsure if Diane was really her name or if it was something else that might have fallen through a hole in my brain before I wrote it down. I did remember Cliff for sure as the male half of this couple. What a gift they were to me. I unexpectedly had a shower, a bed, and new friends. Their kindness added to my growing list of *trail angels* (those who help hikers) on this trip.

A number of years ago, when I was hiking on the AT in New Jersey, a lovely couple I met in a restaurant took me home for the night. My friend, Kathy, back in Washington, said she was afraid that going home with strangers, I would get snatched up by an ax murderer. But I have learned that strangers are just friends I haven't yet met. On the ADT I found stranger after stranger who became my friends.

The next morning, continuing on the Cardinal Greenway, really enjoying the cool weather, I walked five or six miles before the rain started. I walk better in cool weather than in hot. My body felt the best yet, conditioning well, trail legs developing.

The Cardinal Greenway made walking the trail sort of brainless. There were no turns to make, no decisions to ponder. I just needed to get started and follow the path as it wound its way through woods, past large farm fields and by rolling hills.

Bike trails are often built on old railway beds. Railways were made to avoid going up and down, and this one was nearly level, even though the surrounding countryside had hills. I steadily tromped the miles.

Darkening clouds and the smell of moisture in the air announced rain was coming. I made sure everything was secure in the pack. My pack was made of Cuben-fiber, a lightweight waterproof material that is now called Dyneema composite fabric.

I also lined the inside with a black garbage bag and my gear was further organized into Cuben-fiber or plastic bags inside the black garbage bag. A waterproof rain cover was spread on top of my pack. I also wore raingear and carried an umbrella. Even if I got wet through all those layers, my dry clothes and sleeping bag meant I would live to hike another day.

The rain was, well, rain. Walking in rain was something I have had to do on most long-distance hikes. Long-distance hikers are not just fair-weather hikers, or they cannot accomplish long-distance goals.

It rained all the rest of the day. I was very happy to find there were nice clean porta potties along the Cardinal Greenway. Besides their intended purpose, they were my lunch and rest stops, out of the rain. With the lid to the seat down I had a place to sit. There was lots of hand sanitizer in these clean and well-stocked little plastic houses.

I balanced lunch in my lap, and it was dry inside this shelter. I know it might sound gross to non-hikers, as one does not normally eat in a bathroom. But to me, they were gifts as I ate and listened to the pounding rain beating on the plastic roof and walls.

About three miles before Losantville, while the rain was drumming on my umbrella, obliterating all other sounds, I decided to look at my email on my phone. I stood in the little circle of dryness under my sheltering umbrella. Once the phone was on, I saw that Karen and Marc had called. Karen had been my roommate in the Peace Corps in Turkey in 1965-67. I was planning to see them the next day.

Karen and Mary, Old Peace Corps Volunteers

I called them back. Nearly shouting and with the phone pressed closely to my ear, I strove mightily to hear what they said above the sound of driving rain: "How are you doing with the rain?"

"OK."

"We can come get you in Losantville."

What welcome news in the pouring rain, with the weather report saying it would get worse all night. A dry bed and a hot shower? Dinner, too? Sold. My hiking day ended with warmth, me clean and fed, and renewing old acquaintances in pleasant conversation.

The next three days I was blessed by Karen and Marc, who supported me while I slackpacked. A slackpack is a hike with only a day pack's worth of gear: warm clothes and rain gear, first-aid kit, map, T-by-T, and, sometimes, food. I had a shower and a bed in a warm house waiting each night after they picked me up. There was time to talk and catch up a bit on the years that had gone by since we were in the Peace Corps.

The weather had turned wet, and then quite cold and windy. The first slackpack day was a brisk 48 degrees, with bright-blue sky and sun. I hiked with warm underlayers and rain gear to cut the cold wind.

My path led me by blooming pear trees, pink-flowering crab apples, white-blooming apple trees, or underneath Red Bud trees, which arched across the Greenway.

Interpretive signs along the Cardinal Greenway Trail told me of interesting aspects of the countryside, one explaining that round barns have the most efficient use of space but were expensive to build. Indiana has more round barns than any other state. They were quite popular in the late 1800s to early 1900s. But by 1992, only 111 were left. I liked the interpretive signs and learning about odd facts or bits of history as I walked.

The trail passed through Muncie and Marc and Karen met me at Red Lobster for lunch. Before walking on the ADT, I had never been on a trail that went right by a Red Lobster. Walking through towns does have its perks.

On the last of those three slackpacking days, I walked into Matthews on a 40-degree day with a 30-mile-an-hour headwind. A week before it had been 80 degrees. But that day, I wore my rain gear for a windbreak, including my Cuben-fiber waterproof mittens over my gloves. Walking into the headwind wasn't great fun.

What made the day, though, was my time in Matthews. I was hoping to find an early lunch with a restroom, as my T-by-T had the letter M next to Matthews, signifying a possible place to buy a meal. At the junction with Wheeling Pike, there was a closed and boarded-up restaurant on the corner. Hmm? Did that mean I was out of luck for food and restroom?

While I was standing on the corner wishing for a warm indoor place with food and not seeing any, a gentleman drove up and asked if I was a hiker and if I was doing all right with all the strong wind. He told me the BP gas station had good food and was only two blocks away, though I couldn't see it from the trail. Oh, good. I didn't have to hike hungry the rest of the day.

The wind blew me in the door where five or six guys, most of my generation, were sitting at a table having coffee. I obviously was crashing the *good old boys' coffee club*. Their chairs blocked the way to the only empty table, but they asked me to sit with them. I doffed pack and went to the restroom. Nature's needs tended to, I eyed the menu on the wall. Food service was just opening at 10:00 am.

One of the guys, Larry, told me, "If you haven't had the breaded tenderloin sandwich from Matthews, you haven't ever lived."

The esteemed sandwiches came in small or large size, and the men warned me the large might be too big to eat. Even though it was only 10:00, the cold had made me hungry, and I had been on the trail long enough to have a hiker appetite. I ordered the large tenderloin sandwich. It *was* one of the best sandwiches I ever had, and of true thru-hiker proportions. The gentlemen in the *good old-boys club*—by this time up to nine guys—were amazed that I ate it all.

We sat and talked, and I told them about trails and hiking; one of them told me about his wood-carving hobby and showed me samples. They proudly told me that Matthews missed being the state capital by only one vote. It was fun to be invited into a group of locals—one that was obviously gender-specific. And when I went to pay for my sandwich, I found out Larry had already paid for it. I was amazed, thankful and felt a little guilty that I had waited until leaving to ask about paying. Larry just grinned at me when I thanked him.

Three of the Old Boys' Club in Matthews (Larry, in the middle) bought my sandwich

As I left, Larry showed me his dog, a half-coyote mix, waiting for him in his truck. He had raised the pup after it had been caught in a trap. He then prayed for me and my trip, and I found out he was a music minister in a local church.

The old-boys' coffee club in Matthews was a very memorable stop. Good thing. Because the walk was very cold and windy.

PRETENDING

My daily mileage varied: 10, 16, 13 miles. I had not expected to stay with Karen and Marc more than one night, but I was very grateful to have the opportunity for more with such cold weather, besides having such a lovely opportunity to reconnect after so many years. I changed my schedule to end at crossroads instead of my planned mileage, which allowed me to return to their home outside of Muncie each day. All that slackpacking, sometimes longer days than originally planned, meant that after those three days, I had only six miles left to go on a very cold morning (37 degrees at 9:00) as I said good-bye to my friends from long ago.

Lucky me, I had another night inside after those six miles, prearranged in my hike plan, at the College Inn, a bit off the Cardinal Greenway on city streets but scheduled for a re-supply stop. Since I am an older hiker and not up to carrying all the weight of younger hikers, and since I had not expected three wonderful nights with Karen and Marc, I had already made a reservation at the College Inn before leaving home and had sent my re-supply box there.

While I was at the College Inn, A reporter from the small county newspaper came over to interview me and take pictures. The guys having coffee in the *old-boys' club* in Matthews had said they would probably see me on or in the news someday. Of course, I said that wasn't likely, would never happen. The county newspaper was delivered in Matthews, so they might have been pretty good prophets.

The reporter asked how I protected myself on the trail and what were my scary experiences. Everyone thinks I should be afraid. He was not very satisfied with my answer.

I said I tried hard not to look like a mark. I had been told by a counselor in years past that not looking like a mark *was* a protection. The reporter thought that very inadequate and not even a real thing.

A story from my Peace Corps days conveys a learning experience that helped form my coping skills with fear. Peace Corps days are another chapter in my life. At 79 years of age, I am old enough to have lots of chapters in my life's story.

While in the Peace Corps in Turkey, I took leave time to visit Egypt. Another Peace Corps Volunteer was traveling elsewhere on her leave time, but we decided to meet on a specific date at the American University in Cairo. I flew to Cairo, but she didn't show up.

There I was in Cairo, a 25-year-old, single woman. By myself. In a strange Muslim country not at all like Turkey. Instead of having another person to hang out with and be brave enough together to go sightseeing, I was *alone*. What was I going to do? I suspected I would never again be in Egypt. And, from Peace Corps training and living for more than a year in Turkey, I did know *something* about how to act in a Muslim country.

The dormitory of the American University in Cairo was a safe place. While there, I visited the Pyramids and the Cairo Museum, having been given instructions on city transportation by the English-speaking personnel at the American University.

I traveled to the Pyramids by city bus. The busses at the bus stop were often packed and overflowing, with people hanging on to the outside as the inside was already packed. I was relieved that the bus I needed was full but not overflowing. I did not have to hang onto the sides.

The bus with the correct Arabic numerals corresponding to the Arabic numerals drawn on my note by the American University folks, dropped me off at the Pyramids. There were camels there for tourists to ride for a price. That looked like fun, but as a single young woman, I thought it risky to ride a camel by myself as other tourists were doing, as the camels came with camel handlers, and I didn't want such a handler to handle more than camels. But I did get to see the Pyramids and the Sphinx—just by catching a bus.

Then I took the night train to Luxor in the Valley of the Kings. I chose the night train, so I would have one less hotel bill. I was not exactly flush with cash in those Peace Corps days. I expected there to be several other people in my train car. There is safety in numbers, and I had traveled in Turkey on such trains. But no one else was in my train car. That made me even more afraid. What if someone came in while I was sleeping? I didn't get much sleep that night.

I did survive the night. And when the train arrived in Luxor in the morning, I and lots of other people got off the train. Then I bucked up and *pretended* that I knew what I was doing. There were no buildings in sight. But everyone was walking in one direction, which I assumed must be the town. I picked up my bag and purposefully strode off, as if getting off a train in the Egyptian desert was a perfectly normal occurrence for me.

I have a long story about that adventure and staying in a 25-cent-a-night hotel, but the important part here is that I *pretended* I knew what I was doing. I *pretended* I wasn't afraid. I *pretended* I was an experienced world traveler. I left my fear behind, or at least I hid behind what I pretended. And I had one of the most marvelous adventures in my life.

Leaving your fear behind is not the same thing as being fearless. I guess, it's courage. Or maybe courage is just pretending. Courage is not being fearless. It is doing something even though you are afraid. Sometimes, it is *acting like* you are unafraid even when you are fearful.

Acting like I am unafraid sometimes also means

acting like I am not a mark. A mark is a victim waiting to be victimized. I try not to look like I am afraid or uncertain. It is an acquired skill. I stand up a little straighter and try to walk with a look of confidence exuding from every pore. It is acting, like playing a part in a movie. And it *is* a defense, of sorts.

Unfortunately, I did not think of that story for use as an example in that interview with the reporter on the ADT; he absolutely did not understand what I was trying to say. Perhaps he decided not to write the article about me. I don't know. I just walked on the next day.

But acting as if you are unafraid *is* a form of protection in the world of people. So, when I am in strange and unfamiliar situations, I make myself act like I have confidence I may not feel. And I smile. To tell the truth, I have used this technique as a pastor when preaching, too. And after lots and lots of *pretending* not to be afraid, it becomes kinda true.

GIVING AND RECEIVING

The Sweetser Switch Trail began where the Cardinal Greenway ended, both had been railroads converted into trails. The Sweetser Switch was a lovely trail, although only three-miles long. That trail did a lot with the railroad theme. Trail signs looked like RR -Crossing signs. Lots of picnic tables had been placed along the length of the trail and freshly painted railroad cars were parked at Sweetser.

Not everyone owning land along these railroads changed to trails had been in favor of the trails. I had learned there were *holdouts* from Gaston north for a few miles, people who did not want a bike trail to be built. People who owned land there were afraid the trail would turn into a hobo trail. I suppose long-distance hikers do look a bit like hobos. Yet, the Sweetser Switch Trail took on the railroad theme and developed it. I'll bet it raised everyone's property values.

I have also walked the Camino de Santiago in Spain, one of the most popular trails in the world. Some years, 500,000 hikers from all around the world hike that trail. On the Camino de Santiago, the pilgrims (as hikers are called there) have contributed to the economy of northern Spain. Walkers do not spend as much as tourists in cars, but the hiker spending does help the economy.

Granted, we, in the United States, don't have St James's bones to draw hundreds of thousands of people to walk the trails that make up the ADT. But why not promote the trail in some way? Perhaps someday hikers on the ADT could significantly contribute to the economy in the small towns through which it passes.

People see the world through differing lenses. Some focus on all the problems and faults. In this case: "What if hobos/homeless people walk here in my back yard?" Others envision possibilities. In this case: "Let's build this trail into a really cool park so people can walk and bicycle and picnic." I vote for the latter view.

There had been major changes to the route of the ADT since Boston and Cubby had walked it. Instead of going north from the end of the Sweetser Switch Trail and up by Mississinewa Lake, my directions took me south a bit, and then over to Cassville. I kept thinking Boston and Cubby's route might be more scenic, and it certainly seemed like fewer miles. Reluctantly, I turned south to follow my current waypoints on the ADT.

Before I reached the turn to the west, a car stopped beside me; the people inside were a couple whom

I had passed earlier on the trail. Nate and Stacy had pegged me as a hiker on the American Discovery Trail. They had hosted and helped a family on the trail a year before, and now they urged me to stop at their house or camp there. Unfortunately, I thought it was too early in the day to stop.

But when I reached their house, I did stop to use their restroom and to mix my dinner, a dehydrated meal that needed to soak for an hour or so to become real food. As we chatted, they offered to come and get me after I completed my planned miles and bring me back for the night to stay. Now how could I refuse such an offer? Once again, I unexpectedly had a bed and a shower. At that point I had not put my tent up once in Indiana. Amazing!

Nate and Stacy had a very involved special-needs child, much like some children I knew when I was a pediatric physical therapist. I admired their tender care of their child and prayed with Stacy before I left. They gave me tender care and prayed for me, too. Wonderful young people.

Taking me out to my end spot from the day before, Nate told me about raising hogs when he was seventeen. He'd culled the fields after the combines to make feed for his hogs. He squirreled that money away and bought his first house at a very young age. I commented that I enjoyed my walk in Indiana while the corn was not yet planted, as I liked to see a long way. He said he never tired of the view.

After leaving Nate for a rainy, windy walk on a country road, I looked for someplace to have a rest and eat my mid-morning trail bars. I stopped at a house with a sheltered porch and asked a young mother of two young children for permission to eat on the porch out of the wind and rain. She brought out a folding camp chair for me and asked what else I needed. After my rest break, I knocked again and asked for use of the restroom. Eating my lunch on her porch gave her time to get used to me. I try to be aware that long-distance hiking probably seems odd to many people, and I don't want to be perceived as a threat of any kind.

Fear works in two directions. I could be afraid of people I meet, and they could be afraid of me.

Before I left, she prayed for me, and her little girl gave me a scripture wrist band they had from Vacation Bible School. Very sweet. The center of the USA is sometimes called the Bible Belt, and more than other places I have walked in the United States, people are open and expressive about their faith. I accepted prayers from many people on this hike and felt free about offering them too, without giving offense.

Continuing in rain, I needed a sheltered lunch

spot and knocked on a door with no answer from inside. I could hear music playing inside a detached garage, so I knocked there. A 72-year-old man looked askance at my request for a dry place to eat my lunch. He had just finished cleaning the garage floor to a sparkling shine for a birthday party later in the day. He agreed but didn't seem happy about it.

I started to sit my dripping wet self on a small rug near the door determined not to get his floor dirty with muddy water. But he stopped me and told me to sit in a chair at a table across the room. I took off my wet and muddy shoes by the door and did so, happy for the chair and the table.

When someone grants my request, I do not expect them to give more than I have asked, and I try to ask only for what I really need. Many, many times I have been given far more than I have requested. But those are bonuses, not to be expected. No one should be faulted for not giving me a palace when I ask for a shelter. Hikers hike because they want to. We are not entitled to anything. Hikers often are given far more than they ask, but not every time. And a basic need fulfilled is quite enough and is a gift.

After fulfilling my basic need for a dry place to

eat my lunch, this gentleman, after noting that all I was doing was just that, eating my lunch, warmed up and started to ask me questions: Why did I knock on *his* door? (It was the first one after I turned the corner after noon.) How did I know he was in the garage? (I heard music playing inside.) Why was I hiking? (Because I liked hiking long-distance trails.) Where was I going? (To the Mississippi River.)

After I left and walked on down the road, he passed me in his car on the way to his friend's house and rolled down his window to joke about my slow pace. A possibly not-so-welcoming experience ended in friendship, jokes, and smiles. Nice.

Finally, I was within about fifteen feet of the Nickel Plate Trail, another bicycle trail where I could leave the road, when another car stopped. The woman driving enquired what I was doing. She was amazed to know the road she was driving was part of a waymarked trail. Before our conversation was finished, she prayed for me, too.

There were lots of prayers said in one day—mine for Stacy and Nate and theirs for me, and then two different women prayed for me. Interesting. Maybe the ADT in Indiana was a religious trail even without Saint James's bones. God is at work everywhere.

Those who walk long trails are usually self-reliant people. You need to have both gear and the trail knowledge to use it, or make do with what you have. Hikers are pretty independent cusses, or they wouldn't start out to do a long trail. But one of the things most hikers learn on any long trail is to accept the kindness of strangers.

One does not lose the ability to be self-reliant by accepting gifts given on the trail. We learn, and on ADT more than any other trail, I think, we learn to be interdependent, both giving and accepting help. At least I wanted to think there was some interdependence, giving as well as receiving.

I have lots of experience hiking and camping, and I am pretty much prepared for any weather I am likely to encounter. I have hiked and camped in sun, rain, and snow, desert, and mountains, easy and tough terrain. I think I am prepared and self-reliant. Yet I was offered and accepted beds and showers from total strangers on the ADT, more than on any other trail.

That night I rested in my tent on the protected side of a house of very modest means. I had been given water and use of the restroom. Everyone wants to give me coffee, which I don't drink. At this house, they were worried I would be cold, and it was a possibility, as it would be down to 37 degrees in the early morning. They wanted to give me a blanket. I told them I would be warm in my down bag. I was self-reliant. Yet my heart was warmed by the concern of strangers who became friends, offers of more than I needed, and prayers for my journey.

In the morning, the couple whose house had sheltered me so well from the wind were sorry they had not done more for me, though they had met my needs wonderfully with tenting space sheltered from the wind, water, and restroom. What more did I need?

As I walked along the trail, I reflected more on being interdependent. That word implied I was doing something. What was it that I did other than receive on that trail?

In a broad sense, I helped to preserve what wilderness there was on the ADT as on any other trail. By walking gently on the land and serving as an example of respect for the land and its creatures, I was interdependent with the land. But on the ADT, I was also a bit like a trail ambassador.

Virtually no one I'd met who lived near or on the American Discovery Trail knew it existed. People were surprised to know it was there and very surprised to find an old lady walking a goodly distance on it. I brought conversation and smiles, and sometimes people expressed a bit of wonderment at what it was possible for an old lady to do, enlarging their view of what was possible.

Beyond that, it seemed I was completely on the receiving end: for water, for a place to put my tent, and sometimes for a restroom. There usually were no other options for tenting. The Nickel Plate Trail had some *no-camping* signs posted. Besides the issue of legality, rail trails were built on a gravel bed and usually had a ditch on both sides, very often with running or standing water, not good places to put a tent. Beyond the ditches were fences and posted land. And the Nickel Plate Trail, unlike the Cardinal Greenway, had no porta potties, nor did the country roads.

I suppose one service I provided for others was to be a cheerful and grateful recipient. And there is something to that. As a pastor I have sometimes reminded people that letting others do something for them helps others to be generous. Conversely, not allowing others to do something for you deprives them of the joy of giving. And that *is* true.

But I would not want to push that too far. Some hikers carry a sense of entitlement, as if every gift, perk, benefit, and bit of trail magic is their due. No! Every gift of trail magic is a gift. Period. All these gifts are not to be expected and always to be gratefully received. (Trail magic means unexpected copacetic happenings or gifts that come your way while walking on a trail.)

I was a reasonably competent wilderness hiker, but most of the time, the ADT was not wilderness. I was a self-reliant person; but on the ADT, I was dependent on others. Those who helped me were making my trip very memorable. I wasn't too sure what it was that I contributed to the relationships I was having with others. That was an uncomfortable feeling, to be so much on the receiving end of so many gifts.

After nearly fifteen miles of walking, I came to a road crossing with houses. The first door knock got a turndown, but across the street, I met Cynthia and John, who generously let me camp in their yard. They, too, were amazed I was walking the trail. As part of my spiel, I let them know I had a trail journal online, and they could look it up to verify who I was. They gave me water, and I set up my tent and settled in. Then Cynthia came out and offered me a shower, and later, a bed. I could tell they had then read my online journal. I did use the restroom, but I was already snug in my tent for bed.

On my trip inside to use the facilities, John and Cynthia shared a bit of the politics of the Nickel Plate Trail from the point of view of those who have not always had positive relations with the trail organizations. The gentleman across the street, on whose door I had first knocked, may have felt my request to camp was pouring salt in an old wound.

If you didn't want a trail to go by your house because you were expecting hobos to use it, having someone knock on your door asking for a place to camp would seem like just what you hadn't wanted had come true. I was not a hobo, but the difference between hobo and long-distance hiker may have been a nuance he was not likely to get. After talking with Cynthia and John, I could better understand his rejecting my request. But once again, I was blessed by strangers who helped and cared for me.

I woke up at 6:00 in the morning, but my eyes kept closing, and I kept going back to sleep. At 7:00 the sun was shining brightly on my tent, and I made myself get up. I wasn't in a hurry to get moving that day, as I was ahead of schedule.

The night before, Cynthia had told me to come in and get a shower in the morning, if not at night, so I did. We sat and talked a bit as I was not in a hurry. She was having surgery in the afternoon, the same surgery I had a couple years earlier. I reassured her about the surgery and left her with suggestions for recovery. We prayed together— she for my journey and I for her recovery from surgery.

As I made the sign of the cross on her forehead, I was aware I was giving her the gift of pastoral ministry. There are opportunities for ministry even if I'm retired. There are times I realize Medicare Pastor, the trail name I chose several years ago, really is the correct trail name for me. And that was the right house to come to, knocking on the door.

That afternoon turned gray, cloudy, and windy. I was a bit tired of the Nickel Plate Trail. It progressed in a line as straight as a string with very little variation between the hedgerows and woods, trees trying mightily to leaf out against the cold, pewter-colored sky. My mood seemed equally gray and subdued, though I didn't have a reason to feel down.

My lunch stop in a small town was uneventful. No one talked to me beyond taking my order and asking if the sandwich was OK. Two guys sitting there barely gave me a glance. I was just someone passing through, not worth a conversation. No warm vibes here. It seemed a very different atmosphere from the *old-boys' club* in Matthews.

The Grainery in Macy let me get water and use the restroom. I asked to camp at one house and was turned down, so I just kept walking instead of asking further. The town seemed depressed, the people quiet and taciturn. Or maybe it was just my afternoon mood and general weariness.

I found a level place to camp just off the trail. It was a hiking no-man's-land, as there was no fence. I couldn't be yelled at for being on the farmer's land as there was no fence. I couldn't be yelled at for being on the bike trail right-of-way as there was no fence. I wondered how Cynthia's surgery had gone, and I wished I had a way of knowing. A pastor only for a chance meeting, I had no phone number. But I was glad we had prayed together.

In a short six miles the next day, I was at Rochester, a town big enough to have a motel. It was time for a rest day and to pick up a new re-supply box.

It was a cheap motel. The springs in the chair were broken and about to come through the material. The bed sagged in the middle. The towel was small and rough. But there was abundant hot water and the sheets were clean. The room had a TV, a microwave, and a refrigerator. It would do, and the price was right, although when I asked for directions, the nicely dressed woman at the nearby gas station had asked skeptically if I really wanted to stay there. The son of the woman running the motel offered to drive me to the laundromat, which was quite a few blocks away. After I and my clothes were clean, I felt much better.

What do hikers do on a zero day? (zero miles walked) Eat and eat some more. Some hikers have energy to party. I do as little as possible. Although I had experienced unexpected beds and showers along the way, it had been eleven days since my rest day in Greenville. My body craved rest. And food. Hikers eat a lot. I devoured half a roasted chicken, raw veggies and dip, maple cinnamon rolls, and ice cream, then washed it all down with milk. Mm good. And that was just one of my meals.

SEEING

After my rest day, I headed north out of town. The ADT does not go in a straight line, coast to coast. After Elizabethtown, the Northern Route spends a lot of time heading mostly north. As I walked along, I saw farmers out disking and fertilizing their fields. The farther north and west I went, the bigger the farms and the farther apart the farmhouses. Out of town a few miles, I talked to a farmer refilling his fertilizer tanks.

"You have a lot of gear there. What are you doing, walking to California?"

"No, I'm only going to the Mississippi."

"Are you kidding me!?!"

"Nope."

Then I explained that the road was part of the American Discovery Trail, which nobody ever heard of. I enjoyed conversations like this, telling people about the trail, about long-distance hiking, letting them know such things were possible.

I stopped a little early to get water and use a farmer's restroom. As we chatted, the farmer said I could tent on his land across the street. Stopping early, I enjoyed the late-afternoon sun shining on my tent as I rested inside.

In my first book, *Old Lady on the Trail*, I talked about being an aging hiker. Although that is not the underlying theme in this book, it still is true that I am an older hiker. Mornings often found me stiff and sore, and that was not necessarily caused by hiking. A score of pelvic tilts and curls to get the back loosened up were sometimes necessary at home in my own bed. Still, I seemed to get ahead of my schedule, walking twelve-to-fifteen miles a day or so. This old lady could still walk.

The next day, I found a porta potty by a house under construction, which took care of morning elimination needs. I took advantage of such possibilities wherever I found them. I walked, ate and eliminated. And along the way I saw what I could see.

I have always wanted to see what was around the next bend in the trail. It has often made me go farther than I should. But really, what is around that next bend? How can you know without going there?

I am not really a *sensing* person, in Meyers-Briggs terms. (Meyers Briggs Personality Inventory is a psych preference test, which I have found helpful for myself and others.) What that means is I often don't really see/notice details. I am much more the intuitive, focused on what is about to be, rather than on the here and now. I like walking around the next bend to see what might be there.

But hiking does bring out my sensing side, and I then I SEE things. So, what did I notice?

The flash of red on blackbirds wings, the sparkling blue of the lake past the reeds on the bank, fishermen in red jackets out for a morning catch, the red of their jackets a nice contrast to the blue of the water. I saw a large metal turtle in someone's yard, made of cast-off metal parts. I saw seemingly endless fields of corn stubble being disked into fields of good dark earth ready for planting, and the peaceful Tippecanoe River flowing under a bridge, its grassy banks bright as sparkling emeralds.

I heard things, too. As I had my lunch, after asking permission, in the shade of a line of firs in a gentleman's yard, I heard the cooing of mourning doves. They reminded me of the cuckoos in Spain. Their mournful coo seemed even the same tone as the second note of the cuckoos I'd heard on the Camino de Santiago.

I saw a building at the corner I was approaching. I saw cars were parking there as I came closer, and I wondered if it was a restaurant. Nope. A doctor's office. Hey, doctors' offices have nice restrooms. That elimination subject again. I thanked them profusely for the nice restroom and the ice-cold drinking fountain too.

In my youth many, many years ago, I learned how

to walk on roads: Walk on the left on the edge facing the traffic coming toward you. If cars don't give you space, step off the road. This is sometimes more easily said than done. I operate on the general principle that no one really *wants* to hit me. It would ruin their day, as well as mine. But I kept alert with my eyes open when I was on roads. It is also true that no one wants to *preserve* me as much as I do. Walking roads does not frighten me, but it would not be good for my mind to wander too much when I'm out there on the roads.

A PREGNANT CAMEL

When I reached the State Park, I asked about camping there, but I wasn't excited about paying for full hookups at a campground a mile off trail. The ranger lady did not appear to be in the least bit interested in accommodating a backpacker, who only needed a place for a tent. I used the restroom, got water, and moved on, to the surprise of that woman ranger who exclaimed, "But where will you stay?"

Good question. About a mile farther, on busy Highway 35, houses were set back from the highway. By one long driveway I saw some pens with interesting animals and thought that might be a good place to stay. Two young girls up the driveway escorted me to a house where *Aunt Glenda* gave me permission to put up my tent.

Four or five young children watched me, entranced that I had a tent, and that I was camping on the way to the Mississippi. This was my most unique stop. I was added to the menagerie of Z-donks (a cross between zebras and donkeys), horses, Shetland ponies, a kangaroo, two camels (one pregnant), assorted fancy chickens, a little pot-belly piglet, cats and dogs, llamas and Guinea fowl.

The pregnant camel

Most of the animals were in pens. I shared a pasture with the Guinea fowl, a stone's throw from the pregnant camel. The owner, who was in some other town checking out more possible animal additions, wanted to have a petting zoo to raise money for handicapped children. I did not pet any, but thought it cool to be part of the menagerie for a night.

CONNECTIONS

May was a lot warmer than April. Instead of wearing gloves and a headband over my hat to keep my ears warm, I was in short sleeves, and as soon as I hit the bike trail it was shorts and sports bra. I missed the colder weather.

But before I reached the turnoff on the Monterey/Erie bike trail, there was a gas station and well-stocked convenience store. I stopped for the restroom.

Two gents, slightly older than me, were drinking their coffee in the C-store. We chatted as I downed an orange juice. The young lady behind the counter heard I was walking to the Mississippi River, and she wanted to give me two nice big cured sausage sticks, sort of like Slim Jims, only much bigger and better, made at their own deli. I talked her down to one. And she cut it into six nice four-to-five-inch chunks.

I thought I would eat the sausage sticks for a couple of lunches. Nope. A mile down the bike trail I stopped and ate the whole thing along with my trail bars for my mid-morning snack. They were delicious. I could not stop eating them until they were all gone. They were the best tasting sausage sticks I ever ate.

Not too far along the trail, a young woman cyclist came by. I stopped her and asked if she would put sunscreen on the back of my shoulders where I could not reach. We chatted a bit, then went on with our different modes of transportation—bicycle and feet.

About 2:00, I stopped for water. There was no answer at the first house. At first, I thought the second house also had no answer to my knock, but as I walked away, a woman came around the corner of the house and asked if I needed something. "Yes, please. Water?"

"No problem. Do you need to use the restroom, too?"

How nice when someone meets my need before I can even ask.

Another mile or so farther, looking down the bush-bracketed tunnel of the trail, I saw a car and a guy picking up some trash along the trail. When I reached him, he said, "I've been waiting for you."

"Really?" I answered, wondering how he knew I would be coming in this state where the only people I knew before getting there were Marc and Karen way back in Muncie.

The young woman who had helped me with sunscreen was his niece, Morgan. Bruce was in charge of caring for the North Judson section of trail and interviewed me for their club newsletter. He also gave me a nice cold bottle of water. Bruce and I had a long chat while sitting in some shade.

Another quarter mile along, another cyclist, Susie, asked if I was the long-distance walker. She had been talking with Bruce, and she wanted my picture for their newsletter. Well, OK. That was fun. I laughed to think I was getting famous, a joke.

Not quite so much fun was the long, hot slog the rest of the way to North Judson. After arriving there, I found that, though the T-by-T said North Judson had meals and groceries, my waypoints were quickly taking me out of town. I spied a building the next block over that had, GROCERY printed on the wall, so I went there, but they were changing ownership and not open.

There was a person there, though, and he told me where food could be found, only three blocks off the trail. On the way to the food source, I turned the corner at the Fingerhut Bakery, noticing the name was my interviewer, Bruce's, last name. As I walked on a block farther to the Subway, a young man from the bakery chased me down. Morgan had told him about me, and he handed me a bag of donuts. How surprised I was!

All those interconnections happened just because I asked for help with sunscreen. Overflowing blessings came to me.

After eating at Subway, with my free donuts for

dessert, I looked for a house with space to camp. I asked at the most likely looking place and was told the police didn't like him and would object if someone tented in his yard. He referred me to the Railroad Museum.

There were no other likely looking spots, and the trail was about to take me directly out of town. The sun was setting, and I needed a place to be. Bruce also had suggested I ask at the Railroad Museum, but I had been intent on finding food. By the time I was through eating, the museum was closed, so I could not ask for permission. I set up anyway in the large grassy lot near the museum porta potty and hoped the police wouldn't roust me.

What a great day it had been—free sausages to eat, multiple human connections, an interview and a photo, a bag of free donuts, and a porta potty a few steps away from my tent. Life was good.

What Makes News?

On the following sixteen-mile day, the wind kicked up at about 11:00. I wanted a place out of the wind for lunch, and I needed water. An older gentleman at the place I chose to knock had what I always think of as a sailor's beard. He gave me water and let me collapse on his grass to eat, sheltered by his house.

Then he came over to chat, saying he was an Oregon boy transplanted to Indiana. We talked about life and trails. He used to work for the Forest Service in Oregon, and then worked in construction, but broke his back so he couldn't get around too well anymore. He had just picked some beautiful asparagus and offered to give me some, but, alas, I had no way to cook them. This was a rare time I regretted being stoveless. I should have taken some to eat raw. (I take no stove with me to save pack weight, no stove, no pot, no fuel. I just eat cold food I fix myself when I do not find a store, restaurant, or source of convenience food.)

At sixteen miles for the day, I started eyeing houses, hoping for one with an outbuilding to stay in, since it was supposed to rain. Seeing folks digging in front of a nice home with numerous outbuildings, I stopped to chat and ask about staying. The result was a home for the night in a large, sparkling clean tool shed—more like a tool garage. I had use of a restroom in the house and took a sink bath. I even washed my hair, and washed most of what I wear, hanging my laundry on their backyard line where it dried quickly in the wind.

Jean and Larry invited me for dinner and conversation when they were finished digging in the front yard. I had already eaten by then, but found room for more, including a slice of delicious nut bread. The repeated hospitality from strangers on this trail astounded me.

Conversation that night turned to their wonderment that I was walking the ADT alone and their fears for me. I said that I had been greeted nearly everywhere with hospitality and kindness. "But we see on the news every night that people are murdered in Chicago," they cried.

I answered, "But all I have met have been wonderful people."

In the following days, I pondered that conversation. I considered the question: What makes news news? What makes something newsworthy?

The usual answer is that violence and sex make the news instead of anything good. But I don't think that is really the answer. *I* was at least a little newsworthy. At least I was interviewed by a reporter of a small newspaper a few days before and then again for a newsletter, and I had not done anything violent or sexy. That reporter did ask what was scary and how I protected myself on the trail. And he did seem disappointed with my answers, perhaps because I had no tales of fear or danger.

As I have pondered the question over trail miles and years, I have concluded that what makes something or someone newsworthy, is not violence and sex; it is that the person, the experience, or something in the universe, is something unusual. It is not usual for a person to walk across the United States. It is not typical for someone in their mid-to-late seventies to hike long-distance trails solo. It is also not usual for people to kill each other.

As we listen to the news, we find that, yes, violence does happen. So do earthquakes, hurricanes, tornados, blizzards, and all manner of tragedies. But, the vast majority of people do not commit violent acts, and, mostly, our lives are more uneventful than tragic or uncommon. Mostly, our lives do not make the news. The unusual makes the news. The usual, on the trail and in life, is meeting wonderful people. The *unusual* is being threatened by people.

An assumption that contributes to our fears is to think that unusual news events are typical, usual, to-be-expected experiences. We fear that people we do not know will harm us. Probably humans have always feared that unusual experiences or unknown people would cause harm.

I suppose that thought is somewhat like fearing the bears in the wilderness, though statistically, hikers are in far more danger driving in a car than walking on a trail. Bears *can* be dangerous but are not *likely* to be dangerous if we learn about them and act and react appropriately. People *can* be dangerous, though most are not.

The media regularly brings the unusual into our lives, which reinforces our fears. We make the mental leap of assuming that what is on the news is common rather than unusual. I like watching or reading the news. At home, I read my newspaper every day, even though the news can be overwhelming. But I keep in my head that the unusual is reported far more than the commonplace. Reporters look for the unusual, the atypical. That is what makes it news.

On the ADT, I have, time after time, met wonderful people who shared hospitably with a stranger. Could I have had a different experience? Of course. But my usual experience on this trail has been so overwhelmingly positive that meeting the people along the way has become the charm of the trail.

My ADT experiences have taught me that my fallback position need not be fear, rather interest in whom or what I will meet next: from camping next to a house of modest means that sheltered me from wind, to tenting near a pregnant camel, from encountering people who may at first somewhat skeptically let me drip on their clean garage floor as I eat lunch, to those who invite me for dinner and a long conversation. All have been wonderful people, whom it has been my privilege to meet.

That night the rain was deafening on the metal roof of the tool shed, but I was thankful to be dry. In the morning, I packed up and started out with raingear and umbrella, and shortly, a very strong wind forced the umbrella around my face. Wind is not convenient for umbrellas. I held the leading edge with one hand to keep it off my face. A little later on, I made a few clothing adjustments in someone's open barn, displacing the ducks and chickens for a few minutes.

While still in raingear, I tried for a house with a restroom but got two turndowns. I found a more deserted area to take care of that issue a mile farther. Not everyone invites me in at my request.

At lunchtime, the weather was still unsettled, and I wondered if anyone would let me eat on a covered porch. Yes! Beth and her daughter Ashley were outside sorting things for a yard sale and raising money to send Ashley to camp. The year before, they told me, Ashley made a hundred dollars for camp by potting up and selling the volunteer petunias that came up in their front yard. I was impressed by the budding entrepreneur. I should have given her a donation, but to tell the truth, I didn't think of it. I self-centeredly only thought of eating my lunch and chatting.

Later on, I reflected on the turndowns I had received earlier when needing a restroom, contrasted with Beth's warm welcome. I also pondered the culture of fear in which we live. The turndowns were from elderly people in nice houses. Many elderly people feel more vulnerable to strangers as they age. I get that. And that goes a long way toward explaining those turndowns.

But Beth, and many others, while welcoming me, expressed fear that I would come to harm, and amazement when I said I have had no problems. They expected there to be problems. They'd watched the news, and problems make the news. Fear has become embedded in our culture.

When I chat, I am able to give an example of opting out of the culture of fear. I have come to realize that is not an inconsiderable gift, but one of import and consequence, because it makes others think about their own assumptions about fear.

I was again getting ahead of schedule. There was plenty of daylight left when I stopped at 5:00. Daylight was not the limiting factor. My feet were. Pavement is really hard on the feet. My left heel felt like it was trying to develop a compression blister under the callous where it couldn't be seen, although I could surely feel it.

Shortly before the turn on Colorado Street, I saw a farm with large outbuildings. It was supposed to rain in the night again, and I was not eager to pack up in the morning with a tent heavy with wetness. A farm with outbuildings was a good place to try for a stop. My stop the night before with Larry and Jean was different from this stop's outbuildings. Larry was a truck driver who lived in the country. Eagle Rock Farm was a *working* farm. In this outbuilding, I spread my gear in a swept corner near tractors, shop, and office, amid all the dirt that accompanies real farm work. I arrayed my large plastic garbage bag on the floor to help protect my gear, especially my sleeping bag, from unsweepable farm grunge.

Jerry and Susie of Eagle Rock Farm were wonderful folks, rich in family. Most of the extended family were present that night, along with some Ugandan kids who were part of a six-month singing-and-dancing tour from Presbyterian Church Missions. There must have been thirteen-to-fourteen people around the table and in the kitchen, love abounding. They invited me to eat pizza and rhubarb cake with them—my second dinner. Lucky me. They regretted that all their indoor beds were already filled with visitors, but my needs were filled, and they shared joy, love, and hospitality with me. It was all good. Susie even found a needle and thread to mend something that had torn. I no longer remember what was mended, but I do remember Susie scurrying around to find the needle and thread.

Jerry and Susie at Eagle Rock Farm with their family and kids from Uganda

The next day was very foggy. There were no grand views over the fields. Sitting on my pack in a vacant country driveway for my mid-morning trail bar, I watched tendrils of fog chasing through corn stubble past the woods. The rest of the morning, it rained. It was still quite warm, so umbrella and pack cover were all the protection I desired.

The route went through neighborhoods and subdivisions, suburbia. My eyes searched for houses with porches on which to eat my lunch protected from the rain. Then I spied one.

"Sure," the woman said. "You could use the porch. And don't you need to use a restroom?"

"YES."

I had a dry spot for lunch and a rest until the woman came back from taking her child somewhere. I filled my water bottle, and we chatted a bit. She had Lutheran background, and they had been considering finding a church since moving to Crown Point from Tennessee. I suggested they try the ELCA church outside of town. I had discovered it while planning the hike, but it was too far off trail to help me. Maybe it would be good for them.

We chatted a bit about trails and churches, and then I moved on. At the center of Crown Point, I stopped at a very good Mexican Restaurant across from the old court house and chatted with a family at an adjoining table. They gave me tips about the area ahead. Since I had no real idea or knowledge of areas other than my turn-by-turn directions, I appreciated local knowledge, not that I always followed such advice.

BELOW CHICAGO

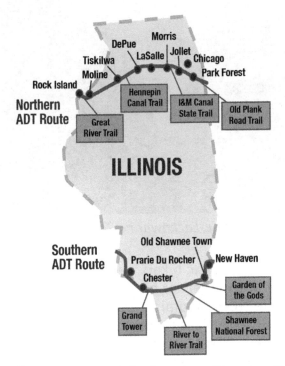

Illinois portion of the American Discovery Trail

After I left the restaurant, I moseyed over to the start of the Erie-Lackawanna Trail—another bike trail. I was rested, and the trail was inviting, so I started walking, even though no one I had talked to knew of good places to stop, and this close to Chicago, it was illegal to camp. Signs proclaimed patrols would be looking for violators of curfew after dark.

Mary E. Davison

Erie-Lackawanna Trail

Joggers, walkers, and bikers were out enjoying the trail, one of the prettier bike trails I had been on, with apple trees blooming, purple lilacs perfuming the air, and pleasing curves winding through well-tended, bright-green grass. I chatted with a runner. Like the family at the restaurant, he was concerned about me finding a place to camp not too far ahead. But then, everyone was always concerned about my walking alone, and I just kept walking, seduced by the smells and sights of the lovely, warm, late afternoon.

The houses petered out, and the trail went on. At the road crossing I had in mind to stop at, just as local knowledge had said, there were no houses. So, I kept on. Another biker told me there was a neighborhood in two more miles. But it was more like three. The sun was getting lower and lower.

I was getting concerned that I would be stuck on the trail and arrested for illegal walking. Who would let me tent in their yard if I knocked on a door after dark?

I finally found a break in the trees lining the trail, with a little walkway to some houses, mostly duplexes. The first door I tried was a guy under house arrest, who thought the cops would not like anyone tenting there.

I skipped a door, and on the next try, I found Kori and Ron.

"Sure," Kori said, after checking my driver's license to see that I was who I said I was. "You're from Washington? I think we can do better than a place for your tent. Go around to the back."

Kori and Ron

In the back was Ron, who had built an elaborate *guy deck* (similar to a man cave) with a roof. The deck was enclosed with plastic to keep the wind from Lake Michigan from penetrating. There was a bar, a flat screen TV with a hockey game on, twinkling colored Christmas lights strung under the roof, and a raised metal firepit he was just lighting.

I camped on the deck while they ate at the bar. And we all had a very good time talking trails and life and gardening while enjoying the fire. We talked way after hiker midnight. (Hiker midnight is whenever it is dark.) They eventually went inside, probably earlier than they would have done without me there, and I snuggled into my bag to sleep by the glowing embers of the fire.

When I woke, I found a nice note from Kori along with the gift of a pretty butterfly stick pin that had been her grandmother's. In our conversation the night before, she had said how much her Gramma would have liked the idea of walking across America. I was honored to be given the pin, and I put it in a strap on my pack. Now there was no question that the pack looked feminine. And I remembered Kori and her Gramma every time I looked at it.

That day, the main attractions on the bike trail and neighborhood streets were the crabapple trees and lilacs filling the air with fragrance and the eye with color. I was very glad I had walked extra miles a few days before, so I had a short day. Before 2:00, I checked in to an upscale hotel right

on the trail (the only one even near the trail).
I had booked this expensive hotel more than a
month ago, as I was nervous about finding places
to tent near Chicago. It was fun to walk into such
a place with a backpack and hiker stink, go up to
the front desk, and announce I had a reservation.
I loved the incongruity of that scene.

My shower was wonderful and very needed. I
couldn't even stay upright after that, though it
was only mid-afternoon. Bed won. My feet were
not willing to stand a minute more, and I crashed
for nearly two hours before moving again. I
hoped my body would recover with extra rest. It
would be a long day to reach the next motel and
a much-needed day off, which would be coming
but had not quite yet arrived.

I had booked a lucky day. Every Wednesday they
had a free dinner/social time for the guests. The
casserole, salad, and cake were delicious. I topped
it off with a hospitality chocolate-chip cookie
warmed in the microwave in my room. And there
was breakfast at 6:00 the following morning. Nice.
The free meals took away my angst about spending on such a pricey hotel while backpacking.

After a good breakfast, I started early for my
eighteen-and-a-half-mile day, my longest of the
trip. The trail was a mix of bike trails and walking
through an assortment of neighborhoods—Lan-
sing, Glenwood, Chicago Heights, Olympia Fields,
Park Forest, and Matteson. I was amazed to find
wooded bike trails so near Chicago. Again, crabapple trees and lilacs added their beauty to trails,

yards, and streets. In an open woods in Glenwood, there was a great display of spring beauties spread like snow beneath the trees.

I found a hodgepodge of comfort stations and commercial establishments to take care of nature's needs. One of these stops was a paint store, and Holly, the salesperson, was very kind and gave me her card with her number to call, just in case I got in trouble.

The afternoon was quite hot, 85 degrees, and the trail took its toll on my feet. I stopped at a gas station for nachos and chocolate milk, perched on stacks of soda cases feeling like a derelict, a stark contrast to the swank hotel the night before.

The hike from the gas station to the Old Plank Trail was tiring and long. Or maybe I was just done. With relief, I reached my motel.

On my rest day, I sat in bed watching TV, doing email, and talking on the phone with my son and daughter. I took two showers and treated a blister on the bottom of my heel, hoping it would heal, and I carved a hole in my shoe insert to give the blister space.

The next day, I started out with much trepidation about my heel. The start of the day was foggy, drizzly, and misty, but the trail was lovely. Lots of greenery and many wildflowers. The bushes flowered white-and-pink honeysuckle. Wild blue phlox bloomed, sometimes in abundance. Marsh marigold and lily of the valley made appearances and May apples shyly peaked out from under their umbrella-like leaves to cheer my walk.

The trail was well used in this area, and I talked with several people. I received two invitations to stay the night, but I already had a stay planned with Sue, a friend of a friend at my church back in Washington.

One bicyclist was very excited to learn I was hiking on a trail. He had thought about doing the AT. Bruce pedaled hard to catch me later, just before Frankfort. He invited me to Mother's Day Sunday Brunch to meet his extended family. I took his number. I wasn't sure what I was doing on Mother's Day until I talked with Sue.

My heel felt a bit better the last few miles, I didn't know why. But I was happy to get off my feet when I met Sue at 3:00. We chatted quite a while and worked out the next day's schedule for Mother's Day. I called Bruce and said I could go to his brunch if he could pick me up at Sue's house and later take me back to the trail, so I could slackpack that afternoon into Joliet.

Sue would pick me up in Joliet and afterward pick up my friend RockStar from the train station. My hike was about to change from a solo hike to hiking with RockStar across the rest of Illinois. Logistics on a long hike are sometimes convoluted and complex, especially with spontaneous additions, but I thought it would be fun to accept Bruce's Mother's Day invitation.

Mother's Day was memorable. I ate all morning, in two places. In the afternoon, I walked an 8-mile slackpack by 4:00, met up with my friend, RockStar and had a social evening. The ADT is very different from a wilderness trail.

Rich, Sue's husband, cooked breakfast, and he and Sue and I had a good time getting to know each other. Then Bruce picked me up to go to Mother's Day brunch.

Bruce had a very large extended family. Tables were set up in the barn. There must have been thirty-to-forty people of all ages, from a two-month-old baby to aged folks like me. Two guys cooked eggs/omelets to order, pancakes, and hash browns. There was also fresh fruit, drinks, ham, bacon, sausage, cinnamon rolls and several other extra dishes. Yep, I ate all morning.

I also talked about hiking. The guys in the family usually backpacked in Wyoming in the summer—with heavy packs. I answered lots of questions, primarily, but not exclusively, from the women. "Where did you start? Why do you hike? Where do you stay at night? How do you find restrooms? Food? Do you take donations?" (That was a first.) "Do you carry a gun? Why not? Aren't you ever afraid?"

One guy was sure everyone should carry a gun. When I explained I refused to let my life be ruled by fear and I had met wonderful people, he countered with, "Fear has nothing to do with it. It's a matter of survival. I have a gun, and I'm not afraid of anyone."

"Then why have a gun? You carry a gun because you are afraid without it."

The look on his face told me he didn't like that, so I changed the subject before we were in an argument, and we talked about something else. One of the ladies came up to me and thanked me for what I had said about fear and guns.

Fear was such a recurring theme on this hike.

Bruce proudly showed me the caboose in the back yard. It was a genuine caboose mounted on a small section of track, bracketed by railroad crossing signs and lights. It looked as good as or better than the exhibits I had seen at Sweetser Switch or North Judson. His dad had worked the railroads, and the caboose was a monument/memorial for his dad, filled with memorabilia. He told me a long story about how they had acquired the caboose and moved it to his farm. I meet such interesting people on the ADT. They all have such interesting stories.

Caboose memorial for Bruce's father

Bruce then took me to the trail at Spencer Road, where I had stopped the day before when Sue picked me up. I started walking beside wet greenery on paved trail, church bells ringing me on my way. Thankfully, my blistered foot seemed to do better.

I reached Harrah's in Joliet and called Sue. Rock-Star called me to say she had arrived and tell me her location. Eventually we all connected, and Sue drove us back to her home where we ate dinner and visited. It had been a very social day.

Our Hike—I & M Canal

My hike became our hike as RockStar joined me for two weeks. Hiking alone has its advantages. Hiking with someone has its advantages. Both are good. They are different.

RockStar on the bridge in Joliet

We started out in rain and wind and had a rocky time the first couple blocks, trying to get over the bridge in that strong wind. RockStar was trying to get settled in for hiking. Her umbrella blew inside out. As she tried to fix it, her just-purchased water bottle flipped loose from her pack and pitched over the side of the bridge (but not into the river). I walked the long way around the end of the bridge and retrieved her water bottle as she fixed her umbrella. We did get over the bridge, turned down Bluff, and were out of the wind.

We enjoyed interpretive displays about Joliet, Limestone, and the history of those towns. Ethnic groups that settled in Joliet included Irish, Serbs, Slovenians, Germans, and Croatians. Different ethnic groups that settled in America first settled in defined areas of the country.

Walking across the country illuminated the multiplicity of our roots as a nation and the sectionality of those initial settlements in detail I had never realized in that way before. Our stew pot has been stirred over the years as people have moved great distances back and forth across the country, added to and stirred again up to the present day. My assumptions of that mix were not exactly challenged, but enhanced by new understandings from the details gleaned from historical markers along the way and the people of diverse ethnicities I met over the years 2015-to-2019 that I walked on the ADT.

When I was a child and realized people came in different colors and from different countries' heritages, I became curious about my own ethnic heritage. I wanted to be from as many different ethnicities and countries as possible, so I could say I was Heinz 57 varieties.

I was entranced with the whole world of people.

I remember being very disappointed when my mother said I was probably just from English, Irish, and German lineage. That seemed humdrum and boring in contrast to my fantasy of a mix of an exotic blend of nationalities and races. I talked my mother into agreeing that perhaps I had some French in me, too. I wanted more. Couldn't I be Scottish, too? Or Welch? Who knows?

Maybe someone came across the channel to England in my line a century or more before or maybe there was a Viking raid or an influx from some farther shore. My maiden surname is from a town on the German/Polish border. I could claim either German or Polish background, depending on the year and where that border lay. Was that a childhood fantasy to be related to the whole wide world? Or reality? Who really knows? I suppose it depends on how far back I could look.

America, though, in the present, has an amazing mix of people from many backgrounds, nations, and races from all around the globe. Sometimes I met people and learned their heritage, or guessed at it, and sometimes I read about early settlers from different lands on towns' interpretive signs. All were interesting to me.

RockStar and I trudged up a hill and found a restroom in a small park. A few more steps and we were on the I & M Canal Trail, which would take us halfway across the state.

It was a very pleasant walk, a green tunnel next to the canal. Sometimes the Des Plaines River was visible on the other side of the canal towpath, water on both sides of the path we walked. We chattered as we walked. It was a pleasant change to have someone to talk to, and I enjoyed hiking again with RockStar, my semi-regular hiking companion since hiking on the CDT in 2013. I had first met her in 2008 on the PCT in California.

Flora and fauna entertained us. We saw many goose families—mom, dad and baby goslings, three-to-four herons, a great egret, lots of red-winged blackbirds, three-to-four furry little animals (disappearing so quickly we could not identify them), one deer, one turtle, and one bunny. There were quite a lot of wild blue phlox and a scattering of other flowers.

At the highway in Channahon, we ate dinner at a Subway and took a nice long break. Just a little farther on we found a campground, mostly deserted. No one was there to take our money, but we set up our tents anyway.

The hot, wet weather below Chicago changed to cold and windy. We wore our warm layers and rain gear. But walking along the I & M Canal was interesting, even if cold. The Des Plaines River on one side of the towpath later merged with the Kankakee River to become the Illinois River.

Our path the next day was a pleasant long green tunnel with lots of flowers - wild blue phlox, violets, garlic mustard, and large sections of red columbine. We saw LOTS of feathered wildlife—at least half a dozen herons, more than eight great egrets, and many turkey vultures. 30-40 cute turtles covered the surface of logs but dove off into the canal when we came closer. Now you see them, now you don't.

Numerous families of geese were seen, different mating pairs defending their territories and families of goslings. The geese honked and squabbled at each other, long necks and aggressive head bobbing expressing their intent to claim their ground and protect their progeny.

It was much easier to answer nature's call on the canal trail than on Indiana roads and bike trails, but we stayed on the trail, as there were tons of poison-ivy plants encroaching the sides of the trail. I pointed them out to RockStar, a Westerner, who was unfamiliar with their identification.

Although it was a lovely day, fourteen-to-fifteen miles was still fourteen-to-fifteen miles, a lot for RockStar just starting out and plenty for my poor left foot, which was trying for another blister. It was getting hard to find non-blistered space on my heel.

When RockStar discovered a motel in Morris, we went for it. That added a mile or so for the day and a mile and a half onto the next day. The motel did not get rave reviews, but we were clean and had beds. We also had dinner at a Dairy Queen.

Sunset from our motel

In the morning, we tried the McDonald's for breakfast. It wasn't a country convenience store, but it did have a large table filled with coffee-club members, this one of mixed genders. They asked us many questions about hiking, and we had fun talking with them.

The weather was warmer than the day before, but the canal disappeared, first into swampy water, and then gone altogether. We missed the egrets and herons. We did see mosquitoes, gnats, a snake, a deer, a bunny, and many squirrels.

At Seneca, we found dinner at Fergie's. "Best burgers in town," the sign said, and we agreed they were very good. We talked to a few folks, who noted our packs. Interestingly, I did not hear much in the way of comments about the possible dangers of hiking after I started hiking with Rock-Star. People seemed genuinely interested and impressed, but not frightened for us. Of course, I was not alone then. But I did make a point of saying that I had come from Ohio alone before meeting RockStar. I don't pass up many opportunities to brag a bit.

After dinner, we asked at the first house past the convenience store if we could set up our tents. I had told RockStar how I asked for a place to tent. She made me go to the door, *since I was experienced.*

An elderly couple named Elaine and Barney were happy to share their yard with us for the night, and Elaine came outside to talk to us as we set up our tents. She was very sweet. She had eleven children, all long grown by now, and she had been a Girl Scout and Girl Scout leader. She knew all about camping and thought our trip sounded wonderful. They offered help with anything we might need.

We were camped right behind the convenience store, which was quite convenient indeed. Restrooms. Breakfast. Perfect. Bright lights that were on all night, quite bright enough to read by, not so perfect. I had to use my eye mask to get any sleep. Still, it was nice to be near the restroom.

The next day we saw a million or so mosquitoes. Up until the day before I had probably seen ten mosquitoes. That day, we each had our own personal cloud following us, and if they were dispersed, they would quickly be replaced, the cloud reconstituted.

That spring had been exceptionally wet and rainy, according to the locals. I had seen swamps and standing water beside most of the trails in Indiana and Illinois. That day we had water over the trail in two sections—one at least three city blocks in length. We had no choice but to wade through, water up halfway between ankles and knees. I hoped we wouldn't repeat that. Although my feet liked their cold bath.

When we arrived in Ottawa, there was a cheap motel right on the trail that I had missed seeing in my planning. It was too hard to walk past a motel. The temptation of beds was too great. We stopped there. It rained all night, and we were glad we had avoided wet tents.

We never made it to the square in Ottawa, site of the Lincoln-Douglas Debates, the most important event in Ottawa's history. An interpretive sign did tell us that the sand in Ottawa was the finest in the world, used for high-quality glass and windshields. The ADT acquainted me with stray facts I would never have known if I had not walked on that trail.

We stopped at Buffalo Rock, at a picnic table for our snack. Then we saw *trail closed* signs. The notice said that floods in 2013 had wiped out the trail, and conservation Rangers were going to be patrolling and handing out fines to anyone on the closed trail. Bummer.

We were tempted to walk there anyway since we knew Boston and Cubby had gotten through in 2012. But the floods signed for were in 2013; we were afraid this washout might have been worse, and we didn't want to find that out after walking four more miles, needing to retrace our steps, so we were law abiding and walked the road for five-and-a-half miles.

The road took us beside the Illinois River. We saw geese in the private-gun-club fields as our reward for being good, but on the road, we got very tired of needing to step on and off the pavement to avoid speeding cars.

We finally reached Highway 178 and turned up to Utica. There was a cupcake shop with a picnic bench in front, a good place for lunch plus a cupcake each for dessert. Utica was a cute touristy town, at least on the south end as one came in from Starved Rock or our road walk.

I was sad that the detour meant I never saw Starved Rock State Park, as pictures I have seen since then are lovely. I learned on the national scenic trails that it is not uncommon for hikers on the same trail in different years to see different sights. Weather, from floods to forest fires, require detours that differ from year to year. The same is true for the American Discovery Trail.

Coming into LaSalle, we met Dave, an 88-year-old gentleman out for his walk on the towpath. He turned around and walked with us and told us tales of serving in World War II, recent hiking trips in Illinois, trips to Lake Havasu, and visiting his children in different states.

When we reached LaSalle, we found a major error in the T-by-T. The route from the towpath to town, although clearly marked with ADT stickers, was completely blocked off with newly built chain link fence, allowing no admittance.

Dave, by this time, was feeling responsible for us and quite insistent on helping us, so he drove us over the bridge to the visitor information building. Never before have I been so welcomed into a commercial establishment. Ariel greeted us with open arms; she and Dave and another customer started conversing about finding us lodging, as well as getting us back to the trail in the morning. Dave was still shepherding us and unwilling to leave until it was all worked out. So, Dave gave us a ride a mile and a half to a reasonably priced motel and promised to bring us back in the morning. Amazing.

We had dinner at a restaurant across from the motel. We were being spoiled with lodging and places to buy food. We enjoyed the luxuries, and I was amazed at how things just seem to work out.

Wonderful people were everywhere. Why were so many people in the world afraid of other people? Or afraid for me? Or think I should be afraid? Why should I be afraid? Wonderful people truly were the norm.

Dave showed up bright and early to take us back to First Street. As we walked, we saw a little tugboat on the river turning around a huge barge, fascinating to two western women who didn't usually see such things.

In search of a restroom, we found Water Street Irish Pub. At that hour, it was not yet open for business, but a gentleman in the doorway told us to go right on in to use the restroom. We admired lots of nifty Irish stuff in the pub. Built in the 1830s, when this spot was as far up the Illinois River as could be navigated by boat or barge, the building was constructed before the canal. Goods were then taken overland to Chicago.

After the canal was built, the town nearly folded, and the buildings stood empty for fifty-to-a-hundred years. Life was now changing with the addition of pubs and eateries in those old buildings.

Winding up through Peru to Highway 6, we *had* to stop when we saw a donut shop. RockStar had a hot cinnamon roll just out of the oven, and I had lemon bread pudding just because I had never *had lemon* bread pudding before. Yum! We ate our way across the miles of the first half of Illinois, as towns and restaurants, fast-food and donut shops were plentiful. This was no food desert.

Highway 6 was pretty busy, but there was a wide shoulder for walking, so it was not too dangerous. While walking past open fields between towns, we felt a few sprinkles. We hurried then and ducked under an awning at a custom motorcycle shop that just happened to have benches.

Turned out, we'd found shelter just as the thunderstorm hit and poured buckets. We waited it out and visited the restroom. We *always* appreciated finding restrooms. That stop yielded one of the cleanest restrooms ever. The whole shop was sparkling clean, not something I would have expected in a motorcycle shop.

At the post office, we retrieved the re-supply boxes we had mailed to ourselves, sorted the contents, and loaded up our packs. As we were walking down the street, the guy from the Irish Pub in Peru drove by and honked at us. We loved the small-town flavor of middle America with towns neighboring other towns, the people neighbors to one another and to us. We found another neat little Irish pub for lunch. It had the best bacon-lettuce-and-tomato sandwich ever, as well as chicken-dumpling soup. We did enjoy eating.

After a trip to the grocery store to stock up for our zero day, we took a taxi to the nearest motel, which was in the middle of nowhere and surrounded by fields of corn stubble. Cleaning clothes, taking showers, and having naps filled the rest of the day. We were really roughing it. We roughed it even more the next day, staying in our motel room.

I usually planned rest days every five-to-seven days. My hike plan called for shorter days in Illinois. My friend, RockStar, liked shorter days. She also wasn't too keen on knocking on doors to find tent spots, and for this section, it wasn't even very necessary to rap on a door as we found more motels as we hiked than I had known about when I'd planned the hike. Not every hiker would take advantage of such. RockStar liked the finer things in life—beds, showers, and restaurants. And when the opportunity presented itself, I was not averse to them.

After our rest day, we taxied (what decadence for a hike) back to Spring Valley, where we had left off. Walking again and passing a Casey's convenience store, we decided on another restroom break and discovered another old boys' coffee club. We, of course, had to tell them what we were doing. They were impressed. It was easy to impress most of the people we met. Hikers, especially older female hikers, were neither found in these parts nor expected to do such things. I usually told them about thru hikers who do so much more than we do. That was even more beyond nonhikers' imagination.

It was a pleasant morning walk along the road next to the railroad tracks, with honeysuckle lining the sides of the route. We saw blooming primroses (the real rose bush kind, not the low-growing flowers sold in pots each spring in Washington) and a scattering of other flowers. We started noticing a tree with fragrant clusters of pea-like flowers. Locals told us they were catalpa trees, often considered a weed tree. We loved their penetrating perfume. In Depue, we had lunch at a Casey's, while we sat on milk crates in the shade behind the store. We frequented what was available, not always sit-down fast food or restaurants.

Going up a hill, we saw a yard with a Penny Farthing (an old-time bicycle with a very big front wheel). The yard also had some whimsical, extra-large, stick figures constructed of long thin logs. There was always something to look at, interesting things not usually seen while in a car.

Unfortunately, RockStar tried to read the T-by-T and walk at the same time, rolled her ankle, and crashed to the ground on the side of the road. She limped onward to rest in the shade of a big silo to eat a snack. Silos give shade as well as shade trees.

We stopped for a lengthy rest and hamburgers at the Ranch House in Bureau Junction. We discovered there was a motel there, too, but they had no vacancy. A gentleman at the bar, Dan, overheard our inquiry and offered his shop building, which had a restroom. He took us to the shop building.

We were indoors, but it was much different from a motel, filled with tools and various pieces of junk, all coated with many layers of dust and grime. But it did have two mattresses in a metal loft. Accommodations on the ADT were varied. We took what was offered and were grateful for the restroom. As we started out the next day from Bureau Junction, we found out there had been a restroom and a place for tents right at the canal. But staying in the shop building was a unique experience.

HENNEPIN CANAL

It was cold the next morning. I needed my rain-coat/windbreaker to start, along with gloves and headband. It stayed cold all morning. Stopping for a break even required my down jacket.

From Bureau Junction, we began walking the Hennepin Canal, which would take us almost to the Mississippi River. The Hennepin was bigger than the I & M Canal, and it was maintained. It had been made with concrete, which was a new thing at the time of its construction. Yet the canal became obsolete for shipping goods even before it was finished. The engineering devised for its building was then used on the Panama Canal. The Hennepin, now, is a long, narrow state park on which we would walk 58 miles.

Hennepin Canal

The highlight of the day was a grand bald eagle we saw in a tree before he flew away from us. We also saw twenty or so herons, several geese, and lots of wonderful birds we nicknamed *acrobat birds* as they darted and soared in aerobatic maneuvers above the splashing water by the waterfalls found at the locks of the canals.

When the sun came out, we also saw turtles. They were shy critters to catch on film. Look, there are ten of them—6-4-2-1-gone.

Ten turtles on a log! Now you see them, now you don't.

The locks, aqueducts, and bridges were interesting, and we camped not far from a lift-style bridge at Lock 21. No, we didn't always stay indoors in motels or work sheds. Nor did we always have short days. That day was just shy of 16 miles, a lot for us.

The next day was shorter, but with a Visitor Center thrown in. RockStar and I both liked Visitor Centers and their interpretive displays. I would not have thought Illinois would be so interesting. But it was.

The woman behind the counter was especially nice. She retrieved bird and flower books to try to answer my questions. The darting acrobat birds we had been seeing were swallows. The yellow pea along the trail was birdsfoot trefoil. The white-to-violet hairy bells I had seen for two weeks were Virginia waterleaf.

I like to be able to identify the flowers. Calling them by name makes them seem like old friends. I was also amazed at the ten-to-twelve different pelts of furry critters that are found along the canal. I had no idea there was such a variety of small wildlife there. We had only identified beaver and seen lots of unidentified furry ends of critters disappearing into canal or greenery along the towpaths, avoiding us.

There was a light but steady rain in the afternoon. The wind also kicked up and felt icy on our skin. We were glad when there were bushes and trees to cut the wind, but some of the canal walk was in the open. We took our breaks that day out of the wind in tunnels as the trail went under roads. We were glad to reach Lock 22 with its designated camping area. We both wished we had brought extra food as the cold weather made us extra hungry. But we had left the areas with towns and restaurants and had only what we had packed with us. That had to do.

Although the first half of the trail in Illinois had many places to eat and sleep, and we had not had to ask for much, there *were* people who helped us in Illinois. Sue and Ron and Bruce as the trail crossed through towns below Chicago, Elaine and Barney in Seneca, Dave near LaSalle, and Dan at Bureau Junction were all in Illinois.

When making my hike plan, I had seen there was a thirty-mile section, which did not go by any houses, towns, or campgrounds, and there was no good place to get safe water to drink. Rock-Star and I are not thirty-mile-a-day hikers. Even though walking beside a canal full of water, it was not water we could safely drink. We knew how to treat water in the wilderness. We could treat bacteria to make water safe. But we could not deal with chemicals in water washed from farm run-off. We did find water at Lock 22, though it was not indicated on our T-by-T. But we needed more along the way.

Shortly before reaching Atkinson Road, we met Richard (81 years old) and his adult daughter, Mary. They were from Geneseo and regularly walked parts of the canal. We chatted a while, and then they went east and we went west. They were to help us a little later on in our journey.

Before that happened, Mark, a friend of RockStar

in years past, solved our immediate water problem by driving all the way from Chillicothe to bring us water at Atkinson Road. There were no doors to knock on for water there, and we surely needed it. We chatted with him a bit and, after he left, we found a place to camp.

After Mark left, but before we had decided on our tent site, Richard and Mary came by again, returning on their way back to their car, a bridge or two farther west. They offered to bring us water at Lock 26. So, our supposed thirty-miles-without-water access completely disappeared, and in its place was campground water we had found at Lock 22, water delivered to us by Mark and then water delivered by Richard and Mary. How cool was that? We didn't die of thirst and had new friends, too.

Back where we stopped at Atkinson Road, the unmowed grass was two-to-three-feet high, which we carefully and methodically stomped down for a place to pitch our tents. Unfortunately, the tall grass was also a home for ticks. After settling into my tent, I found a tick on my leg acquired while knocking back the greenery. Fortunately, he hadn't burrowed deeply and was easy to remove and kill. Our tents had mosquito netting on floor and door. So, unless we brought more ticks or creepy crawlers in with us, we were fine. Just us and some annoying gnats in the tents after I dispatched the tick.

The cold weather turned into hot the next day. Putting on a backpack and walking increases the body's temperature even on a cold day. On a sunny and warm one, with many long, shadeless sections, it seemed brutally hot. We hoisted our umbrellas for shade after only an hour of walking, and we kept them up until afternoon when haze finally obscured the directly beating sun.

And the gnats were fierce. I don't know their use in the greater scheme of creation, but we did not appreciate their efforts to fly all over us. They didn't taste good or breathe well, either. We did not eat or breathe them intentionally.

When we reached Lock 24, where there was supposed to be water, we found the drinking fountain did not work. No water. It was a very good thing Richard and Mary were bringing us water at Lock 26. Even at that, I wanted more water than I had. Finally seeing a house a couple miles before Lock 26, I walked over with two empty bottles and asked for water.

The gentleman at home filled the bottles with cold water from his refrigerator. It tasted *so good*. Rock Star laughed at me out loud when I returned with our water. She said the man probably hadn't been expecting a sweaty, white-haired, seventy-three-year-old lady in a black sports bra with a bandana headband that made her hair stand straight up. I probably had looked a fright. I hadn't thought about how I looked. I just needed water, asked, and received.

Arriving at Lock 26, we found shade without tall grass or obvious ticks. Richard and Mary arrived with our water, and we chatted for a while before they went off for their canal walk. There was even enough water to get clean after such a sweaty day, and a lock waterfall on the canal beside us provided white noise for sound sleeping.

The next day, we met Traveler, who said he had hiked the American Discovery Trail in 1996 and the PCT in 2012. He had seen us from the road up ahead where it crossed the trail and pulled into a parking spot to talk to us. It was extremely rare to meet another hiker on this trail. Traveler wasn't exactly hiking on the trail, but he had been a thru hiker, and we talked of all the trails the three of us had hiked.

We had a pleasant, short-and-shady six miles into Colona, admiring geese and flowers along the way. Arriving in Colona at the Subway by 9:45 in the morning, we had a very early lunch. After eating, we backtracked a couple short blocks to go through the traveling carnival set up along the trail. What impressed us both was a pit of fifteen, or so, horseshoe games going on simultaneously. I never knew before that there were horseshoe tournaments. I had never seen so many people playing before.

After watching horseshoes being pitched at stakes, entertainment over, we commenced a very hot section of road walks. The route travels north and even a little east to walk around Moline. We would rather have walked straight to the river. Oh well, we did not design the trail, but it seemed strange to walk sixteen miles to get somewhere only about five direct miles away. What we didn't realize was that our crossing of the Mississippi would be a good bit farther south than hitting the Mississippi on a straight line. And trails don't always go straight from point to point.

When I did the planning for this hike, I knew we needed a way to get to the airport at the end of the hike. So, I asked at church if anyone knew anyone in Moline. Why yes, Debbie had a brother and his wife (also named Debbie) who lived in Rock Island, right next to Moline. They would help us. Perfect.

We met Parker and Debbie at 20th and 3rd, and they drove two very hot-and-tired hikers to their house in Rock Island, giving us tours of the sights on the way. They were superb hosts, and soon we were clean, as were our clothes, and we were wined and dined as well. We also had three kinds of ice cream and chocolate-chip cookies for dessert.

Mom and teenage geese along the Mississippi River

On our last day, after a wonderful breakfast feast given to us by Debbie, and attending church since it was Pentecost Sunday, we headed out for a walk along the Mississippi River. We saw thirty or so turkey vultures sitting on electric towers, and enormous numbers of goose families walked the paved bicycle path with us. Geese at the beginning of the ADT in Illinois had been baby goslings. The geese were now growing up. They looked like teenaged geese along the Mississippi River, but still traveled in family units.

It rained off and on that afternoon, but not enough to ruin the day. We crossed the bridge to Arsenal Island and then the next bridge over the Mississippi River to Davenport, Iowa. Spring hike complete!

I had a taste of the ADT that year, 2015. It was a very different kind of hike, but one I enjoyed. There were no mountains in that section. Yet it had its attractions and adventures, as well as allowing me to see old friends and in-laws I had not seen for many years and may never see again.

Yes, it was flat, and yes, it was mostly on pavement of some kind. Yes, those hard surfaces blistered my feet. In some ways, of course, it was the easiest possible trail with smooth and level hiking. Asking to stay in someone's yard to camp was a challenge. But meeting the people whom I had to ask for help in tenting, for water, and for restrooms created lasting impressions in my memory. Meeting the locals along the way turned out to be a joy. I remember the people, far more than the countryside. I treasure the memories I have of those people, their kindness, and generosity.

So, the biggest potential challenge of this section of the ADT had turned out to be the biggest blessing of the trail. Because it was a necessity for me to meet and talk to people, I repeatedly discovered the goodness of the people. The ADT, more than any other trial I have hiked, also opened my mind to ponder the subject of fear, fears I have had and fears that others have for me. That thread of thought was to continue over the next years of walking the ADT.

HikaNation

HikaNation was the predecessor to the American Discovery Trail. Personal photos, Club memos, and newspaper articles about HikaNation can be found on the internet under HikaNation Progression. The following summary was gleaned from those sources:

In 1978, Bill Kelmsley had suggested a hike across America to make a publicity splash for the newly formed American Hiking Society. The plan was to start in California and end up on the steps of the Capitol in Washington DC, with a welcome by President Reagan.

An article went out in *Backpacker Magazine* asking for interested hikers to contact James A. Kern, president of the American Hiking Society. As Jim Kern and the American Hiking Society realized what a big undertaking this was, the hike date was postponed to 1980. An amazing amount of organization was necessary before then.

By March 15, 1980, 86 people had expressed the desire to hike the entire distance. On April 12, 1980, a crowd of hikers gathered in the Polo Field of Golden Gate Park, walked along Ocean Beach, and then the Embarcadero, to a campsite near the off ramp of the Oakland Bay Bridge. On April 13, 1980, a huge crowd gathered and crossed the Oakland Bay Bridge, the first time pedestrians had been allowed to walk across since it was built in 1936. The Official sponsors of HikaNation were the American Hiking Society, Postum Instant Grain Beverage, and the United States Department of the Interior.

The purpose of HikaNation was to show the size of the American hiking community, demonstrate the pleasure of hiking, encourage hiking as an energy efficient sport for all age groups, dramatize the need for more trails across the nation, and gather information on trail opportunities currently available at that time.

HikaNation was widely publicized, and individuals and groups, everyone from the Boy Scouts to various hiking clubs, were invited to join the walk, for an afternoon or several days, as the hikers moved through the states on their routes.

This was an incredible undertaking with massive logistics to be worked out along the way. HikaNation was in the days before the invention of ultralight equipment, and the average pack weight for a hiker was 55.6 pounds.

On May 13, 1981, these intrepid hikers walked down Pennsylvania Avenue in Washington, DC.

I found it interesting to read memos and newspaper articles of HikaNation in research for writing. For all the publicity surrounding it, not a word had penetrated my life at that time. I was then concentrated on survival as a single parent, having gone through a divorce, trying to keep myself together, and raising two young children. My children and I did go on hikes on the slopes of

Mount Rainier during this time, but news of this hiking feat was simply not on my radar.

HikaNation was the forerunner of what eventually became the American Discovery Trail.

2016

American Discovery Trail

DELAWARE

Delaware portion of the American Discovery Trail

In 2016, I decided, since I had so much enjoyed my first experience on the ADT by simply plucking out a nice flat section in the Eastern part of the United States, perhaps I should start at the beginning.

As I read of other ADT hikers who posted stories of their journeys on Trailjournals.com, I saw that most of those who walked the ADT began at the beginning, at Cape Henlopen, Delaware. (A second choice was to begin at Point Reyes, California and walk east.)

I planned to visit my daughter and her family in Virginia in the spring, and after that visit, to rent a car to drive to the beginning of the ADT for my yearly spring hike. The nearest place to Cape Henlopen to check in the rental car was Rehoboth Beach and the nearest lodging to the beginning of the ADT was in the town of Lewes.

I stopped in Lewes before taking the car to Rehoboth Beach. It was a good thing I did, as the 88-year-old proprietress of the B&B I had found online had forgotten that she had agreed by email to pick me up at the car rental. However, when reminded, she was quite agreeable to do so.

I unloaded my gear to my room while she checked where the Budget Rental was in Rehoboth Beach, and she led me over in her car, an aged Caprice Station Wagon. She patiently waited while I gassed up the rental car before turning it in to the rental agent.

Patricia then drove me back to Lewes and the B&B where I promptly discovered I had left a Ziploc bag with some medications in the rental car. The bag of medications must have jumped under the seat when I was eating lunch and rearranged things in my backpack. Patricia was a real gem. She just loaned me her car to drive back and get the meds, which the rental agent had found for me.

Deciding to pick up some fast food at Taco Bell for dinner while I was out, I rolled down the driver-side window of the old Caprice. Big mistake. The window fell off its track and it took about fifty tries to muscle it back up straight. I bet Patricia never opened that window, and indeed, I recalled it was the passenger side window that had been open when she had been driving. I was glad I was able to return the car with its parts back in the right place.

The King's Inn B&B did not get rave reviews on the internet, but I figured it would do fine for a hiker. Yes, the proprietress was getting hard of hearing, forgetful, and probably didn't even see the dirt along baseboards and in corners. The carpet was not sparkling clean. But the sheets and towels and bathroom were clean.

There were cute furnishings, if elderly; some, perhaps, were antiques. The shower curtain had brightly colored flowers. Flower pictures hung on the walls, flowers decorated bed coverings, and complementary freshly cut daffodils and tulips sat on the bedside table for cheerful decor. Patricia was more than accommodating in helping with my needs and my minor disaster losing meds. I hoped I would be that functional at 88.

My first trail day was an eight-mile day with only three miles of actual trail progress. I simply walked to the beginning of the trail, waded in the Atlantic Ocean, walked all around the state park, visited the nature center and a museum, and ended up back at my B&B in Lewes.

Mary wading in the Atlantic Ocean

Lewes was founded by the Dutch East Indies Company in 1631. It was re-founded a couple years later, after having been wiped out by Native Americans. Eventually, Lewes became predominantly British, but the Zwaanendal Museum, with its distinctive Dutch roofline, and all the blooming tulips in town proclaimed Dutch heritage. Did you know the actor Marlon Brando was Dutch? He was listed in the museum with many other famous people of Dutch heritage.

Coming back to the same B&B meant a second breakfast with Pat. It also meant we were even more comfortable with one another and had a longer conversation. Pat was an interesting woman, the daughter of a woman who had worked for the State Department in Washington, DC. Pat had married an Afghan and had lived in Kabul. She had also lived in Ghana and Venezuela. She had many stories of adventures and lots of spunk. And as she told me tales, her eyes sparkled.

Patricia, proprietress of my B&B

Leaving Lewes, I found Delaware had flat farmland and rivers, a nice beginning to a spring hike. Lunch was a bit early, but how could I turndown Hopkins Farm Creamery with picnic tables, porta potties, and a chocolate-banana-walnut icecream cone for dessert. Yum.

A few miles before Milton, a car stopped. The driver was a young woman named Lydia, daughter of the Delaware ADT coordinator. They lived nearby, and she told me to call her father and he would pick me up when I got as far as I wanted to go for the day. I would have a bed and a shower. Sweet! I did.

Before the end of the day, coming down Front Street, I passed an African American family outside enjoying the sunshine, and we laughed together about all the exercise I was getting. A couple houses farther, an elderly African American gentleman sitting on his porch asked me how far I was going. I said I was looking for somewhere to eat and hoped it wasn't much farther, as my feet were hurting from all the pavement. He gestured down the road, and the next thing I knew, he was on his bicycle guiding me the last couple blocks to make sure I found the restaurant. How very kind he was.

I grew up in the 1950s in a suburb of Denver, Colorado. In those days, perhaps from the redlining real-estate practices of the time, African Americans generally only lived in certain areas of Denver.

(Redlining is an unethical and unlawful discriminatory practice [legal until laws passed in 1968 and 1977] of systematic denial of services to a certain race or ethnic group. The term generally is used for describing a situation in which a particular ethnic group or race is denied financial services including mortgages, insurance, or loans in a particular area.)

I personally experienced a similar practice at the time. My family was interested in building a home in a new development by an attractive lake; the contract included a requirement that the buyer of that property could never sell it to a person of color. My family refused to sign such a stipulation and instead, we looked for a mountain property without a racist requirement.

The church we attended for a time was in the central part of Denver. My brother, seven years older than I, was in the youth group, and my parents stepped up to be the leaders of the group. They encouraged the youth group to meet once a month with the local Baptist youth group, which happened to be African American. Holy *you know what* broke out over that, and we changed churches. Even though I was seven years younger, that uproar was known to me.

My mother, in Denver-wide Christian Women's Groups, continued to work with groups and encouraged conversation across racial lines. Yet, in my youth, I had few opportunities to know those of a different color than mine as people of a mix of colors rarely lived in the same towns.

In my adult life, my childhood fantasy of being related to more of the world became true. While I was in the Peace Corps, an African American family became part of my extended family because a small girl in a predominantly African American Church my father was serving at the time, started calling my mother Grandma, and the relationship grew with the adults as well. Even though I was not present when Ethel became my Sis, she attended my seminary graduation and sang at my ordination. I also had the honor of presiding at one of her daughter's weddings, and they have been my base in Denver when walking on the CDT. There are ways to be family that go beyond blood relations.

My son married a beautiful young Japanese woman from Tokyo, who proudly claims that she is Japanese. My daughter married her junior-high and high-school sweetheart, whose name and lineage came from Finland. My childhood wish to be related to the world is a little closer now than when I was a child.

Over the years I sometimes have had opportunity to know others of diverse heritage, and I treasure those relationships. So meeting those of diverse heritage or color along the ADT was very meaningful to me, perhaps especially because of my parents' desire for understanding, paradoxically combined with such sparse contact when I was a kid, living in a world of racial separateness, though I'd had a childhood wish to be related to people different from myself.

America's mix of people of diverse backgrounds is a gift. When writing this book someone suggested to me that mentioning African Americans as African Americans or Black could be seen as racist as I do not mention other people I met are white. It seems to me leaving out those words is ignoring them and even more racist. Walking across the country brought gifts to me in all the people I met including African Americans. Not to specifically mention African Americans in writing about the many people I encountered would be to miss part of the America that I discovered on the American Discovery Trail and memories I cherish. That an elderly African American gentleman so kindly climbed upon his bike to guide me on my way to rest and food is one of those cherished moments.

After I had walked a couple miles past Milton, I called Lydia's father, Howard, the husband of the ADT coordinator for Delaware, and he picked me up and took me to his home. After I had a welcome and needed shower, we went to the restaurant where Lydia was working. Howard ate his dinner there and bought me tea and dessert, a scrumptious bread pudding.

On my third day on the trail, I passed a farm with three miniature animals in front. The first was a dwarf wart hog who was so ugly he was cute. He wagged his tail like a dog and seemed all ready to play. Two miniature goats were very cute without being ugly first. The day before I had seen a fox. There were both domesticated animals and wildlife in Delaware, though I had not expected the latter.

On this third day, it became apparent that I had not done enough conditioning before beginning this trek. My feet hurt. My knee hurt. My back hurt. A trail is a trail, even on pavement. But the jarring of feet on pavement was not friendly to my body.

On this section of the ADT, just like my first experience the year before, the people were charming. A driver stopped to chat with me, and he even knew about the ADT. I also talked to Djin Din, a gentleman fishing from a wooden bridge, his name and appearance suggested to me that he was of Central Asian heritage, another facet in America's mix. I met another gentleman out raking leaves, who also knew about the ADT.

Most of my first hike on the ADT, several states along, people had not known I was on a trail. Perhaps hikers begin the trail and then quit for a variety of reasons. Or they take the lower route through Missouri and Kansas instead of the Northern route I had chosen that first year on the trail, skirting below Chicago then over to the Mississippi River at Moline. For whatever the reason, the ADT was more *known* in Delaware than Ohio, Indiana. or Illinois.

That evening I asked a friendly gentleman mowing a very large yard if I might stop and camp in his yard. Lloyd did not know he lived on the ADT, but he was just fine with me setting up my tent in his yard and granted me bathroom privileges in his house, complete with shower.

Door Knocking

I had learned the patter I used in asking for a tenting spot in my first year on the ADT. But it occurred to me that I had learned to knock on doors many years ago. In a different day and age, some sixty-five years ago, or more, I was a Girl Scout and there were cookies to sell. I had fallen in love with Girl Scout Camp and some small portion of the price of the cookies helped me get to camp. I sold Girl Scout Cookies door to door, forty-nine cases of them one year, if my memory serves me correctly.

In this day and age, I am not sure Girl Scouts go door to door. Is that really because the world is such a much more dangerous place, or is it that our fears have multiplied exponentially past reality? I cannot answer that question, but I observe the difference. I buy Girl Scout Cookies at church or in front of stores these days.

Many teenagers of my vintage babysat for spending money. I wasn't too successful at that. The first time I babysat for a family, I fell asleep on the couch after tucking my charges into bed. I slept so soundly that the parents had to wake up their own children by rapping on their bedroom window to let them in the door they had carefully locked before they went out, leaving me the key. When back inside their house, they woke me up. I was not a popular babysitter.

On my second babysitting job, I suspected the

father wanted to groom me for something other than babysitting when he took me for an ice-cream cone very late, at midnight, on the way home. Not everyone in the world was, or is, trustworthy.

Many hikers write online about paying attention to intuition, their *spidy* sense. As a teenager, I did pay attention to mine. When I talk about leaving fear behind, I am not talking about not paying attention. Intuition is a thing. When you are uncomfortable, it is best to listen to what your spidy sense is telling you. There may or may not be something real to fear in any situation, but only you know what your intuition tells you. In that instance long ago, as a teenager, something about the situation did not feel right. I had no desire to babysit for that family again.

I found another way to make a little money as a teenager. I sold cards, wrapping paper, and stationery going door to door. It didn't make me a great deal of money, but it was something I could do by myself. I earned enough money to buy Christmas presents for my family and, combined with my allowance, enough to go to Scout Camp. I really did not aspire to make more money than that.

Those teenage jobs, while not very lucrative, probably set a foundation I would rely upon so many years later.

As a pastor developer, (a pastor who is intentionally trying to develop and grow a church) I also had more recent experience knocking on doors.

I was somewhat effective in reaching out to the unchurched community, many of whom became part of our growing congregation. Being a pastor developer is not a piece of life experience that most hikers have had, nor, probably, have many hikers sold cards and stationery door to door as a teenager. But those activities were part of my experience. On the ADT knocking on doors was not an entirely new experience. I had met interesting people behind doors on which I knocked before I started the American Discovery Trail.

A word to those amazed or intimidated at the idea of knocking on doors and interacting with people on this very different kind of trail or in other instances in life: One does not have to be an extrovert to knock on a door. In fact, it is a rather solitary sort of thing. It is just me knocking on a door. How I do so is mostly under my control. I do not/did not have to be able to chatter at length with anyone. I only had to think through what I planned to say and say it over and over again each time I knocked on a door. The same has been true on the ADT. My verbal patter when knocking on a door has few variations other than responding to the unique and different people I encounter who answer the door.

I am not an extrovert. I have always had some difficulty maintaining a conversation in social situations. I admire people who have the gift of drawing others out in conversation. I have the gift (sometimes curse) of talking about myself. Since I have done some things a bit out of the ordinary and have some interesting stories,

I tell them over and over again.

Since, on the ADT, I met new people each day, I could tell the same stories each day to different people. It is pretty self-centered of me, but there you have it. Think through what you want to say when knocking on a door and say it. And a world of interesting people will talk to you and ask you about yourself and what you are doing. They will also tell you something about their own lives and broaden your perspective on the world.

MARYLAND

Maryland portion of the American Discovery Trail

A really good rest that night helped various body parts. I did multiple sets of thirty curls and moved very gingerly changing positions. My back was still tender, but much more reasonable in the morning. It does help that I once was a physical therapist and have some knowledge of body mechanics and what to do for ailing body parts.

As I walked along the road in the morning, a guy in a car—Gary—stopped to talk with me. We chatted for a bit, and he drove off but came back again. He and his wife lived nearby. He offered to have me call when I was through for the day, and he would come and pick me up so I could stay in the playhouse behind their house. He told me he had hosted other hikers. It was nice to know I could have a place to stay and a shower at the end of a hot day. No buzzers of a spidy sense went off in my brain or my emotions. I had learned to accept offered help. A place to stay and a shower sounded good. I walked on with that promise for the end of my day.

In the heat of the afternoon, I stopped at a farmhouse to get water. The woman who gave me water thought I was very brave to be hiking alone, which led to a discussion about fear. I told my story of not packing for my fears, and she said she wished her daughter could learn to give up some of her fears; she was afraid of so many things.

It is not that I am never afraid. I have another story I frequently share. I am a Lutheran pastor. But before I was ordained, when I was a pastor *wanna-be*, the clergywomen in my area had a retreat, and they invited me, a seminary student, to come.

That evening as we sat around and talked, the discussion was about the state of the world and how horrible it was that women could no longer walk anywhere alone at night. This was in about 1989 or 1990. Although I am unsure of the exact date, it was a distinct moment and memory in my life. I did not say anything in that discussion. After all, I was the new person in the group. But I clearly remember sitting there, saying to myself, "I *refuse* to live like that! I refuse to have my life ruled by fear. I am just too darn ornery to agree to that."

Please understand that did not and does not mean

I am never afraid. But I do refuse to have my life *ruled* by my fears. That is a conscious choice. This story, along with the backpack illustration of leaving fears behind, are my standard stories about fear, which I shared many times along the ADT. Leaving fears behind *can* be a conscious choice. Orneriness helps.

The woman who gave me water liked my stories. Perhaps she shared them with her daughter.

Hiking on, I made it past the Delaware line, and Gary picked me up at Bates Road. After I was cleaned up, we went out to eat and then to his family's creamery. They had ice cream to rival Farson, Wyoming. (The tiny town of Farson, Wyoming has the best ice cream ever, which I had discovered while walking the CDT.)

Gary knew who lived in every old farmhouse we passed and told me stories of the area. Did you know that area of Delaware produces more fryer chickens than anywhere else in the USA? I enjoyed a local guide telling me all about the area. Delaware had been mostly flat farmland after leaving the Atlantic, pleasant but not spectacular walking. But Gary, and the others I had met had been gracious, helpful and very interesting people.

Gracious and helpful people continued to meet me the next day. Not far from Denton, I sat to rest, leaning on a brick driveway pillar. The daughter of Gail, the lady who lived in the house down that driveway, drove by and saw me sitting there. She was worried and called her mother. Gail came out to check on me. We introduced ourselves and she graciously offered the use of her bathroom. That was wonderful, as I had just been contemplating the need to take a trip into the woods where there were no inviting woods to be seen.

After leaving Gail, I had an early lunch at the Subway. The guy making my sandwich had been an Appalachian-Trail hiker and was a thru-hiker *wanna-be*. We talked trail talk, and he put my sandwich on his employee tab. Why, thank you very much! People in Maryland were as kind as people in Delaware.

By the time I left the Subway, it was hot, and I kept inventing reasons to stop in the shade. A dentist's office along the road provided another restroom in air conditioning and ice-cold water. In the afternoon, high clouds formed, which helped a lot, dissipating the sun's rays.

Reaching Ridgely, I had dinner from a C-store and used the restroom next door at the laundromat. I ate my steak-and-cheese sub in the laundromat as they had chairs and the C-store didn't. Dessert was an ice-cream sandwich. (The availability of food as I went along meant I did not have to carry as much food and have as heavy a pack as would otherwise have been necessary.) Ridgely was a pleasant town with old period houses—some nicely repainted and cared for, others not so much. This trail was not wilderness, but it was still interesting.

I decided to go on past Ridgely before stopping for the night. But then there were no habitations, and I wondered if I would be able to find a place to be. Remember, since I planned my hike by the miles in the T-by-T directions, I really had no idea what would turn up or what sort of neighborhood or countryside I would see when I needed to find a place to stop. The first two doors I knocked on did not yield a place to stay. One person worried because she did not own the house. Another worried her shelter dog would be upset and cause a problem. Those were good reasons to turndown my request. But I really needed to find a home for the night, which was fast approaching.

The third door I approached led me to Mike and Ruth and their adult daughters, Shannon and Jenny. Mike and Ruth had hosted hikers before and also camped and kayaked themselves. Those lovely people showed me the best place to put my tent, offered me a shower, which I was happy to accept, and would have fed me dinner, too. I declined dinner as I had already eaten.

Mike was a retired Federal Agent who was writing personal safety tips for runners and day hikers on the AT. We shared hiking tips. The two young women were both recovering from some serious surgeries. They were in my prayers.

Continually meeting people who helped me furthered my reflection on my role, my obligation in return for receiving their help. At the least, my job was to be very appreciative of any help offered. Words like please and thank were to fill my sentences.

Besides appreciative receiving, a hiker provides novelty and entertainment. People helping hikers generally wanted to ask questions about the trail and why I was hiking. Hikers usually love to talk about their experiences. I enjoyed being a *trail ambassador*. Sharing trail stories is part of the job in return for water and places to camp, showers, and bathrooms. A recommendation to other hikers on the ADT: Count on spending some time with those who aid you. It is a fun thing to do and a little repayment for all they do for you.

Since I am also a pastor and a child of God, prayers for those in need and prayers of thanksgiving, even if silently said, are often my response.

Unfortunately, social time in pleasant chats does cut into either walking time or sleeping time. The rest of the world does not operate on hiker time. In hiker lingo, *hiker midnight* is whenever the sun goes down, and hikers should be asleep. Electricity in normal life means people assume there are hours to talk. And I enjoy talking, telling stories, and listening to stories. It was hard to break away and head for my tent. And once in my tent, I needed more time to write of my travels and thoughts in my journal. Visiting with gracious people was almost too much of a good thing. But I wouldn't trade those experiences for anything, even sleep.

It was difficult to get a good night's sleep for other reasons, too. I had not had such a physically rocky start to a long section of hiking for nine years. In 2007 I had begun hiking the Sierra with a torn meniscus, though I did not realize that was the reason for my pain. In 2016, I seemed to have done something to my good knee on a spring-training hike.

My knee didn't hurt consistently, but it tweaked at me a lot. I also was having back issues beyond the relatively normal stiffness of aging in the morning. That night I found it very difficult to find any position that did not cause something to hurt. As a former physical therapist, theoretically, I knew how to properly position myself for back or knee. Nothing I knew helped. If one body part was comfortable, the other one complained.

There were problems during the day, too, but that I expected. I needed a good night's sleep for my body to heal and be ready for the next day's challenges. Getting that sleep was a challenge as big as walking each day.

The next morning was cooler, though, and I liked that. I had been walking in a major early-spring heat wave. I was glad for the change in the weather, but to be counting the hours until I could take my next pain medication was not a good thing. I was having serious doubts about completing what I had begun, though I soldiered on.

Flat Delaware was a good way to start out a hike, especially since I seemed to be having some physical problems. Maryland gave me slight rises through farmland interspersed with woods. I found a nice bench to rest upon beside the little lake in Tuckahoe State Park and watched the geese and ducks.

Trees were trying to leaf out. Spring growth was trying to emerge on branches and on the ground. I again enjoyed seeing May apples spreading their umbrella-like leaves across the ground in wooded areas. I talk about them every spring when hiking in the East. They are one of the recurring, pleasant, familiar sights in Eastern Woods. My trail was mostly roads, some quiet country roads, some highways with heavy traffic. The former were more enjoyable than the latter. One long stretch on a highway had very wide shoulders for safe walking. I sang songs loudly to keep myself going on that road. No one was near to hear my singing and the distraction of the songs and their rhythm kept me moving.

I was blessed by people. One guy came down a long driveway from a farmhouse when he saw me walking along the road. He had a bottle of water in his hand to give me and asked if I needed anything else.

Hmm, "Restroom?"

"Sure."

"Thanks!"

Sometimes roads required eyes alert for traffic as shoulders were narrow. Much of the traffic was friendly, giving me a wide berth and a friendly wave. A few drivers coming at me carved their half of the road with no give at all, even with no oncoming traffic in the other lane.

I fixed my dinner and ate it about 5:00. I was looking for an excuse to stop and rest. Still, I had put in enough miles for an old lady and was ahead of my schedule. I looked for a friendly house at which to camp. There were no likely looking houses until I reached George and Kathy's house right before Joseph Boyle Road. George and Kathy were a younger couple with three small children.

They gave me water and the use of their restroom. I then collapsed on top of my sleeping bag in my tent for nearly an hour before moving for any reason. I was very tired and looking forward to a day off, coming up soon.

When on a long trail, my tiny tent becomes my home. I pitch my tent very quickly and equally quickly unload my gear and pack into the tent. I crawl in and sit down, everything within reach. It is my private space wherever I am, though I have walked in public space all day. Especially on days I am truly tired, it is a welcome retreat in which to crash. It is home.

Boy, was I tired *that* night! I was horizontal, if not always asleep, for twelve hours. It did wonders for my old and ailing body. I was more inventive with positioning to prevent pain while horizontal, and when I woke in the morning my back seemed more its usual aging self. A bit of morning stiffness only required a few pelvic tilts to loosen up. I knew I needed to remain vigilant with self care, or the pain could return, but it was nice to just feel normal morning achiness. I was also encouraged to know I had only a short day to walk since I was ahead of schedule.

An interpretive sign about Civil War days gave me my day's history lesson while I walked through Queenstown. The year before the Emancipation Proclamation, the Union Army was drafting Black slaves and paying their owners $100 per slave. Many slaves ran away from their owners to join up, too. Maryland, a border state, between North and South, had many families split in allegiance between Union and Confederacy. Civil War and slavery remain a painful part of our history in America, with lasting effects to this day.

A bit past Queenstown, a sign commemorated the Battle of Slippery Hill, a mild skirmish with the British in the War of 1812. Revolutionary War, War of 1812, Civil War—reminders of all can be found while hiking in the East.

Walking on busy roads, most of which did not have shoulders or sidewalks, I wondered how anyone could walk this route with a cart, pushing or pulling a wheeled cart as I know some have done. It was annoying enough on foot, needing to step onto uneven ground off the road, yielding to approaching cars. The idea of dealing with a cart seemed to me a nightmare. Even with a knee problem, I was more nimble with a pack on my back, than I could have been with any sort of cart.

Arriving at my destination by 11:00, I met Diane, with whom I had talked on the phone making my reservation while still in Washington. I checked in and then headed for local creamy clam chowder at a nearby restaurant.

In the afternoon, after completing laundry and shower, the remainder of the day was for rest, and the day after was an unexpected zero day (zero miles walked). This motel was where I originally had wanted a zero day when writing out my hike plan, but I had decided the weekend rate would be too pricey, and I planned my rest day for two days later. When the manager heard of my original plan as I checked in, she gave me the next day for the weekday rate. I quickly changed my reservation farther on and got my rest day when I wanted it. Yay!

ANNAPOLIS

The day of rest was good for me. Ready to hike again, Diane gave me a ride over the Bay Bridge, which did not allow pedestrians. The weather was cool, but beautiful as I walked by pink-flowering trees. Approaching Annapolis, I stopped at a little deli for lunch. A couple there pegged me for a hiker since I was carrying a backpack, a little strange in the East unless you are near the AT. This couple struck up a conversation with me, and I had a very pleasant lunch break talking with them.

As we talked, they looked at my maps and my plan for the day, recommending I not stop in the neighborhood I had planned at the end of my day. They recommended that I stop earlier. They didn't really tell me why, and I did not ask. I walked on to Annapolis, crossing the Severn River, looking down on the Naval Academy over blue water and flowering trees.

US Naval Academy

While I was walking, I thought about the conversation in the deli. I wondered if their cautions to me were about race. Now, I don't always take advice given. I didn't want to cut my miles short, as that would just leave the need to increase my miles somewhere else. I had a schedule to keep with lodging arrangements and re-supply boxes farther on. I did not want to get behind on my schedule.

Other thoughts were intruding in my mind, as well. As a pastor, I stand in the pulpit and preach that God loves all people, of all backgrounds and all colors. And I believe that with all my heart. If a conversation containing friendly cautions to me were rooted in concerns about a neighborhood predominantly African American, how could I justify stopping early to avoid them? I couldn't. I had to walk the walk I talked. How did I know that caution was about people of color? I have no idea, but my intuition said it was.

Yes, it did turn out to be a neighborhood where all the people I saw were of the color black. It wasn't a bad neighborhood. Nice-looking rentals, duplexes, quadplexes, eightplexes stretched in all directions. Rentals were not usually the best places to ask for tenting space, as people could be hesitant to agree when someone else owns the home. Now, every night I was a bit nervous, as I wondered what would happen when knocking on a stranger's door. But my nervousness seemed increased that night.

The people of color I have known, I knew one by one in personal relationships. Except for one brief period of cross-cultural experience in Oakland, California while in seminary, I was not used to being in a community that was predominantly one of a different color than my own. My feet were about to take me past that neighborhood into a commercial area. A commercial area would not be a good place for my tent. So, I screwed up my courage, and, at the last set of duplexes, I knocked on the door.

Larissa met me at the door after a kid inside yelled in evident surprise, "Hey, there's a *white lady* at the door." Larissa was the Grandma and matriarch of the family who lived there.

"Yes," she said, "Of course. We would be *honored* to have you stay in our back yard."

Honored? Wow. I hadn't had anyone say *that* to me before.

We chatted for a bit. Then I put up my tent, had my dinner, and they let me use their bathroom. Practical needs tended to and conversation over, I crawled into my sleeping bag inside my tent and went to sleep.

Sometime later, probably after 11:00 at night,

I woke up with a start, sat up, and grabbed my tent pole, because, as I sat up, the tent started to fall down around me. A man had been peering into the tent, and as I suddenly sat up, he had jumped back in startled surprise and tripped over the center guyline, the main tie-out supporting my tent.

At my sitting up and the tent collapsing, he was shocked. It seemed to me at first like a scene that might have played well in a sitcom. As I took in what had happened, it struck my funny bone. Perhaps I have an odd sense of humor. At any rate, I was not used to meeting strange men in the middle of the night looking in my tent that was collapsing.

A tent in that location might have been out of the ordinary. Carl was on his way to work at the local Target in the commercial area just ahead. I seemed to have put my tent in the short cut to that commercial area. Curious at a new, unusual thing in his neighborhood, he had investigated. When I suddenly sat up as he was looking in, I think I scared him half to death.

Carl started babbling, "I'm sorry, lady. I'm sorry. I'm sorry. I'm sorry I broke your tent. I'll fix it. I can pay for it. I have a job. I have two jobs. Actually, I have three jobs. Here's my card. I can pay for your tent. I'm sorry, lady. I'm sorry."

I told him, "Hey, it's OK. See that silver thing in the grass?" pointing with my free hand and shining my headlamp's beam on the tent stake not far away. "Can you give it to me?" He handed me my tent stake, and I put it in the guyline loop and gave it to him, saying. "Here, pull it out as far as you can; and stick it in the ground. There. Tent fixed."

Carl and Mary

Then Carl and I had an interesting conversation in the middle of the night about long-distance hiking and the American Discovery Trail. Before he went on to work, he begged to take a selfie with me, as *no one* would *ever believe* why he would be so late to work. I too took a selfie of the two of us, heads together in the doorway of my tent. And if you need to have your car detailed in Annapolis, I have his card, and I'll recommend him.

That night I learned from personal experience what white privilege is. It's when someone of another color is *honored* to have you stay in their yard, and when someone of another color who accidently kicks out your tent stake and sees you're *white*, feels they have to justify themselves as being super responsible by saying they have three jobs.

Sometimes I get past fear by knowing I have an obligation rooted in my faith, and my values demand it. I cannot preach God's love for all people without living that, even by knocking on someone's door asking for assistance when they are different from me in color of skin.

I'm glad I pushed past my nervousness and any fear I had in that unfamiliar neighborhood. I was rewarded greatly by meeting Larrisa and Carl. My journey and life were the richer for having met them, just as my life has been richer for meeting others, mostly white like me, on this trail of discovery.

While walking on the American Discovery Trail, one of my joys of discovery has been noting the history of various ethnic groups that make up America, from the Dutch settlement of Lewes, Delaware, Serb, Slovenian, German and Croatian people of Joliet and Limestone, the Irish in LaSalle, Illinois. The African American community on the west side of Annapolis was also an important part of America for me to discover.

I hate to admit there is still a color barrier in the United States and in my life. Yet, honestly, I was more hesitant to knock on a door in an African American community in an unfamiliar city than my regular nervousness in knocking on other doors, all of which were unfamiliar to me as I walked across America. I suppose that isn't a surprise, as America has a long history of separation between people of color and those of the color white.

I am a product of years in my past and years before I was born. But in Annapolis, a combination of my faith and my need pushed me beyond that hesitancy, that fear I had to knock on that particular door. I'm glad I did.

I have learned that experiences and people previously unknown, different, or unusual in my life and on this trail are not to be fearfully avoided. They are gifts to become known and treasured, chance meetings holding new lessons, or old lessons learned again. I'm still learning. I don't have it all down pat and continually need new lessons.

One of my most memorable experiences on the ADT was meeting Carl on the west side of Annapolis. My first reaction was to see it as a slapstick, funny incident of surprise for both of us amid a collapsing tent. And it certainly was that. But there was more to it than that. In reflection, how sad that I was warned away from a whole neighborhood.

Why should Carl have had to feel he needed to justify himself by telling me how many jobs he had to prove he had the means to fix my tent? Yes, I'm glad my tent was so easily fixed as a replaced tent stake. I'm also glad Carl and I talked in the middle of the night, and he learned something about long-distance hiking. I'm glad we both took *selfies* together before he went off to work.

But this incident, like my memory of a family I spoke with below Chicago, stays in my mind with a mixture of joy and sadness and many *whys*. Why must we fear each other? Why cannot there be the real freedom to know and be known across perceived racial lines? Why cannot African Americans in America be as free to Discover America on a long-distance hike as an old, white-haired, white grandma? Why should it be fearful or a surprise to be in each other's neighborhoods? Why don't we live in neighborhoods together more often than we do?

I remember talking to a wonderful African American family on that bike trail below Chicago on my first year on the ADT. They were fascinated with what I was doing, and the guy said he thought that would be a wonderful thing to do. I wondered at the time, although I didn't write about it in my journal, what kind of a reception he would have if he went up to a door and knocked and asked for water or a place to put up his tent.

Carl, met in the middle of the night, might someday decide to go for a walk across America. He was very interested in what I was doing.

What would his reception be?

I yearn for the day when people of color have as good a chance as I for acceptance and wonderful experiences on the trail. I yearn for an America in which we do not fear each other, no matter the shade of our skin, our differences.

At various times in the years I have been doing long hikes around this country I have observed that African American long-distance hikers are few. I have a book on my bookshelf, *The Adventure Gap* by James Edward Mills, which added to my understand of the difficulty people of color have had to be included in outdoor recreation. I have had the good fortune to meet a few hikers of different races and ethnicities and I rejoice to see the numbers of people of color increasing on long-distance trails, though they are still far outnumbered by white faces.

Two years later, in 2018, Sharon (the ADT Coordinator for West Virginia) and I talked about this issue. She had been in contact with a young woman of color who was starting out on the ADT that year. She told me the young woman was searching for places to stealth camp (camp without being seen) as she was fearful of the reception she would have if she knocked on doors. I did not catch the name of that young woman then.

But in the fall of 2018, I rejoiced to learn that a young African American woman named Colleen became the **first** African American to complete the ADT, and she did it as a thru hike. It may or may not have been the same person Sharon told me about. But my hat is off to her. Well, my hat is off to anyone who completes this trail, thru hiker or not, person of color or not. But I do recognize that it might have taken extra courage for her to have completed a trail such as the ADT.

May adventure gaps, color barriers, and our fears of meeting others who are different from us disappear. May we leave our fears behind.

The Sunday morning after I met Carl, walking by St Phillip Episcopal Church, I saw on their street sign that their early worship service was just beginning, as it was 8:00. I used the facilities and stayed for the service. I plan extensively for my hiking trips, but often the most wonderful experiences are the unplanned. There is no way I could have planned to arrive at a particular church along my route just beginning a service as I walked by.

Following the service, some of the people chatted with me, and we took pictures together. They wished me well as I left upon my way. A month or so later, while I was showing that picture to someone, my finger inadvertently deleted it. Oh no! Electronics are sometimes unforgiving to old ladies. I wish I still had that picture. I loved all their beautiful faces surrounding mine. Like the *old-boys' club* in Matthews, I had been accepted into a community of people different from myself.

When I was asked to officiate at the wedding of the daughter of my God-sis in Denver, my daughter and I flew back and stayed with Ethel and her family. At one point, Ro, my daughter and I were sitting on a bed comparing color shades of skin on our arms placed on the bed next to each other. We ranged from Ro's dark chocolate brown to my very tanned arm to my daughter's pale white. I thought them beautiful together.

I love the diversely colored flowers I find in nature along my trails. I also love diversely colored people of differing ethnicities and backgrounds. All are gifts.

Arcane Art

After leaving Annapolis, it was a long walk—first through woods, then by nice houses, then passing mansions with acres and acres of precisely trimmed lawns, extensive enough for a development or two or three on their grounds. Then came more woods, more houses, and more farms. There was no opportunity for a restroom from 10:00 to 4:00. And there was quite a bit of traffic on the roads and thick poison ivy in all the patches of woods.

Time for the FUD. Ok, this is another bit of *too much information*. Feel free to skip this part if you don't want to know about the arcane art of women peeing. But it is an important issue for many women hikers.

A FUD is a feminine urinary device. They can be purchased online. I had gotten a couple models in the past at the recommendation of another woman hiker and used one a few times the previous year. But I really wasn't happy with either model, so in 2016, I made my own.

Just get the smallest plastic salad dressing bottle you can find that has a long neck and cut it in half lengthwise. It was a bit hard to cut through thick plastic, but I was able to do it with sharp knife and strong kitchen-sheers. I covered the cut edges with a narrow strip of duct tape for comfort. To use, loosen your pants. Hold the half bottle on the appropriate body part slanted down and away from you and pee into it. Using a FUD enables a woman to pee standing up like a man.

Why in the world would you want to? For days like that one past Annapolis. I could walk a little way down a long driveway in the woods. There was not enough cover for squatting with my butt showing. But there was enough cover to stand behind a tree and use the FUD like guys stand behind a tree to pee. Your pants are not lowered much, and a passing car would not notice anything. (They *should* be watching the road when they drive.)

The most difficult thing was to convince my old body that it was OK to pee standing up. Women have years of cultural training saying otherwise.

A FUD can also be used in a tent or outbuilding where you have no restroom privileges, by peeing through the device into a Ziploc bag. The bag can be emptied under cover of darkness or at a more appropriate time. I liked my version of FUD better than the ones I had purchased. It was a little wider and not as prone to leaking or overflow.

OK, that is more than enough on that subject. But it is important to know what to do when you have several hours of hiking with no other good options. Many women hikers simply prefer using a FUD everywhere, although it is not my favorite technique in the arcane art of women peeing.

On to Washington DC

Farther on, there were many towns, houses and people between Annapolis and Washington DC. Commercial establishments were many, too. I opted for a motel since there was one, a rare occurrence to find right on the ADT.

That day after Annapolis was a long one, 18.8 miles, plenty long and then some for an old lady. I didn't plan on it being quite that long, but that was how the miles worked out.

Stopping to ask for water while passing University of Maryland agricultural land, I met Randy. His job was to walk around in the woods collecting and identifying native species. Tick bites were common in his line of work.

Randy told me he was making concoctions of herbs Native Americans likely used to counteract Lyme disease. The principal ingredient was the fresh root of goldenseal. He said goldenseal, however, was bad for your liver. Another herb could be taken first to improve liver function. He thought the two herbs balanced out problems with liver function, while giving protection from Lyme disease. The science of natural remedies used before we began taking antibiotics may help us today, old remedies becoming new again.

I had planned to stop on Ridge Road but was discouraged after three turndowns. I knew the Greenbelt Park would have a campground, and I just kept walking until I got there, even if it was longer than I wanted to go in one day. My directions were a bit fuzzy, and I was glad I had my GPS to find my way. The ADT is a waymarked trail, but it is not a marked trail. That means I had dots in my GPS in my hand indicating my trail, but the paths/roads between those dots were not always matched with ADT signs and directional signals on the ground.

Walking around a lake on the way, I chatted with a woman who said she was meant to hear what I shared with her about my travels and about fear, as she feared approaching seventy. If I could long-distance hike at seventy-four, she decided she should get over her own fears and enjoy her seventies. Her statement made my day, making up for the turndowns earlier in the day.

I finally reached Greenbelt Park, and eventually found the campground just at dusk. There were no official people around. I just chose a campsite and threw up the tent. They didn't even have a sign at the Iron Ranger telling me what the fee was. (An Iron Ranger is a box on a post with a slot in it to put in your campsite registration and fee.) I wrote down my Golden Age Passport number on the registration and dropped $5 in, hoping that was close.

I was so tired I could not even wash my body, sticky from the long, hot day, even though there was both hot and cold running water in the restroom. I had a place to be horizontal, and that was all I wanted. I crashed. Waking up in the middle of the night, I washed up when I went to use the facilities, and no one was around. Then I went back to sleep, clean at last.

Surprisingly, to me, the Washington DC area of the ADT was on bike trails by rivers, the Northeast Branch of the Anacostia Tributary Trail System and then the Northwest Branch.

I also saw the East Coast Greenway Trail, which goes from Maine to Florida. Every year I hear of new trails. If one of the goals of HikaNation was to highlight and spur the development of more trails in the United States, either it succeeded or that vision was caught by those who may not have heard of HikaNation. Trails multiply every year. And people use them too: hikers, runners, walkers, bikers, people out for an afternoon stroll. Much of America may be obese and out of shape, but there are those who follow a fitness drummer, and I saw them as I walked those trails into Washington DC.

My target that day was the Totten Metro. I confess I had been nervous about knocking on doors in Washington DC, and I had played the Lutheran card. In planning my hike, I emailed a letter asking for assistance to about ten Lutheran churches and heard back from two people who attended Augsburg Lutheran Church in Georgetown. The Totten Metro was right on the trail, and it took me to a stop near their house. Yes, the ADT is different from wilderness trails. I didn't hop Metros at trailheads on wilderness trails.

One of the things that raises up fear in my old brain is public transportation with which I am not familiar. From my point of view, walking in the woods and dealing with bears is easier. But I do know how to ask for help. I told the guy at the ticket booth that I was out of state and didn't have a clue, but I needed to get to Dupont Circle. He assigned me a guide, who instructed me how to buy a ticket and pointed out the right train. Thank you! Just what I needed.

My hosts in Washington DC were Megan and Luke, their thirteen-month-old, and Megan's mother, Judi. They had friends also visiting, Jan and Edith, so we had quite a party that night. The next day I hopped the Metro back to Totten Station and walked through Rock Creek Park and on a few other roads to the beginning of the Chesapeake and Ohio (C&O) Canal in Georgetown. I then walked back to my hosts' house. I felt like I should wear a sign saying, "I rode the Metro and survived." Different people are afraid of different things.

I was directionally challenged in Rock Creek Park, as the signs were more for the people in cars that drove through than people on foot looking for trails. As a result, I spent time wandering and added more miles to my day than planned, but it all worked out fine with a little help from another hiker who knew the area. The park was beautiful. Tulip trees were blooming, and some branches with blooms were blown down on trails and roads. Yes, the blooms really do look like tulips in green and orange, which I found quite charming.

I had planned a rest day and had sent my re-supply box to Washington DC. I stayed two nights with Megan, Luke, and Judi and entertained their baby with my altimeter watch hanging on a carabiner and my headlamp. She wanted to keep them both for her own toys, but I needed to take them with me. I had a delightful stay with hospitable company and great conversation. Then it was time to move on along the C&O Canal.

C&O Canal

Denise (also from Augustana Lutheran) picked me up at 6:15 in the morning and drove me to the C&O Canal. I felt it was a lot to ask for just a mile and a half. But by the time I got to Swain's Lock that night my knees were quite grateful that I had not walked a mile and a half more than I did.

C&O Canal through Georgetown

The ADT stretches along the C&O Canal for more than 156 miles of honest-to-goodness trail underfoot, not highway, sidewalk, or paved bicycle trail. I found it interesting from the very beginning as it proceeded between old stone walls on the way out of the city, a reminder of its original construction long years ago.

Mary E. Davison

One of the most unique sights was around mile three, when I saw turtles copulating. This was not from prurient interest. Have you ever wondered how they did it with the hard shells on their backs? Me neither. It was not something I had spent time considering. Walking along, I saw something ahead in the canal that I could not identify. In fact, I could not identify it even when I got closer and looked right at it. Eventually, I identified flippers and a head, but it did not resemble anything I knew. I finally guessed turtles, but I wondered if turtles could somehow be conjoined twins at birth as sometimes happens with humans. Finally, I was able to distinguish two bodies very closely entwined in an embrace. It was a very interesting and curiously moving sight.

About then, they separated. Yep, two turtles and not conjoined twins. Then they went at each other again and were locked belly to belly in a tight embrace. It couldn't be anything but turtles copulating. I certainly had never seen that before. I was later told there often is great ferocity in this act with turtles, but the pair I saw spent a lot of time floating, serenely engaged in a flippered embrace. There was no privacy for the act. I took their picture as they floated together in the waters of the canal.

I also sighted six herons and a deer, and late in the day, at least a dozen geese with many multiple goslings. Turkey vultures were harassing goose families, probably trying to steal eggs or goslings. The world of nature is not always peaceful and can be violent.

The towpath, which was my trail, was sandwiched between canal and Potomac River. If I tired of looking at one, I could look at the other. Sometimes the Potomac ran wide and deep with the power of enormous amounts of water flowing beneath the surface. Sometimes it spread out around islands or through flood plain forests. At the end of the day, the Great Falls of the Potomac were a grand sight with crashing falls of white water. Seeing them was worth the side trail.

And there were flowers. Some of the reviews of my first book complained about all the flowers I listed. Other reviews were glad I told about them. Different strokes for different folks. I love the flowers. Starting out there was mainly garlic mustard (an invasive part of the mustard family with white blossoms) and a few Buttercups. Then I saw my first wild blue phlox of this trip. The striking blue phlox grew in abundance, lining both sides of the towpath. There were also dogwood and wisteria blooming in nearby woods. I saw blue spiderwort and white and purple violets. The main flower show was the wild blue phlox, sometimes in sharp contrast against the dark water of the canal as it wound through green forest. Absolutely lovely.

Swain's lock campsite was my destination for the day. All along the C&O Canal, there were campsites every five-to-seven miles. You must camp in the campsites, not make it up as you go along as you might do in the wilderness, but it was nice to know there were sites. Most campsites on the C&O had a picnic table, a chemical toilet, a fire pit, and a water pump. They were free and available on a first come, first served, basis. Maybe those campsites would be crowded in the summer, but in the spring, there was plenty of open space in every campsite I saw.

The next day was a Saturday, and I was surprised to find a 100K walk/run sponsored by the Sierra Club, which meant there were lots and lots of walkers/ runners going from Georgetown to Harpers Ferry in one day. Wow! That impressed me.

It would take me four days for the same distance. But then I was seventy-four and carrying a backpack. There were at least three different sponsored runs (deduced from different styles of numbers worn on folks going different directions) as well as lots of independent runners/ walkers, bikers, bird watchers, photographers, and a wild-flower-lovers' group. (See, I'm not the only one who loves the flowers; sometimes whole groups of people walk to see them.) People were on the trail for long or short distances, all enjoying the canal. The flavor of the afternoon was much different, only a few bikers and walkers shared the trail with me.

I had a long conversation with Lucy and Suleyman. Suleyman was from Turkey. Among other things, we talked about the trails now in Turkey. I surely would have liked to walk the Lycian Way when I was in Turkey. I don't believe the waymarked trail existed when I was in the Peace Corps. America is not the only country sprouting hiking trails in my lifetime.

New flowers of the day were trillium, Virginia blue bells, blooming May apples, wild geranium and ginseng. Spring is a lovely time to go for a walk on the C&O Canal if you like flowers.

The weather, however, had changed. The first ten days or so of my hike in 2016 was in a heat wave. Once on the C&O Canal, it rained. Every day. Or night. Or both. It rained a little or a lot. Every day. Or night. Or all day long. It wasn't necessarily cold, just wet. I don't mind walking in some rain. With pack cover on and umbrella up, it was not too unpleasant, and I usually stayed dry. But putting up my tent in rain and taking down my tent in rain was never fun.

I continued to see deer, herons, egrets, geese and turtles. I also saw bicycle riders. A popular trek for bicyclists runs from Georgetown, right next to Washington, DC, to Pittsburg, Pennsylvania, most of it along the C&O. One biker I talked to had come all the way from Alaska to bike that trail, a nine-day trek for him.

I liked seeing where the ADT and the AT crossed, a trail I had seen in years past when walking the AT. I had a friendly feeling following white blazes again as I took the bridge to Harper's Ferry to pick up my next re-supply box and stay for the night. At the AT Conservancy, along with my re-supply box, I found my picture in the 2008 hiker-picture book. They took my picture again as an ADT hiker. The AT continued south toward Springer Mountain, Georgia, and I retraced my steps over the bridge and continued on the ADT on the C&O Canal.

The river constantly changed color. Gray water raced over rocks. Green, placid water stretched beneath trees. When the sun came out, the water sparkled blue, and back at my campsite it turned green. Filtered sunlight dappled the trail—when it wasn't raining.

Some nights I was lucky enough that the rain stopped for a potty run in the middle of the night. On one such nightly trip, a wasp was attracted to my headlamp and flew in the tent with me. I flailed around trying to get the wasp out, and it stung me through my shirt. Nasty bugger! After I succeeded in displacing the wasp from the inside to the outside of my tent, I fell back to sleep.

Later, I woke briefly, hearing sounds of feline-like snarling while something was evidently having something else for dinner. But it wasn't me, so I went back to sleep again until I woke to the sound of the bird chorus. While contentedly listening to the pleasant alarm clock of birds singing, I saw the wasp on the outside of my netting, searching for a way in. Not finding a way to inflict further harm, he finally flew away.

When giving presentations about my hikes, people have often wondered how I can go back to sleep after hearing snarling or scaring off a bear. They say they would not sleep a wink after such an occurrence. Well, I need sleep. I cannot hike without sleep. My body cannot heal from the day's exertions without sleep.

Steven Scarano, trail name Hamburger Helper, a trail angel on the PCT, is a new internet friend and a former Marine, who now gives corporate-leadership courses, including a module on fear. A tip he offers is when you are afraid, "Do the next right thing." In other words, think of what you would do if you were not afraid, and then do that. I like that line. I do not waste time being afraid when I need sleep. If I were not afraid, I would be sleeping. Besides, whatever animal woke me up was taking care of the situation, not asking my advice or coming at me.

Walking through woods along the Canal and the Potomac was pleasant, but I got a little tired of the green sameness. I didn't need a lot to be entertained, but I needed something—a new flower, rocks, people, houses—something.

Something was provided at lunchtime when Della, a seventy-two-year-old bike trekker, who had also hiked the AT came pushing her bike up to the picnic table at which I was having lunch. After lunch, as I headed on, she was going to unload her bike and work on the back wheel. One needs a whole different set of skills to do trekking on a bike.

The Big Slackwater came next. Instead of blasting a canal out of solid rock beside the river, the canal builders made a dam to back up the Potomac, making the river manageable for canal boats. Only a towpath just big enough for the mules needed to be carved through the solid rock. Canal boats were pulled along the Potomac for thirteen miles before canal and river separated once again.

In 2012, a concrete footpath parapet was constructed to replace a flood-prone towpath, an interesting and beautiful walk around a big horseshoe bend in the river on a concrete pathway next to cliffs. And I saw my first red columbine of the year.

When I was still three miles short of my campsite, dark clouds gathered. Earlier, I had heard thunder in passing storms, now I heard it once again, closer. The sky had deeply darkened. I walked those last miles as fast as I could. Arriving at the campsite, I had time to use the facilities. Then I hurried to set up my tent and unload into it. The rain began just as I got into the tent, raindrops hitting the back of my legs as I dove for cover. Wow. That was close timing. I ate my previously hydrated dinner while I listened to the storm.

I finally made it up to the water pump in a rain break following dinner and a little nap. But I found no water at the pump. I pumped vigorously for seventy-five pumps and only heard a few distant, half-hearted burbles. It wore me out. Getting water was not worth having a stroke or heart attack. Well, I had enough for my meds and a small amount for morning. I would have mid-morning snack for breakfast and breakfast for snack when

I found more water. (Breakfast took more water than my snack.)

The Potomac reminded me of a Robert Louis Stevenson poem set to music as a Girl Scout Regional song:

> Dark Brown Is the River
>
> Dark brown is the river.
>
> And golden is the sand.
>
> It flows along forever
>
> With trees on either hand.
>
> Green leaves a-floating,
>
> Castles of the foam,
>
> Boats of mine a-boating—
>
> Where will all come home?

I sang as I walked along and admired the flower of the day, dames rockets, a tall phlox in pink or white, which lined the trail. I met a bike trekker who had also done the AT and Long Trail. We had a nice chat, and he gave me a bottle of water when he heard my water supply was almost out. Thank you. I had been short of drinking water, but my sleeping bag was damp from all the water in the air. It would do for another night or two, but I wished I could get it dry. Dry weather was in short supply. I laughed. Just before I got to DC, the weather forecast had said: three days of rain followed by nicer weather. But I kept getting the same forecast every day for a week, three more days of rain to be followed by nicer weather. Day after day after day, it said the same thing over and over again. When I reached Williamsport, to dry out, I decided to stay in lodging, if such could be found, though it had not been in my hike plan to do so.

At the turn to Williamsport, I stopped at an interpretive center on the advice of a biker and watched a short video. Did you know George Washington was the first to dream about a canal past the Great Falls of the Potomac? George Washington was president of the first Potomac Canal Company.

I walked to the Desert Rose Café and had red beans and rice for a late lunch. The owner of the Desert Rose was a young woman named Desert Rose. She said she had hippie parents, hence the name. She seemed very young to me, but she had teenaged kids. Importantly for me, she volunteered to drive me to the Red Roof Inn and even stopped at the Dollar Store on the way. Very, very nice. She had done similar things for other hikers and bikers. She told me she gets her livelihood from those who hike, bike, and visit the canal. Giving rides is her payback. Someone wrote in a trail journal I read, that Williamsport was not a hiker-friendly town. I very much disagreed. I was glad to be in town and dry, and Desert Rose had been exceedingly friendly.

The day out of Williamsport was a very wet one. About lunch time, I came to a house near the canal with a large porch veranda. Hooray, a place to eat out of the rain. I rang the doorbell several times to ask permission to eat there. When no one answered, I helped myself to the space. It was such a nice place to eat lunch in the dry, while rain poured all around the porch.

When I was nearly done, a young man came out. He had been in the basement and hadn't heard the doorbell. He had no problem with my eating on his porch. He also gave me water, so I could cold soak my dinner, and he let me use the bathroom.

While hiking on the C&O Canal, I had not had to depend on local people to meet my needs until Desert Rose in Williamsport and my lunch on that broad porch. But when I had the need, here again were lovely people. Knocking on a door, talking to the owner of a café, ringing a doorbell, or just talking to hikers and bikers on the trail, I found again, a world filled with congenial and helpful people.

Large white dogwood blossoms, like open hands on spread-arm branches, said *hello* in the woods. Honeysuckle edged the canal and towpath. I loved the view of the canal, black-looking water under gray skies, contrasting strongly with white honeysuckle drooping down the banks to the water's surface.

The ground cover in the woods featured an abundance of white violets, creeping charlie, and queens cup, so, white and purple. White-and-pink dames rockets, wild blue phlox in shades of pale blue, little white daisy/asters and yellow, smaller daisies added variety. Patches of blooming May apples' green umbrellas laid carpets under trees. I do love the flowers.

North of Williamsport, it seemed wilder, with thick understory growth. A deer peered at me through greenery. There were bunnies and squirrels, too, but the coolest wildlife were always the turtles.

It had been so cloudy and rainy that it had not been turtle weather. But after about six miles that day, the sun came out, and I glanced toward the canal, which at that point was slow-moving, nearly stagnant water with green pond scum and many logs sticking up through that green goo. With the sun out, I expected to see turtles. Boy, were there ever! I must have seen a couple hundred turtles in about 200 yards of trail. Every log had ten-to-twenty-five turtles on it, sunlight glistening off wet turtle backs. Delightful.

I met Mark who was bike trekking to his youngest son's graduation in Missouri. There are many ways and reasons to trek across the country. We stood mid-trail and talked. He was full of enthusiasm for his bike trek, eager to share his joy of the trail, as was I.

I was tired by the time I reached Hancock. I had

walked the first six miles without poles before both knees insisted that I use them for the rest of the day. At the motel, I quickly shed clothes, showered, and headed to Pizza Hut for dinner. Then came serious horizontal time. Sleep is the body's powerful elixir, mending body and mind.

Old hiker tip: it's all about recovery time. Recovery time is important for all hikers. But much more so for older hikers. The trick is to find the right pace and right number of hours to hike each day to be tired at night but not so tired you cannot get full recovery overnight.

Young dudes can do twenty-to-thirty miles a day, sleep exhausted, but wake up in the morning refreshed and ready to go again. Every year I find the need for rest greater than the year before. If I do not get enough rest, my fatigue is cumulative. Rest days were serious blessings and much needed. It surely felt good to relax in lassitude past 7:00 a.m. on my zero day. I did get up before the motel breakfast closed. Food is at least as important as rest.

I must have looked tired and disappointed when I found out there was no laundry at my motel. They offered to do my laundry for free when housekeeping arrived on my rest day. I happily left a tip for the laundry, and with clean pants the next morning, I went to church. I had been Episcopalian for an hour two weeks earlier. In Hancock, I was Methodist. God loves us all.

After my rest day in Hancock, I stepped out with

a sprightly step and a good attitude. I didn't try to hurry, but the miles ticked by in a satisfactory manner. The flower of the day was dames rockets. They put on quite a flower show, growing thickly up both sides of the towpath, as well as continuing back into the woods.

Gary

At White Rock Campsite, I stopped to use the facilities and met Gary. Bike Trekker, homeless, and character are all words to describe Gary. He lived on the Canal—year-round. His speech and mind rambled as he talked. I gathered from him and later from a trail worker named Shayne, that the local Rangers and Conservation Corps folks tried to keep an eye out for him, bringing him in to town when it snowed. His soul shown behind his blue eyes, and I was glad I'd met him.

I knew it would rain in the middle of the next day, so I loaded up my PB and jam roll-up and put that and my cheesy crackers in a plastic bag tied to my belt. I ate under my umbrella as I strolled along. Later, I replenished my plastic bag with jerky, dried pears, and candy and walked some more.

In the afternoon, a mower mowing the middle of the towpath, followed by a truck, approached me. Shayne, the guy driving the truck, talked to me for quite a bit. They were part of the Civilian Conservation Corps of West Virginia, though they were working on the Maryland side. Shayne and his wife were facing a transition in jobs, and he asked me to pray for him. Holding his hands through his truck window, it was my privilege to lift Shayne and his wife to the care and direction of God. One does not have to be a pastor to pray, but I am always ready to pray for someone who asks.

In my tent that night, my phone told me it was supposed to rain that night and in the morning, too, so I wouldn't be dry when I packed up. Boo Hiss! It was supposed to rain the rest of the next day, too. Boo Hiss, Hiss! I reminded myself that I liked walking in cool weather. But I wouldn't have minded seeing a little sun or staying dry. Turtles liked the sun, too, and I liked seeing turtles.

Yes, the next day was wet, but it wasn't all bad. Pink-and-white flowers once again thickly lined the trail and ran up the banks past the canal. The canal was still, blackish water that perfectly reflected the trees, bushes, and colorful flowers.

Mary E. Davison

For a while, I had difficulty making forward progress as I wanted to take pictures of everything I
saw.

My last day on the C&O Canal was wet again. No
surprise. It also had another adventure in store
for me.

The soggy trail became even muddier, with lots of
puddles, as I approached the Paw Paw Tunnel. The
towpath narrowed as the canal ran between hillside cliffs and the towpath. The towpath mutat-
ed to a boardwalk ledge. The opposite bank had
a mudslide at one place, nearly filling the canal.
Water rivulets and waterfalls came off the hills on
both sides of the canal and path.

When I had dressed in the morning, I should have
left my headlamp around my neck where I wear
it at night. (It's easier to find around my neck
than placed loose somewhere in my tent.) But
I had taken it off in the morning, and as usual,
had stowed it in my pack, thinking I would take it
out again before I reached the tunnel. But at the
tunnel entrance with the headlamp in my pack,
there was no dry, safe place to take off that pack,
nor had there been as I walked to the tunnel.

At the tunnel entrance, there was no ground between the boardwalk and the murky water of the
canal. The boardwalk had spaces between the
boards, water below. And it extended over the canal straight from the vertical cliff wall at a slant
toward the black water of the canal flowing by,
and under. I did not want to take my pack off

when there was any chance my water bottle or something else could come loose. Under those conditions, anything loose would have rolled into the canal and been lost forever.

I looked in the entrance and could see the dot of light at the end of the long tunnel. It didn't look as far away as it really was. "I can do this without a headlamp," I said to myself. And I started in. It was OK for a few steps, and then became very, very dark indeed. I could always see the dot of light at the end of the tunnel, and I could sometimes make out the railing beside me, just barely. What I could not see, was where I placed my feet.

I did have my poles. I slowed my pace, and it reminded me of the book the women's Bible study read the year before: *Learning to Walk In the Dark.* (Good book, by the way.) The writer had a lot to say about darkness, real physical darkness, and what she had learned over time about that and other things, too. OK, here was my opportunity to learn to walk in darkness.

The path was three-to-four feet wide, and the tread uneven. I could hear water dripping from inside the mountain. I stepped in a few puddles. But once committed, it was either go back and take off my pack and risk losing something off the boardwalk or go on. Choices, choices. I went on.

I did OK. I just took my time and depended on my poles, not my eyes, to find my footing. I wouldn't recommend that mode of tunnel traverse to anyone else. Get your headlamp ready long before you get to the tunnel. But it was an experience I won't forget and a nice challenge to overcome. There was nothing particularly dangerous about that experience—just challenging and spooky to walk in the dark. Little children are afraid of the dark. I reminded myself I was not a little child, and as my Marine friend said, I did the next right thing. I walked.

On the other side of the tunnel, there was a sign that warned walkers to have a flashlight. Well duh, yeah. Walking in the dark without a flashlight for almost a mile was not recommended.

Now the history: The Paw Paw Tunnel was the single biggest project in making the C&O Canal. It took fourteen years to complete. There were cave-ins doing it. And it was all done with pick and shovel and black-powder blasting. It was lined with 6 million bricks. It was 3,118 ft long. (Nearly a mile). It was completed in 1850. I walked it in the dark before breakfast.

Paw Paw, the town, not the tunnel, seemed too far off trail to go to for my breakfast, and the picnic tables at a nearby camp site were soaking wet. So, I made my trail breakfast under a road overpass. I felt a bit like a bum.

As I walked along in the rain under my umbrella, I concluded I stayed drier and cleaner than the bikers, some of whom were covered with mud as they passed me. Even if it took me longer to cover the distance, I didn't have a wheel throwing mud at my behind. I did see turtles that day, 200-300 of them. They came out at 60 degrees Fahrenheit, even in the rain. On a sunny day, I bet I would have seen thousands.

I reached Oldtown before 4:00. Thanks to reading other hikers' journals, I knew about the School-house Kitchen restaurant. Since the school closed in 2000, the school building was a privately owned restaurant. I also knew they let hikers and bikers stay in one of the old classrooms, if asked. I was ready for a dry night. The food was good, too.

Sleeping in the same building as a restaurant meant breakfast was easy and good: eggs and bacon and biscuits and gravy, hiker favorites.

WEST VIRGINIA

*West Virginia portion
of the American Discovery Trail*

Good-bye C&O Canal. Good-bye Maryland. Hello, West Virginia. Good-bye, level towpath. Hello, country roads and mountains. I crossed the low wooden toll bridge over what was left of the Potomac and had a nice chat with the lady in the toll booth. I did not have to pay the toll since I wasn't in a car.

I started out without pack cover and umbrella. It was misty, but it wasn't raining. The clouds were obscuring the tops of the mountains and dropping their tendrils into the valley, but *it wasn't raining*.

When I turned on Donaldson, banks of red columbine hovered over the creek. Donaldson Road had a 600-feet elevation gain. Well, alright then, flat walking was left behind on the canal.

There were people, though. John was getting his mail. He knew nothing about the ADT but was very encouraging. I talked to Jane later, who had helped many ADT hikers. She made me wish I needed something. She was such a sweet person to talk to, I wanted to talk to her longer. About 2:00 I heard thunder rumbling, put on the pack cover, and had my umbrella at the ready. And then it rained most of the rest of the afternoon.

I stopped for dinner at Fort Ashby. Did you know Fort Ashby was one of a string of forts founded by Colonel George Washington before the Revolutionary War?

Moving past the town after I ate dinner, the skies were dark. I walked over the bridge, turned left on Baker Road, and thought, "I *have* to find somewhere to stay! And oh, I want it to be dry."

One of the first houses after that turn had a large covered porch. An elderly gentleman with a cane had just arrived and was unloading his groceries.

"Sir," I called out, and introduced myself and my need as a hiker to sleep on his porch.

He seemed startled (Isn't everyone every time I do this?) but gruffly said, "Won't hurt me none."

Did that mean yes? I wasn't really sure, so I ran through my little spiel again, ending with a request to sleep on his porch, hoping for a bit more clarification about my welcome.

He said again, in the same gruff voice, "Won't hurt me none."

Since I needed a dry place to stay and really wanted to stay on that porch, I decided "Won't hurt me none" must mean *yes*. I expressed my gratitude profusely and followed him onto the enclosed porch. He continued inside with his groceries.

After a few minutes he came out and said in that same gruff tone of voice, "Going to see my son."

"OK," I answered, somewhat perplexed. It almost sounded like he was asking my agreement or at least implying I was entitled to know what he was doing.

While he was gone, I set things up on my two plastic garbage bags to protect my gear from greasy dirt covering the floor. Then I saw the broom hanging on the wall and I swept his porch room of the winter's grime.

About the time I finished sweeping and was settling down on a rocking chair on the porch, he came back with his son. I could tell at first glance his son was not entirely comfortable with this situation. I went through my introduction again and produced my driver's license to prove I was who I said I was. We then had a very long conversation about me, the trail, and long-distance hiking, something they had never heard of before. Until it became obvious we were going to be friends, I kept worrying that I would be turned away into the dark of night. Knocking on doors after it is dark is not a good idea. Whoever would give me a place to be if I asked after dark? I talked a bit like a used car salesman, selling myself as harmless.

I give kudos to Bill for including his son in the conversation, safer for him that way. And kudos go to Tim for being the good son and checking it out with his Dad.

I asked if they had ever seen hikers with backpacks going down the road. Tim said, "Yes. But I just thought they were lost." They were incredulous to know there was a real waymarked trail that included Baker Street.

About an hour later, Bill, Tim, and I were friends, and they knew a whole lot more about long- distance hiking and the ADT. Funny how this trail and the need to ask for a place to stay makes friends from total strangers.

Oh, and Bill's short, gruff way of talking? Tim told me he showed up at his door with the gruff statement, "There's a woman stayin' on my porch." Tim didn't know quite what to make of that statement, either. After Bill said it the second time, Tim responded, "Well, make sure she cooks you breakfast." That's just the way they talk in these parts; at least, it was the way Bill and Tim talked.

So, I had a covered place to stay, Bill got his porch cleaned up a bit, and his son was going to follow my journal to see if I made it to Clarksburg. And

I had another favorite memory. I smile at Bill's gruff statements every time I remember this story, and I treasure that I met him.

Bill did not ask me to make his breakfast, but he did let me use his restroom before I headed out in the morning on West Virginia roads.

The connecting small roads were nice, with very little traffic. Then I came to Knobly Road. When he had looked at my map the night before, Tim had said Knobly Road was the only straight road in West Virginia. Well, it wasn't exactly straight, more like wavy, both up and down and side to side. But it was straight enough for cars to go faster than on more winding roads. When walking a road with no shoulder, that is not a good thing. One does have to pay close attention to avoid being squashed.

I stopped for water and to eat lunch on a porch at the house of Joyce. She was a horsewoman, ran a stable, and led trail rides. I was always meeting interesting people. After I went on, she passed me a couple miles farther, driving a truck and hauling a horse trailer, and she wished me a good journey, just like the standard greeting on the Camino de Santiago—Buen Camino, only her salutation was in English.

I also met Lawrence, who had helped several hikers. One of his friends had seen me walk by and had called to tell him there was a hiker on the road. He drove out to catch up with me, and we talked in a driveway. Again, I was sorry I didn't need anything and already had a reservation for the night at the Candlewyk Inn in Keyser and my re-supply box was there. But we stood and talked quite a while.

Just as in the West, the mountain ranges of the East are geological folds running roughly north and south, more accurately, northeast to south-west. Knobly Road, which I traveled for some time, ran just east of the ridge which my map labeled Knobly Mountain, a small range just before the Allegheny Mountains.

When I reached my day's end at a junction, I tried to call Fred, my contact at the Candlewyk Inn. I couldn't get through, no reception. Nick, a geology student, was out taking down campaign signs from the recent elections to use the material in other ways. He was happy to give me a ride into Keyser.

While resting in Keyser, Fred discovered I was a retired Lutheran pastor. It is easy to discover since my trail name is Medicare Pastor, which often leads to the question of which brand of pastor. He and I hatched a plan to take a long slackpack and stay another night at the Candlewyk Inn. He said I should meet Pastor Sally, pastor of the Lutheran Church in town. I called Pastor Sally, and she agreed to pick me up the next afternoon and bring me back to the Candlewyk. Fred would take me to the trail junction in the morning. Both ends of the transportation arranged, it was a plan.

Fred drove me out to the junction. I got out of

the car, waving good-bye as he drove away. Then I put on my pack, buckled my chest strap, and realized my two water bottles were back in my room. Oops. What to do? Fred's phone didn't work, still no reception from that spot. Well, rural West Virginia was not desert or wilderness. Something would work out. In my experience, keeping on keeping on eventually solves lots of problems.

About two-and-a-half miles down the road, I passed a chapel, and it was Sunday. The first two cars pulled into the little country church parking lot, and people unlocked the church. Perfect timing.

"May I use your rest room?"

"Of course."

There were paper cups in the rest room, too, and I drank my fill. OK, that would be good for a while.

Another three-and-a-half miles down the road, I came to the House of Prayer, another little country church.

"May I use your restroom?"

"Of course, and we're just finishing our after-church dinner, are you hungry? Would you like some dinner?"

Now how could I turn down that kind of offer? I didn't. I had a big ham dinner, mashed potatoes and gravy, beans, macaroni and cheese, and cake. And when they learned I had left my water bottles behind, one guy jumped in his car, drove home, and brought me two water bottles. Norma, one of the church ladies, and I, chatted all the time I was eating. She prayed for me, and I prayed for them. I was helped by Pentecostals that Sunday. I may be a Lutheran pastor, but I get around.

A day with no water yielded a ham dinner and two water bottles. God will provide. Many hikers would say, "The trail will provide." But I'm a Lutheran pastor and think I know who really does.

Pastor Sally from the Lutheran Church in Keyser picked me up in Martin. I was happy to meet her and happy to have a pickup. It was a very ecumenical day. She also volunteered to take me back to that spot on the trail the next morning.

True to her word, she picked me up bright and early in the morning. This was an act of extra kindness. The night before, after taking me back to the Candlewyk Inn, she had needed to take her sister to the hospital with heart problems. Yet she showed up to take me to the trail. She and her sister were in my prayers all day. *Thank you* seemed very inadequate under the circumstances.

I walked on. It was a beautiful day for walking, crisp and cold, with a beautiful, bright-blue sky and bright green of various shades all around me. Turning up aptly named Greenland Gap Road, I walked beside a rushing mountain stream coming from a pretty falls. Lawn mowers were humming as I walked along. Everyone was taking advantage of the sunshine. All the rain had encouraged the grass to grow quite tall. This sunny day was their chance to cut it back to manageable height before it rained again.

Richard was the first lawnmower guy I encountered. He insisted on shaking my hand and calling me his hero. Silly. I was just a hiker. But he probably didn't know any other hikers.

In the afternoon, I walked on freshly laid blacktop. Each step gave a little, which my feet and knees liked, but I wondered how much black stuff I was picking up on my shoes. Eventually I caught up with those laying the blacktop. Fresh blacktop is very hot and crackly when it goes down. I managed to walk on the small shoulder and avoided stepping on the steaming blacktop and becoming part of the road.

At the end of my day, Will, also out mowing, gave me a friendly wave. Finding level, dry ground for my tent was not going to happen. But Will offered a trailer he and his wife, Brenda, had converted into a camper. I considered the cot in the trailer luxurious. When the rain started again in the night, I was dry.

WILDERNESS

My host had warned me he was not an early riser, so I had no restroom in the morning. A mile and a half down the road, I found the old Streby school-house with an old, but still functional (and used), outhouse. Perfect! It even had room for my pack inside, just barely, so I could keep everything dry while tending to my needs. It didn't take much to excite this hiker on a rainy day, just enough dry space to do business. I appreciated the small things in life.

Trail disguised as a stream in Dolly Sods

Although I had the opportunity to camp all along the C&O Canal, I was getting to the main wilderness attraction of that year's trip: The Dolly Sods

Wilderness. Dolly Sods did not reward me for the climb with grand vistas, but with rain, cold, and fog. I obviously was not in charge of the weather.

There was a 2,300-feet elevation gain up to the Sods, nothing particularly hard about it other than a long uphill walk on a well-graded gravel road. But it was 2,300 feet up, and so required some energy and time.

The challenge of the day was finding a way to maintain correct body temperature while staying dry. Walking with a pack on your back makes you hot. But it's cold to start. However, if you exert energy and effort with too much on, you will sweat, making your warm, dry layers wet. I began with a long-sleeve shirt over a short-sleeve shirt, rain suit, and umbrella.

First, I took off the long-sleeve shirt, leaving on my short-sleeve shirt, and not much later I took off the rain jacket. That worked well until I stopped for snack or lunch. At 45 degrees and raining it was hypothermia weather. Stopping required me to immediately add warm layers. And all this changing needed to be done carefully, under my umbrella, while it was continually raining. Maintaining correct body temperature is sometimes a difficult art.

The Dolly Sods is a unique area in West Virginia. The terrain at that altitude resembled Canadian tundra. Where there were trees, they were pines and spruce. Even though I couldn't see very far through the cloud I was walking in, I could see enough to tell it was a pretty spot. I wasn't the only crazy person recreating in the rain. I passed eight cars parked at various trailheads on my way to the campground.

The pit toilets in the campground were nice big Forest-Service-type pit toilets. I left my pack in the dry, enclosed pit toilet, selected my campsite, and pitched my tent. The ground was very soggy. There was no trouble getting my tent stakes into soupy sod. I hoped they would hold the tent in the rain that night. I was dry and reasonably warm inside my tent.

Turtle, an AT hiker in 2014, who was also camping, but with wheels, walked across the campground road and invited me to his campfire. We talked trail, and he wanted to feed me, but I had already eaten by then. I did take a banana for breakfast. Then I snuggled back in my tent to listen to the patter of raindrops above and around me.

The Dolly Sods was sodden. Totally. I woke up to rain. No surprise there. It had been raining ever since I left Washington DC. Dolly Sods had snow a couple days before I reached it. At least it wasn't snowing while I was there. In the morning, the ground under and around the tent was even more sponge-like than the night before.

Still, I managed to pack everything up inside the tent and take the pack to the nice restroom to keep it dry while I took down the tent. Finally loaded, I asked Turtle for some water to refill my second bottle and started off into the Sods in the rain on a boardwalk. The boardwalk ended as soon as I was out of sight of the trailhead, and the fun began.

There were lots of rocks. There was lots of water. There was lots of mud. I kept my feet relatively dry until the second river crossing. I could just barely make it across the first river crossing by rock hopping.

At the second river crossing, the crossing rocks were all under water. I rolled up my pant legs and then I rolled up the rain pants. I decided it was more important to move safely and securely than quickly. I was very careful, making sure I had good foot placement and a secure stance at each step, even though the icy cold water went over my ankles.

Shortly past the second crossing, two young men blew by me, headed out on the Red Creek Trail. They moved with youth and testosterone to spare. The same could not be said about me. It was difficult hiking, with mud pits, bogs, and water running in pathways. I didn't try to stay dry anymore. After all, my feet were already fully baptized at the last crossing.

But I still tried to be sure of each foot placement. I didn't want to fall. I didn't want to break any-thing. I was being very careful not to twist my knee. Sometimes the mud was extremely slippery clay. I did not move quickly, and I did wrench my knee once during the day, but, all in all, my knees performed admirably, although I hiked slowly.

A young couple hiking toward me warned me of muddy trail ahead. Do tell. And then I came to the third river crossing. It was even more dicey to cross—a lot of water moving fast, and all the stepping-stones were at least six-to-eight inches below the surface of the water. On each side of the underwater stepping-stones, the water looked quite deep. I managed to cross the river without falling in. Thank you, God!

A while later, the trail stopped looking much like a trail and looked more like a fast-moving stream. There was water everywhere. It was as if the mountain was an enormous sponge and someone kept pouring buckets of water over this already too-full sponge. My supposed trail was complete with many merry waterfalls. All that wading of rivers and walking in ankle-deep water on trails was done with temperatures in the low forties. My feet stayed warm, if soggy, as long as I kept moving. Stopping for a rest was out of the question. I would chill.

After a junction, I started down what must have been a forest road many years ago. It didn't look much like a road, just a conduit for more water. Eventually though, the water road came to a maintained road. No more trails or roads were disguised as rivers. After reaching a real road I just worked at churning out the miles to catch up with my schedule. Inclement weather and wilderness had definitely slowed me down.

I had planned on eating dinner at Caanan Valley Lodge and then moving on to find a campsite a mile farther on. But I was wet and cold from my adventures of the day, and I didn't reach Caanan Valley Lodge until 6:00. I opted to spend the money to be dry and clean even if short of my itinerary goal. After wondering if I might fall in the river and be lost in the Sods, I stayed in the lap of luxury. It seemed surreal to be in a high-class hotel so close to soggy wilderness challenges.

Sometimes hikers skip, walk, or ride around the Dolly Sods Wilderness. In spite of the somewhat grueling day, I was still glad I had not skipped it. It was good to see there was wilderness, even though I saw it in fog and rain. If I had not done it, I would always have thought I missed something. Was it easy? No. Was it do-able? Guess so. I did it.

After an excellent dinner, I was clean once again, and all my soggy gear was festooned across every available surface in my room to dry.

The next day was a dry day. Amazing. I started out from the lodge, and there was blue sky, well, not all of it. It was partly cloudy, but for this trip, it was glorious. Even my feet started out dry, although they didn't stay pristinely dry as I was soon walking through wet grass.

This was another day of mostly trail, real trail. There were bridges over creeks. I did not have to wade. I enjoyed walking through Eastern hardwood forests, the lower canopy a bright spring green. I hit the one mile stretch of FR 13 and walked on dirt/gravel graded road.

When I started up the Davis Trail, trouble began: more mud bogs and trail cleverly disguised as a flowing stream. It was nothing compared to the day before, but my pace slowed as I danced around the streams and bogs. Mostly I stayed dry, but it was slower going. I had to keep watching where I put my feet as it became muddier, with more puddles of water.

At a trail junction with a shelter, trails headed out in four directions from the signpost, and down each choice of trail stretched lengthy sections of trail filled with water. Take your pick: mud, puddles, and bogs in every direction. There *was* a nice boardwalk to the shelter, but all around the shelter and the boardwalk there was standing water. It resembled a boardwalk in a lake. I ate cheesy crackers sitting on the short boardwalk to the shelter, the driest spot around and in the sun.

The names of trails on my T-by-T directions were different from the names of trails on the signposts. Without both the waypoints on the GPS and the compass directions on the T-by-T, navigation would have been difficult. A mile or so after the shelter, the trail improved to a pleasant path by a stream and entered Black Water Falls State Park.

Reaching Black Water Falls Lodge at 2:30, I found the dining room had closed at 2:00 and would not open until 4:00. Bummer. I had been planning to eat there. Oh, well. I did find water to make my dinner and fill my water bottles, and I left, munching on jerky and almonds.

I wished the T-by-T or some sign had told me to turn right at the road near the stables. Not knowing that, I followed waypoints and missed the falls after going through all that mud and muck up north for that attraction. That was disappointing. But by the time I realized my error, I was not going back.

I turned left at the waypoint on my GPS, though the trail was unmarked. It was definitely the railroad grade described. Although unmaintained and neglected, it seemed alluring to me. This forest was quite different from the other side of those same mountains. There was abundant fir instead of hardwoods. The forest floor, including the trail, was soft duff with very little mud. Firs make a forest smell *right* to me. I camped not far from a rushing mountain stream on soft forest duff, my favorite campsite on that year's hike, sleeping soundly, lulled by the white noise of the stream.

In the morning, I had the pleasant task of packing up a *dry* tent. Imagine that.

But soon the trail worsened. I reached a trail junction close to the next supposed shelter, which would mark the trail to my next waypoint. It looked like the first shelter trail junction had looked, a swamp. I was very glad I had camped on forest duff instead.

The T-by-T did not mention that trail junction. Not a word. Nor did I see a trail headed to my next waypoint. Well, maybe I did, but what I saw was a very big and deep puddle swallowed up by rhododendrons on all sides. I didn't take that large mud-puddle trail. The trail to the right at least looked like it might be passable, and after consulting my GPS several times, I deduced that it would also get me to FR 13 about a mile and a half past three other waypoints. I chose to go my own way.

Passable meant different things at different times on that trail. Sometimes it was rather nice, and sometimes it was a complete bog. I danced on little rocks and roots and skirted edges of bogs by pushing my way past rhodies. (For those that do not know, the principal vegetation in much of the East, and especially the Southeast, is rhododendron.)

Hiking on those trails was a constant decision-making process. What was the best way around or through a large puddle? Was there a little more room next to the rhodies on the right or on the left? Wait, is that a rock or two showing in the middle? If I lean on my poles, can I stretch my legs safely far enough to reach it? Do those rocks get me across? Choices, choices, choices. And I lived with whatever choices I made. It was like a giant puzzle. Or much like life. As soon as one puzzle was solved, one choice made, there was another puzzle to solve, another choice to be made, and more trail to travel.

When I reached the forest road, I turned south and walked the mile and a half to old FR 422. That old road was a very pleasant walk—broad, with flowers and grass on each side.

WONDERFUL PEOPLE

Finally, I hit the highway and eventually made my way to Hendricks. I asked at one of the first houses I came to for water. They very helpfully gave me water and a small, cold energy drink, too. I had been walking without water for a few hours as I had mistakenly thought roads on my map would equal houses, which was not the case. I chatted with those gracious country people, who also let me use their restroom.

From there, I took T-by-T directions on the highway to Parsons. There was a lovely bike trail by the river, which it seemed would have been much more scenic than the highway. I hope the ADT updates its directions to include that trail.

Three or four people in Parsons stopped me to ask about my hike. The owners of the campground drove by and identified me as the Mary with the reservation, who was to arrive and pick up a re-supply box. Before I reached the campground just outside of town, I stopped at a fast-food place for a quick dinner.

At the campground, the host met me in a golf cart with my re-supply package and drove me to a covered pavilion. I gratefully set up home as a cowboy camp (didn't put up my tent) in the middle under that large pavilion which would keep me dry in the coming rainstorm. I reveled in the amenities of the campground, especially the shower.

It poured for a good portion of the night, drumming deafeningly on the metal roof of the pavilion. I was very grateful for my dry and dusty spot under that roof. When I woke in the morning, the rain had stopped. In the month of May, there had been, maybe, two twenty-four-hour periods of no rain. And there was no sun in the forecast. 2016 had turned out to be an exceedingly wet hike. Even I was getting discouraged by all the rain. I expected some. I did not expect it to rain *all* the time.

To expunge my whiney mood, I reflected that many people have far more adversity in their lives than hiking in the rain. Hiking was entirely voluntary. I have sometimes reminded other whiney hikers that they don't have to do this. So, I reminded myself, not with the intent to quit hiking, just to stop whining. Attitude adjustment underway, I headed out of Parsons on a steep 600 foot elevation gain. But it was on paved road, not muddy, boggy trail. I could do this.

Part way up the hill, I saw a lovely bit of orange from a wild azalea growing in the middle of a barren cliff, a nice symbol of growing and being beautiful in adversity. I enjoyed the greenery, and I enjoyed the flowers and waterfalls. Rain made very cheerful waterfalls in every brook.

I stopped to ask for water at a house at a V road junction. The couple there was most gracious. Several hikers had stopped at their house before. It was refreshing to meet people who knew I was walking on a trail.

Past another nice, but narrow, valley dotted with farms, a severe rain squall doused me. It came down in such bucket-loads I couldn't make forward progress. While the heavens opened, and it poured, I just stood there under my umbrella and ate the PB&J roll ups I had made at breakfast time for just such an occurrence. But I really needed to sit down and rest.

After the rain eased, and my roll ups were a memory, I moved forward and shortly saw a nice house with multiple porches and decks, lights on inside, shining welcome on the gloomy day, and a car indicating someone was at home. (Asking for something requires not just a house but someone at home in that house.) I asked for permission to eat on the covered deck, but they invited me into the upstairs kitchen.

Surprise, they were related to the gracious couple who had given me water earlier in the day. Tina, my host, was decorating a cake for her daughter's birthday, getting ready for a family bar-b-q. I finished my lunch, had a good time chatting, met her husband and two adult kids, and visited the restroom twice before heading out. They had hosted several hikers in past years. Good folks. I wished I could have stayed, but then I would have had too many miles to go to reach Philippi the next day.

OK, up the rest of that mountain and then a long descent on the other side. Twenty beautiful white doves perched on a barn roof I passed. The people there told me they used to have 100, but hawks had gradually thinned the flock. They were very beautiful birds. I was always seeing unique and unexpected sights on the ADT.

Following two more severe thunderstorms, I reached the near end of Valley Furnace and looked for a place to spend the night. I spied an outbuilding behind a low rambler. It appeared to have open space alongside farm equipment. I was getting good at spying out dry places to be. I had a lot of experience doing so on this hike.

I stopped at the house and asked Gladolene if I could stay in that dry space for the night. She invited me in out of the cold and rain and asked about my hike. She was pretty certain I could stay in the outbuilding but would not make that decision until her husband came home. We chatted companionably, though I was getting concerned about approaching darkness and not having a decision. But all went well when her husband came home, and I was again cowboy camped in a dry place, that time next to a mower, trailer, and miscellaneous other smaller farm stuff.

Interestingly, as we had talked, she asked where I had been staying and who I had seen on my travels. It turned out she knew many of the people who had given me water or let me stay in their yards, all the way back to Maryland. Not only do I make connections on this trail, the people I meet can be connected as well. Our world is a smaller place than I would have imagined. Simply knocking on doors looking for a place to be, I had made friends of friends of friends of friends. The world is a much less fearful place than I might have imagined before the ADT. Friends of friends of friends were not scary at all.

It rained during the night, but not when I needed to be up. Although it rained as I left my sheltered spot, the weather soon settled down to a sputter of wetness and just looked threatening as I walked. I was happy not to have a wet tent, even if I did have a wet umbrella as I walked through rolling hills.

Another Sunday had rolled around, which meant my restroom needs were taken care of by churches. The first church at which I stopped was a fairly large nondenominational church. They were gracious in the use of their restroom, although they really did not understand the *American Discovery Trail Thing*.

"What was I hoping to discover?"

Whatever is around the next bend was not an answer they understood. They were gracious with their welcome, but I had the impression they felt I was a bum or weirdo. Or maybe that was just me, aware of my sweaty self and duct-tape-patched rain pants in contrast to their Sunday best. I did not tell them I was a retired pastor.

That might have been more confusing.

The other church at which I stopped later in the day was tiny—there were exactly five people present that Sunday. But after my use of the facilities, they were very interested in me and my hike. It always makes me happy when people are honestly interested, and I can tell them trail stories. They wanted to know my remaining route. And Darwin said, "Hey, you will walk right by my house." I pulled out my itinerary and discovered, yes, I would be walking by his house near the end of the day in two days hence. I more or less invited myself to stay there, but Darwin had a twinkle in his eye, and I thought I might have a place to stay and dinner. too, especially since the pastor told him he surely wouldn't turn me away hungry. All this conversation was spoken with good humor and fun.

*The whole congregation (June and
Darwin in red and blue)*

I enjoyed talking to those five people. They were of a Pentecostal bent, and I am sure there were many theological points about which we would disagree. But we met on a human level because of my very human need for a restroom, and we enjoyed talking with one another.

My 2016 hike had quite an ecumenical flavor, worshiping with Episcopalians and Methodists, being helped by Lutherans in DC and Keyser, stopping by a nondenominational church, and helped by the hospitality of two small groups of Pentecostals. I prayed for them, and they prayed for me.

Then I set off for my motel, which was then only a mile and a half away. I definitely needed a rest day. My right knee was feeling very stressed from mile pounding on a paved road. Shower, laundry, horizontal time before dinner, and a rest day beckoned. Yay.

Sharon, the West Virginia coordinator for the American Discovery Trail, took me out to lunch during my rest day. This was special. Since I was planning to stop for that year's hike at Clarksburg, and she lived beyond that, she had to drive a distance to meet me. We had a lovely girls' time out, a great time talking about many subjects. I think we both enjoyed ourselves.

ABUSE OF HOSPITALITY

Our conversation touched on an important and somewhat troubling subject: hikers abusing hospitality. I know there is sometimes a sense of entitlement in those who walk long trails. It is not a new problem and has been discussed many times on PCT and AT chat lines. I suppose these days it is discussed on Facebook.

There have been people who claim they are hiking the trail yet make only three-miles-a-day for days on end, while staying multiple days at each stop, sponging off the hospitality of kind people. I know, I know, hike your own hike. Hikers aren't supposed to make negative comments about other hikers. Hiking your own hike is quite enough to worry about. But when I hear of people obviously taking advantage of others, I am appalled.

Yes, I knock on doors and ask for places to put my tent, for water, for a restroom. But that is just not the same thing as showing up and *telling* someone you plan to stay for five days—in their house, using their facilities, eating their food, and then have the rudeness to complain about the housekeeping of their hosts. REALLY!

Hikers are supposed to hike. And if people are gracious enough to help us when we need help or even offer far more than asked, they are to be profusely thanked.

Hikers are doing a voluntary activity—*taking a*

vacation, personal challenge, enjoying themselves. We are doing this because we *want* to. We are not *entitled* to anything. Anything we receive is a *gift* for which to be grateful, *not* something to be expected.

The day before, when Darwin had first exclaimed that I would walk right by his house at the end of a planned day on my itinerary, I sort of *invited myself* to stay there in a covered shed. But we were all laughing and joking about it. There is a line crossed when such things are commanded or expected instead of taken as gifts, with thanksgiving. Those who take advantage of their hosts give all hikers and the trail a bad name.

The hostels on the Camino de Santiago enforce strict time limits on the number of nights a hiker may stay. Many established trail-angel stops on the AT and PCT have had to enforce limits, as well. Unless there is some extenuating circumstance, such as illness, injury, or the good fortune of staying with friends you already know, staying for a night or two is plenty. Hikers who wish to visit on an extended vacation can pay for other lodging.

Besides buying me lunch (a gift, not an expectation) and sharing conversation, Sharon took me to the other side of the river to see the Covered Bridge. Although the T-by-T takes you within a block or so of the bridge, it doesn't mention it, even though routing through Philippi was for its historical interest.

Philippi was the site of the first land battle of the Civil War. I did not recall ever hearing the name Philippi in connection with the Civil War. But when I saw the sign telling me Philippi was formerly called Booth's Ferry, that did ring a bell in my memory.

One of the reasons the Covered Bridge is of importance is the apocryphal story that late in the Civil War there was a secret meeting between the Confederacy's Jefferson Davis and President Lincoln on that Covered Bridge. It was a nice little nugget of history on, well, *near* the trail. But you have to walk across the bridge or drive around to see the interpretive sign. Covered bridges look a bit like a barn one drives through. They are bridges over water with roof and, usually, solid walls. The solid walls provided concealment so the meeting would be secret,

Leaving Philippi, I had a lovely walk along the Tygart River. Flowers were blooming and the sky was blue. Pink and white dames rockets, purple asters, a deep blue something else, and a wild white rose bloomed, the rose casting a sweet fragrance to enhance the walk. Butterflies were everywhere around me. There were so many butterflies I felt like I was in the movie, *Bambi*, and Thumper would surely join me any minute. I reached Arden for lunch, and the Methodist Church had a covered picnic area beside the church where I ate my lunch, though no one was there.

The river turned to roaring rapids, and I passed a large rock. I learned later, the rock was nicknamed Party Rock, big enough for many people, and many people were there, one young man jumping in the river on a smoother-flowing side. That still seemed dangerous to me, with fierce rapids all around except for that one side. Ah, youth. I am pretty sure none of those sun bathers was more than twenty-five. I met one person who was eighty-plus years old and walking on the road, a pleasant but more sedate pastime for those who do not think they are immortal, blithely leaping into backwater pools near rapids.

At the top of a hill past Moatsville, I came to the home of Darwin and June. I walked in and was immediately presented with an incredible feast of huge quantities of fried chicken (best I ever ate) and everything to go with it, including pineapple-upside-down cake for dessert. June cooked big meals, and various extended family came over throughout the evening to take some home to share.

Darwin and June were the patriarch and matriarch of a loving extended family. I was honored to meet them. I was quite taken with the country love that was obvious in this family and they shared with me. Love is love, but West Virginia country folks have their own flavor, and I loved it.

Two of their grandsons thought a push lawn mower and a weed eater were fun toys. They were busy weed-eating and mowing Grandpa and Grandma's yard for fun. Grandpa Darwin had taught them how to use his woodworking tools, too, when they were very young. One of them had banged together a bookshelf to take home. They obviously adored their grandpa. The oldest grandson also liked talking to adults, including me. He was a very mature young man at 12 years old. I was quite impressed.

This family had a down-home West Virginia flavor, folks who had lived within two stone's throw of each other for all their lives. Darwin had worked in the coal mines. He also had done some hay farming. His son-in-law was raising grass-fed animals for the Washington DC market. That son-in-law grinned ear to ear when talking about his farm. In love with being a farmer, he also clearly loved talking about each aspect of his life and farm decisions with his father-in-law.

Darwin and June knew Gladolene, in whose outbuilding I had stayed the day before I had reached Philippi. I was getting the impression everyone knew everyone else in West Virginia.

I *couch surfed* that night, giving thanks to God for the privilege of a glimpse into their lives. Darwin and June fed me extra well for breakfast: bacon and eggs, toast and oatmeal, all of it delicious. Darwin had frozen two bottles of water for me, too. How thoughtful! The weather had suddenly turned hot instead of cold and rainy. It was at least 84 degrees that afternoon, and that cold water was wonderfully appreciated. I said goodbye and thank you. I had met a very special family, sad to think I probably would never see them again. Nevertheless, it was time to leave.

That morning started an up-and-down day, a countryside of mountain and valley farms. There is a reason the West Virginia nickname is the Mountaineers. I liked the morning roads in spite of the up and down, seeing only four cars in nearly three hours.

While I had lunch sitting on a wire-gated stone driveway that led into woods, a ground hog ran across the road right at me, intending to come up the driveway where I sat. He didn't see me at first, and then he did. He froze for several long moments. Freezing in place seemed to be his first line of defense. I didn't think that would work very well with cars. After *freezing* for a while, it appeared I wasn't leaving, so he did, scurrying off in another direction.

Cicadas were out on the road. I had begun seeing them just before Philippi. They are harmless, don't live too long, look like a gigantic fly with beautiful bronze wings, and have a very long (years) life cycle as nymphs and a very short life as mature cicadas. Although I had heard of them before, they do not live in Washington State. Cars mashed a lot of them on the road.

Squirrels and chipmunks were out in abundance. All the woodland critters were tired of hiding from the rain and out of their lairs, enjoying the day with me.

I camped that night in a city campground, in an

area that appeared unused. It was so hot I couldn't take my Ziploc bath until after 7:00, when it finally started to cool down. If taken earlier, in all that humid heat, I would have just sweat more under the layer of water used to wash. Hiking in shoulder season, neither summer nor winter, means any kind of weather is possible, and I had hot to rain and cold to hot again.

The next day was hot as well. A woman hanging laundry in Hepzibah gave me water for my bottles. Interestingly, she said she wouldn't have given me any if I were a guy. I guessed there might have been layers of story behind that statement that I did not learn.

People are often afraid for a woman to travel solo. But I seemed to get a lot of perks both by being female and by having white hair. I have read journals of other hikers, some male. They too met interesting people on the ADT, as I have done. Because I am an older hiker, I do not hike as fast or as far per day as others on this trail. That means I have had more need and more opportunity to meet more people. That has not been a bad thing.

One more treat awaited me. Near the end of the day, I took a picture of a view. As I turned around, a walker approached. She asked where I had started my hike and where I would end the day. We talked trail a bit and she gave me an invitation to stay on their deck that night. After finishing her walk in the other direction, she caught up with me again. The offer of the deck morphed into an offer of a bed and a shower as we walked and talked.

Sarah and Larry were both musicians. Sarah was the music director at the biggest Methodist Church in West Virginia. Larry was an organist who taught at West Virginia Wesley University. Sarah and Larry were very different from Darwin and June, but equally gracious and interesting people.

Larry and Sarah were wonderful capstones to my travels for the year on the ADT. I had only a little way to go the next day to my motel near the airport and my spring hike of 2016 on the ADT would be complete.

Larry and Sarah would have gladly cooked me breakfast, but I ate a trail breakfast as I wanted to get rid of my food. However, it was a leisurely breakfast, as it was so pleasant talking with them. I could have stayed hours, reveling in sharing my tales and hearing theirs.

Sarah and Larry

The sun, however, was getting higher. I walked down the hill and into the lovely valley. The only problem with those scenic rolling hills of grass dotted with houses and farms is that there were no trees and was no shade on that road. Before long I was very hot.

Along my way, I met a guy out using his mower to do battle with his tall grass that had grown so well with all the rain. He told me Lewis and Clark had passed through this valley on their way to the Ohio River and then on to the Mississippi. He was quite proud of his 210-year-old house.

I was very glad I had a short day. I was dripping sweat. I was better off dealing with rain than heat. Fast food and restaurants came before the Microtel. Stepping inside a building holding several brands of fast food, air conditioning hit me full blast. Some people there were complaining about the strongly blowing, rather frigid air. I thought it was wonderful even though it nearly froze me, since I was so wet with sweat.

I had a Little Caesar's lunch special and loved every salty, fatty bite of it. I followed that with a Blizzard. How convenient to have all those brands together under one roof. I would have to start watching what I ate the next day, flying back to Washington State, my body toned by long- distance hiking and my mind filled with memories of wonderful people met along the way.

PERSPECTIVE

I get a little full of myself, especially when I think I have discovered an important truth. After two trips on the ADT, I had met so many wonderful people by stepping past my fears. I had so many great stories of people I had met on the trail. I was sure I needed to tell everyone I saw what I had observed and learned about fear and my conclusion that the world was filled with wonderful people. I wanted to encourage others to move past their fears, refuse to fear, be open to others, even those they did not know. I had a gospel, of sorts, about leaving fear behind.

Rosey Eagle, another retired Lutheran pastor who was a hiker, sent me an email, after reading my online hiking journal. He dubbed me the Apostle of Unfear. I liked the name and it inflated my ego even more.

Back in Washington, while filling in to preach at a church at which I have old friends, I was pontificating to one of my friends about my experiences relating to the topic of fear and unfear. She was interested in that topic too, but from an entirely different perspective. She was being stalked.

That took me off my high horse in a rather quick hurry. I could not solve all the world's problems. I could not take away her fear, nor would it have been a good idea for her to leave all fear behind regarding her stalker.

Are We Never Supposed to Be Afraid?
Is Fear Always Bad?

Fear can be a good thing. Being afraid can keep us from danger and keep us safe. It can also rule our lives and keep us from living full and abundant lives. It is not always easy to discern whether fear or unfear is the right choice in any one moment.

Life is a dangerous sport. We are born into this world and even our innate growth processes put us in danger. Babies can roll off changing tables. Children move. Moving bodies of any age can fall. Even natural development is dangerous.

When my daughter was learning to walk, we lived in a house in Texas with an uncarpeted floor. She learned to pull herself up to furniture and loved standing at the open dishwasher. But when she tried to move away from things she could hang onto, out into open space on her own, she fell, and bashed those nice sharp baby teeth through her lip.

That experience made her slow to learn to walk independently. She *feared* having that happen again. And it did happen again, on the sidewalk in front of our house. Fortunately, growth and development are powerful forces that overcame her fear. Those bad experiences slowed her for a while, but she did learn to walk and run and even has a Bachelor's Degree in Fine Art and Modern Dance. Now, she chases her own eight children, rather well. Fear of falling did not keep her from living fully for very long.

When we learn to walk as toddlers, we learn to take risks. The simple act of walking is a continual process of risking, losing balance, almost falling, and catching our balance again with each step we take. You can *see* that process if you watch a toddler learning to walk. You can *see* that we have difficulty with that process as we age. Keeping or catching our balance becomes more difficult as we age. And along the way, in between the time we are babies and the time we are aged, we have a lot of opportunity to take risks and then to catch our balance, in walking and in living.

Fear can keep us safe. We fear putting our hands in fire or on a hot burner on a stove. We fear being burned. That is a good thing. We understand the consequence of heat touching skin and avoid it. And fear can hinder our living, like keeping my daughter from walking, for a while. Sometimes fears are rational and needed. Sometimes fears are irrational and restricting. And sometimes it is hard to tell the difference between rational and irrational fear. It can be hard to tell when to keep our fears and when to give them up.

My perspective on fear and unfear, on risking, knocking on an unfamiliar door when on the ADT, or any other risk I choose to take, is just my perspective. Yours may be different. But it is my hope that sharing trail stories about the

American Discovery Trail and my life experiences, might make you stop and think, as it has made me stop and think, about our fears and the *possibility* of unfear, leaving fear behind. Discerning which fears to keep and which to leave behind is a lifelong challenge.

2017

While visiting my daughter, son-in-law, and their family in 2016, I had questioned aloud how I would get those western states on the American Discovery trail done after completing the CDT. I liked to hike at the best time of year for each section of the United States that I hike. But what in the world would be the best time of year for Nevada? My son-in-law suggested April, so I tried Nevada in the spring of 2017, with mixed results. The ADT in Nevada is not part of this description of the ADT from the Atlantic to the Missouri River, but I mention it since my attempt to do Nevada in April was the reason I did not continue hiking the ADT in the East in 2017. Those who like logical progression following years would notice the gap.

I also took the most serious fall I have ever had while on that hike in 2017 when I was 75. Falling has increased my caution on steep terrain. I am 79 now as I write this book. My strength, reflexes and balance are still good for my age, but not as good as when I was younger. I do have a fear of falling like that again. My fear is not enough to keep me from hiking, but it is certainly enough to give me pause going down steep hills. Hopefully, this fear, a good one to have in moderation, will inspire some caution and help prevent me from falling again. Remember, fear sometimes has good uses.

My friend who had been stalked takes precautions now that she may not have considered in her life before. I take more care with steep hills and where I place my feet than I did when I was younger. Both of us try harder to be more aware of our surroundings, for different reasons. Leaving fear behind does not require leaving your brains behind, nor ignoring all precautions. Neither one of us has abandoned all risk. All of life is a risk. There are no guarantees, regardless of precautions.

I know long-distance hiking is good for me, good for my physical health, my mental health, and my spiritual health. Neither my friend nor I let fear rule our lives, although risks and fear affect us, in differing ways. My choice is to keep on hiking. All choices carry possible consequences, possible joys, possible opportunities for learning, and possible dangers. And just as a choice of footfall on a mucky trail means a risk of slipping, once you make your choice and commit to that foot placement, you live with the consequences.

Some of the risks I choose to take are risks others may not choose. Risks others take may be risks I do not take. Fear does influence the level of risk taken, for good or ill. And although I have some fear of falling, fear of people whom I do not know has greatly diminished while hiking the American Discovery Trail. The consequences of my actions have brought me great joy and less fear, also more caution with where I place my feet.

Mission of the American Discovery Trail Society

According to its website, The Mission of the American Discovery Trail Society is to create, manage and promote the American Discovery Trail as a national resource for the enjoyment and benefit of its users. The Society will achieve this mission by:

Developing and managing an off-road trail (wherever possible and feasible) across America for non-motorized users.

Providing support to local trail groups to enable them to develop and manage their section of trail and increase their constituencies.

Creating a national constituency to support and protect the Trail.

Providing informational materials to its members and the public for use on the Trail.

Providing educational services concerning the ecological, historic and scenic features along the Trail route.

The ADT incorporates trails designed for hiking, bicycle and equestrian use. Because it connects five national scenic and twelve national historic trails, 35 national recreational trails, and many other local and regional trails, it is the backbone for the national trails system. It passes through metropolitan areas like San Francisco and Cincinnati, traces numerous pioneer trails, leads to fourteen national parks and sixteen national forests and visits more than 10,000 sites of historic, cultural and natural significance.

The ADT is all about **connections**—people to people, community to community, urban areas to wilderness. It provides the opportunity for the most adventurous to travel from coast to coast, truly discovering the heart of America. More importantly it provides millions of people access to a trail system that improves quality of life and protects our natural resources.

The above statements and paragraphs come from the American Discovery Trail website. My experiences on the ADT resonate most clearly with the statement about connections, connections to the people I have met along the way and connections of trails to roads to other trails. I am a section hiker. My hiking goals have never included going from start to end of a long trail in one long trip. I do connect sections of trail, sometimes years after leaving spaces between those sections already finished. I like the emphasis on connection on the ADT as it fits me and my preference in style of hiking.

2018

American Discovery Trail

In the fall of 2017, I completed the CDT and the Triple Crown of long-distance hiking. Over the winter of 2017, I wrote my book about that experience, *Old Lady on the Trail*. After completing the Triple Crown, both my annual spring hike and my annual late summer/fall hike could be devoted to the American Discovery Trail.

In the East, I had walked from just before Cincinnati

to the Mississippi River. I had also walked from the Atlantic Ocean to halfway through West Virginia. It was time to connect those two sections in the spring of 2018.

TRAINING

Training for a long-distance hike as an older person presents increasing challenges each year. In 2018, I walked too far, too fast, causing an injury in my left foot. Eventually, it healed up enough to start training again. But an older person often heals by calcification. In other words, a torn tendon on the side of my foot healed by becoming bone. Fortunately, my podiatrist and I figured out a specific way to pad the insert in my left shoe to relieve pressure on that part of my foot. I could still hike.

The weather in the East is quite variable in the spring. I kept looking at weather reports while visiting my daughter in Virginia, prior to beginning my hike on the ADT in mid-April. It snowed in Clarksburg, West Virginia, yet the next day it was 64 degrees. In Charlottesville it was 85 degrees, and the week before, it had snowed. The weather is what the weather is. April can be hot or cold, difficult or glorious in either direction on your outdoor thermometer.

I was known as Outdoor Grandma to my eight grandchildren in Virginia. In 2018 I had to be serious about walking most days while visiting them, hoping I could get feet and body in shape to hike. Some of my grandchildren walked with me. We walked in their neighborhood, to Still Meadow and the river. We walked a fitness trail in Pen Park. The three-year-old twins walked with me to see pinwheels in a yard about a mile and a half away from their house. One of the twins was a great walker. His answer, when given the choice of going more or going back home, was always "more!"

My daughter and I set up their very large tent in the backyard and she, the children, and I slept in it for two nights, all eight grandchildren, including the eighteen-month-old in a Pack'n Play in a sleeper under a blanket and the rest under sleeping bags.

Training with grandchildren was the best! But my foot injury had put me behind where I should have been in conditioning. It was too late to worry about that. I had an airplane to catch to get to Clarksburg.

WEST VIRGINIA

West Virginia portion of the American Discovery Trail

In the Bridgeport Airport, I assembled my gear into my pack from the duffle-bag which was checked luggage on the airplane, hoisted pack on back, folded the duffle on top and walked out of the airport through the town of Bridgeport. While stopped outside a gas station for dinner, Darren walked up to my table and asked if I was hiking the ADT. Darren's sister, Tangent, was a hiker working on her Triple Crown. Amazing. A Triple Crown to American Discovery Trail connection and a person to person connection on the very first day. It was a great way to begin a hike.

The rest of the day was a navigation challenge as my T-by-T directions had an error. I created my own route to a waypoint a little farther along and think I had a nicer walk than the one on the

T-by-T. Being flexible is good. Since it was fast getting dark by the time I was once again on the ADT, I settled for the leaves on a poor shoulder of the trail with firm mud in front of my tent. Beggars can't be choosers. At least I was found and not lost, and I had a place to be.

The next day, I met up with Sharon again, the Coordinator of the West Virginia section of the ADT, whom I had met in 2016. Sharon provided me with some lovely trail support to begin my hike. She suggested changes to my schedule to be able to see more of me, and those changes were all to my benefit. Thanks to her support, I could do one overnight and then day hike for a couple days without carrying all my gear or heavy food.

Sharon

The weather was ideal walking weather, a little cold in the morning with blue sky all day, though it never got really hot. The ADT in this section was on the North Bend Rail Trail, through woods, small hamlets and meadows. Rail trails are trails that once were railroads. The first half of West Virginia, which I had walked two years earlier, was on roads up and down mountains. Rail trails don't go up and down mountains because trains don't go up and down mountains. They go through them. This half of West Virginia had tunnels. I walked through two railroad tunnels that day, briefly needing my headlamp on. The first tunnel was dry and would have made a good shelter, provided the wind wasn't blowing through it. The second one was wet, requiring a bit of dancing to dry spots, avoiding puddles.

My trail stayed close to highway 50, tread on grass or bicycle aggregate, good underfoot as it coursed through woods, by small hamlets, over creeks and rivers on bridges. My left foot did pretty well until the last mile of the day. My left knee was a little swollen though. At 76, some body part was always getting out of whack.

As I exited my third tunnel, I met an older hiker looking for his glasses, lost from his coat pocket a day or two ago. As he gave up his search, I asked what I should do if I found them. He said to post the information on my journal. I also told him, if I found them, I would leave them with Sharon and Paul. Unfortunately, I failed to catch his name.

After the tunnel, I took a long lunch break after

chatting with two ladies who were enjoying the day as they took a walk. It was a great day for walking and for resting. After eating my lunch, I stretched out with my head on my pack and my umbrella up to keep sun off my head. The welcome sunshine soaked into the rest of me as I lay there, road noise deadened by a hill separating me from the highway. I blissfully enjoyed my closed eyes, knowing that on my short day, a nap would cause no problems.

A mile or so farther on, I found the man's glasses lying on the trail. I put them in my soft glasses case in my pack pocket and hoped they would eventually reach their rightful owner.

Reaching Salem, I picked up a couple things from the IGA for breakfast and stopped at the Dairy Queen for dinner. That night I stayed in Crystal's garage. She had been recruited for me by Sharon. Hikers have few needs, other than a little space to throw a sleeping bag and some water. Restroom privileges were a bonus. I appreciated Crystal's hospitality and we enjoyed talking. She was hoping to help out with other hikers who might come by on the ADT.

Two little baked apple pies purchased from IGA were my breakfast, eaten before heading out of Salem, my progress noted by barking dogs at each house I passed. The day was overcast but warm. I walked through woods of leafless trees, white sycamore trunks contrasting with the brown trunks of the rest of the forest. Purple violets, yellow dandelions, and occasional spring beauties bloomed.

I saw my first stand of wild blue phlox for the year. (Yes, I know I have talked about them in the two previous hiking years on the ADT, but they were equally beautiful in each succeeding year.) Red cardinals flitted through the trees along with a few sparrows. Four turkey vultures perched on high trees over the trail.

That day's tunnel was wet. The east side had an interesting creek, shale like rock and deep valleys below the trail. The west side had a picnic table with highway traffic close by. I thought the picnic table should have been on the scenic east side, but no one asked my opinion.

A guy and two young dudes passed me on the trail that day. Their car had run out of gas, embarrassing the mature adult as they continued their impromptu hike. I passed a fairly new large gas and oil plant. I later learned the weight of the big trucks connected with the gas and oil plant were breaking up country roads. Much of the money paid by the gas and oil industry to the state was not being used to fix the local roads, to the chagrin of local people.

In Smithburg, I sat on a park bench to send an email but ended up only reading one sent to me. My eyes fighting an urge to cross and close, I yielded to fatigue, stretched out and closed my eyes for a short nap, a vagrant hiker sleeping on a park bench.

On my last three miles, three groups passed me walking or biking. One asked me if I was the famous person in the local paper who had hiked all over the place. I said I did not know if I was in the paper or famous, but I *had* hiked all over the place. Sharon had sent an article in to the local paper. She does many things to support the ADT. A great trail angel, she certainly helped me with support as I started that year with my still ailing foot. Saying good-by to Sharon and Paul the next day, I headed out from Pennsboro at no great speed as my body gradually warmed up to the idea of trail walking.

TALKING TO, PRAYING FOR STRANGERS

Not too far out of Ellenboro, a youngish man walking a section of trail on his lunch break, caught up with me and started a conversation. Ryan and his wife had ten kids (even more than my daughter) and had bought a farm a few years prior. No one had lived on that farm for 60 years before they moved in.

Needless to say, they had a few things to do to bring it back to life as a working farm. They raised two kinds of dogs and a small breed of cattle. Garden Grove Farm was now doing well, and Ryan was contemplating quitting his outside job. Finding my trail name was Medicare Pastor, he asked for prayers as he and his wife contemplated this change in their lives. We held hands and prayed there on the trail. That moment caused me to recall another.

One of my memorable moments while walking on the Camino de Santiago in Spain was meeting a young man from Brazil. As we walked along together, we exchanged the usual, "Buen Camino" and "Where are you from?" greetings. Then he asked me, "What have you learned from walking the Camino?" The Camino is a trail where such questions are asked and more than surface answers are given in return.

I don't recall what I answered him, but I vividly remember what he shared of his learning on the trail. He said, "I learned I can talk to people I don't know. I talk to people I don't know every day on the Camino." He went on further and said, "I have never talked to my neighbors at home in Brazil. When I get home, I am going to introduce myself to my neighbors and talk to them. I no longer fear talking to people I do not know."

On the National Scenic Trails in America, hikers meet hikers they did not know before, and strangers met there become friends too. On the Camino, my young Brazilian friend learned how to introduce himself to strangers and the joy of conversing with people he did not know before he made the effort to meet them. Maybe everyone should walk a long trail to learn to talk to strangers. On the Camino, other pilgrims and I debated the benefits of a requirement that heads of state should be required to walk the Camino to learn to talk to people of different countries than their own.

My young friend on the Camino, having learned to talk to strangers, aimed to go back home to talk to his own neighbors who were still strange to him, and would be so, until conversations made them friends.

I too had learned to talk to strangers, even pray for them. I chuckled to myself, recognizing that I, a retired pastor, had found a widely dispersed congregation on trails and roads across America, sharing prayers in holy moments of connection with people I had not known before.

Ryan and I had paths that soon diverged from our chance meeting and the brief connection of our prayers together as I went on and he retraced his steps back to his work and then his farm and family. As in my conversation with my Brazilian friend on the Camino, we had learned from each other and had supported each other in new connections.

The rest of that day had no other major interesting events, but it did have scenic interests. There were three more tunnels as the trail gradually but steadily climbed higher in elevation, pines and firs among the predominant deciduous trees, rock and winding rivers to view.

Reaching Cairo (pronounced like the syrup, not the town in Egypt) I stopped at the Bike Shop plastered with American Discovery Trail signs. DJ graciously filled my water needs and told me of two covered shelters in the town. The bigger one had two moveable picnic tables made of metal mesh. I moved them around and pitched my tent with their assistance under the playground picnic shelter before the rain started.

A Little TMI and Other Problem Solving

Skip a few paragraphs if you don't want to read one of my tales of too much information. But really, one of the most difficult parts of the ADT is finding a way to take care of nature's needs.

I had a place to put my tent, sheltered and out of the rain. But there was no porta potty there. I wondered how I would solve my problem.

After writing my journal entry for the day, it was still light out and children played outside, houses were nearby and a road with some traffic was next to me. No one was interested in talking to the lady with a tent in the park. I closed my eyes and snoozed, waiting for darkness. At 9:00 I sat up and brushed my teeth. But there was no concealing darkness. There were streetlights. And it was raining. And there were barking dogs if I tried to walk to the shadows to relieve myself. *Everyone* would look outside their windows at the sound of dogs. No one had seemed interested or friendly and I had not knocked on any door. My need was urgent. What should I do?

I hoped everyone was inside having dinner or watching TV, intent on their normal every evening concerns, not looking outside. Sitting on the edge of a picnic bench I peed into a gallon Ziploc bag. Other than the bag underneath me, a casual glance would just have revealed an old lady sitting at a picnic table beside her tent, tent and mesh tables barely disguising a necessary act. That tactic worked at 4:30 a.m. too.

At 6:30, it was too light with natural light, and people were moving about. I had to take care of that issue in the tent before I took it down, harder to accomplish there. I know not everyone wants to read about me peeing. But, honestly, doing so discretely was one of the biggest challenges on the ADT.

As I left Cairo, a lady commented on my umbrella, liking my hands-free arrangement. My umbrella kept the space between my back and my pack dry, as well as most of me. My hands were free to use hiking poles, as the umbrella handle went under the chest strap of my pack and then into my bra, a woman's solution. Everyone always laughs when I tell them how it's done. Guys are envious.

It rained all day. That about summed it up. I saw no one on the trail all day. Who wants to hike in the rain except long-distance hikers who just hike, no matter the weather? At Walker, a guy at a house near the trail let me get water from a spigot on the side of his house. He didn't offer anything else, so I just got water, crossed the bridge, quickly set up my tent beside the trail, and dove in just as the rain picked up again.

My last day in West Virginia, I had to pack up a wet tent. But it did not rain most of the day, though overcast. Squirrels liked the lack of rain and scampered through the forest. Birds sang cheerily as I walked down straight sections of rail trail. There were no more tunnels but quite a few bridges over brown water creeks overfull with spring rains.

Leaving the rail trail for Parkersburg, it was evident roads were not as flat as railroad beds. The shoulders of roads were small or nonexistent and the roads went up and down steep little hills.

I begged a bathroom at a welding shop. After leaving the men to continue their welding, rain started up again and I struggled with my umbrella on a tiny shoulder of road. Cars whizzing by turned the umbrella inside out. The guy in the welding shop had suggested I walk the railroad, a real one, not a rail trail. I did not do that. I do know how to walk on the left side of the road, carefully watching cars, but I was glad to reach sidewalks.

My motel for the night and my re-supply box were a mile off trail. I was craving pizza all day and picked up a Dominos about a block before my motel, the cheapest motel in town. The sheets were clean. Water was hot. Electricity charged my electronics. It was good enough for a hiker.

It was also time for a zero day. The nearby Rite Aid was stocked with food for the microwave. The laundromat was across the street. Needs for cleanliness and food were solved. I fiddled around with gear, duct taped a couple tiny holes in my raingear, and made sure electronics were charged and gear and clothes were dry. I packed away the contents of my re-supply box, and mostly laid around resting with my feet up, entertaining myself with a little TV or the news on my cell phone. A zero day is made for resting.

While out purchasing my food, I was inspired to stop by Ace Hardware to see if something struck my eye to resemble the tent stake I had lost in piles of leaves on my very first night from Clarksburg. They sold tent stakes, but they were huge, not something I wanted to carry. I looked at the prongs in the pegboards holding merchandise and asked if they sold those.

The guy at the store showed me one for sale, and I asked if he could snip off the end and the two stabilizer prongs. He did that and smoothed rough-cut edges on a grinder. Voila. Two new tent stakes. They were a little heavier than titanium but not bad at all. I felt very clever. Mainly, I was happy to have two more tent stakes, one to replace the one I had lost and one spare. Funny, but one of the things I like about long hikes is solving little problems when they arise, nothing big like war and peace, just little problems, like how to make a tent stake.

The motel owner found me an envelope and contributed postage for me to mail home my first set of maps. The motel may have been a bit worn, but it had everything I needed including an owner with thoughtfulness and generosity.

Setting out the next day, my bad foot told me the surfaces I was walking were not to its liking. It was teaching me nuances of pavement and trail

I had never noticed before. A slight slant down-wards to the left was much more comfortable than a slight slant uphill on my left. Sidewalks often slant slightly downwards to the road. That means sidewalks on the right side were the ones I walked. Roads generally slant downwards from the middle. With no sidewalks, I walked on the left side of the road for the better slant for foot comfort. Fortunately, the left side of the road was also the correct side to walk to face oncoming traffic.

OHIO

Ohio portion of the American Discovery Trail

Crossing the bridge over the Ohio River, I left West Virginia behind. I held fond memories of West Virginia and stepped sprightly forward to see what Ohio would offer. I immediately thought it smelled and looked like Ohio. It was a beautiful day, and everyone was outside mowing lawns.

The ADT doesn't go through the choicest bit of real estate in Parkersburg, but Belpre, on the Ohio side, was lovely. Many people were out enjoying a paved walking trail in the city park by the river.

As I walked by, an older gentleman in a car was enjoying the view with his windows rolled down. He struck up a conversation with me when I smiled at him, and said he used to run marathons. In fact, his last marathon was in Oklahoma at age 75, where he was the oldest one on the course. That day, definitely older than 75, he had breathing problems and sat tethered to oxygen, but still enjoyed the view. He encouraged me to keep hiking while I still could. Good advice. I high fived him for his marathon at 75. I cheered for him and he cheered for me. He was glad to have memories of his accomplishments though he could not run anymore. I was glad to have met him in the park.

Leaving the park, a steep hillside was thickly covered with lavender phlox. Intentionally planted flowers are beautiful as well as wildflowers. My lunch was in a pleasant covered pavilion at picnic tables provided by a picturesque white Presbyterian chapel on the outskirts of Belpre.

After Belpre my road immediately went up and down hills, no more level rail trail for me. Ohio, particularly southern Ohio, is known for its hilly nature. It may not be the Rockies or the Sierra but up and down works the same way on hills or mountains. I was no longer going through mountains by way of tunnels, I had to walk over them.

Stopping to ask for water at a white house, I met Thelma, age 89. She said she used to walk a lot but not anymore. Her husband had worked for the B&O Railroad, and she had raised five children. Thelma wanted to give me cookies or granola bars, but I declined as, with a fresh load of food, I wanted to eat only what was in my pack to make it lighter. I did take water and mixed up my dinner to soak, thanking her for her generosity.

I was cheered at all the smiles and friendly waves I was getting. At least fifty drivers waved at me in Belpre and nearly that many more on country roads before I stopped for the night.

After reaching my planned stopping waypoint, I looked for a house and knocked on a door. Tammy, an adult woman, said she would ask her mother, Patty, who was the owner. Not only did they let me pitch my tent, they offered use of their shower. After I was clean, we talked. Patty was grieving the loss of her husband the last November. They had been married 54 years. I'm glad I knocked on her door so that she might tell me of her love and grief for her husband.

After we got to know each other, Tammy disclosed that when she had told her mother of my request, she had said, "She's OK, Mom, you could take her." I was glad I had not had a fight to get a tent spot and I thought the statement quite funny. It would have been quite a sight, two little old ladies in a tussle.

In the morning, as I walked around Veto Lake, my foot felt very good. I often feel 10 years younger when I set out in the morning. Too bad I can't feel that way all day. It was a day of up and down rolling hills of farmland. Mid-morning, the wind began to blow. I hiked in shirt sleeves, down jacket and wind breaker, with sun hat, ear band or nothing on my head, and with gloves on and off, all in one day.

Stopping in Vincent, I ate my mid-morning snack sitting in an old rocking chair in front of a dilapidated old church, which had become a senior center. My energy was flagging before lunch, and the wind was cold, so I asked at a house if I could eat on their porch, sheltered from the chilling wind. In the afternoon, my foot decided to hurt, so a number of miles were made limping.

A group of Amish had recently moved into the area, bought old properties, and cleaned them up. They used tractors and chain saws, but also horses and buggies and wore traditional dress. I passed two horses hitched to a buckboard rolling on rubber tires, lawn chairs placed in the buckboard for seating. The menfolk were cutting down trees and loading wagons with wood. The women had fresh wash hung on lines. Later, another horse and buggy passed me. Nice horses and good-looking people.

I learned about the Amish from a local woman out clearing the roadsides of trash. She was a gem, working at a never-ending job, just because it needed doing.

My last mile of the day was cold and windy, the sky full of dark, threatening clouds. The forecast said *no rain*, but those dark clouds seemed to say otherwise. I was limping markedly, my focus fixed on completing the last mile to my scheduled road crossing to stop for the day. Achieving that, I knocked on the door of the nearest house.

What luck! Vikki, Greg, and thirteen-year-old Jill

were just back from vacation. They had hosted hikers before and invited me to stay inside. Since the forecast was for a night in the low thirties, I was thrilled. They were a joy to meet. Vikki and I hit it off and talked about trail, life, religion, and, more gingerly, politics.

I was certain my politics did not match that espoused by many of the people I met on my travels. I tried to talk about other things with people who were being so kind to me. Neither side of the political aisle is filled completely with ogres. We do indeed live in two different Americas though, our thoughts and opinions forged differently, one contributing factor clearly which news source is dominant in the areas in which we lived.

Fear, politics, and points of view are forged and reinforced by how often we experience, hear, or repeat statements to ourselves. I was in counseling many years ago, and my counselor cautioned me to change my self-talk, mental comments made to myself. I did not think such comments carried impact, but I discovered I repeatedly called myself stupid, jerk, or dummy when I made mistakes. What we hear or even repeat to ourselves has power. Realizing that is true, we *can* choose to say, hear, and experience different things. I can, at least, recognize the process happening to me or others as I, or we, process and absorb fears or political points of view.

I charged electronics, scored another shower, and Vicki volunteered to wash my socks, undies, and both shirts—even if that was all I had that needed washing. How thoughtful and how sweet. I didn't get to bed until well past hiker midnight, but I had an enjoyable evening. It was cold outside, but I was inside, and life was good.

On a blue-sky morning, I walked away from Vikki and Greg on a road lined with flowers blooming brightly in the bright-morning sunshine. It didn't take much walking with a pack on my back to warm up, even in the morning briskness.

Approaching the Shin Covered Bridge, I peered at its barn-red sides through branches of leaf-less trees. Past the bridge, I walked by a winding creek in an almost park-like setting. At one turn, two rivulets emptied into one culvert, racing over many layers of shale before plunging into a hole. It reminded me of creeks I'd played in as a first grader in New York State, outside of Buffalo. As I ate my lunch perched on an old log chunk near an abandoned house, I remembered all those many years ago.

At 79, I have had a lot of life experiences, and wherever I walk, memories travel with me. I am always seeing something that reminds me of some other place I have been or some other circumstance or stage in my life.

Water splashing over many-layered shale by a culvert can take me back to playing in a creek in first grade. Some experiences have not been so pleasant. All life experiences added up together contribute to the views each one of us have on life and fear. Long trails give a hiker both time to reflect and intensity of experience. Every stop at night, every kindness along the way, every meeting with each of so many diverse people, are to me like the many-layered shale, my life the waterfall, each person or experience along the way beautiful in the sunlight of my memory, although passed in quick succession, one to another, or so it seems, in my life's history.

Coming into Chesterhill, I stood on a corner checking my GPS and a car full of teenaged boys passed me and then backed up to ask if I needed help. They told me Ernie's Café, still marked on my T-by-T, had closed a couple years ago, but a new restaurant had opened. They pointed in that direction. A Lady behind the library told me the new restaurant closed at 3:00 on Sunday. Shucks. It was 3:30. She said to go on over and ask anyway. They might fix me something.

I did and they did. What a nice flavor of small-town America. The owner of the Triple Nickel Diner fixed me a feast of what they already had made and hadn't sold, a wonderful chicken salad sandwich made with halved grapes, with sides of coleslaw and applesauce, and dessert of cherry pie. I sat at the bar and talked trail talk with the owner, Kathy, and her daughter, Rosie. They told me about starting a new business. They had only been open a year and were already doing very well. Kathy refused payment when I tried to pay for my fine meal, saying they were closed for the day anyway. Great food. Great people. Great generosity. I hope many hikers and bikers stop there to reward them with their business.

When I had left Vikki and Greg in the morning, they said to call if I needed a place in the evening, as the temperature was forecast to be in the low 30s again. I could really handle that weather in my tent, but the temptation of another night with them was too great to resist. I called, and they drove out to find me, even though my directions were not entirely accurate. I enjoyed another shower, more talk, and a warm indoor night. Give a hiker an inch and they will take a mile. They did tell me to call though, or I would have found some place to pitch my tent.

Looking at the frost on the grass outside the window in the morning, I was very grateful to have slept inside. I surely did enjoy both nights with Vikki and Greg. Vikki liked trail stories and I liked to tell them. It was a match. In the morning, she drove me back out to Hoffman Road.

The sky was blue and the walk in the woods pleasantly warming. A sign on my road said, Road

Closed. I had come to similar signs before and locals had told me that meant cars, not foot traffic. So I didn't give it much mind as I continued on. A number of stream crossings on Hoffman Road slowed my steps. I didn't want wet shoes, so took the time to change to crocks for each one. That was time consuming, and I fell behind on my miles in the morning. Still, it was a nice day and a pleasant walk.

At the next waypoint, there were logs felled across the trail and threatening signs saying anyone on the trail for any reason would be prosecuted and cameras were watching. Oops. Well, I had walked slowly enough that the gendarmes could have caught me, but no one did. Perhaps a different routing for the Buckeye Trail [BT] and the ADT should be made. The Buckeye Trail, a blue-blazed trail that circles the state of Ohio was then my route. The ADT followed the BT through southern Ohio, beginning not long after Chesterville.

As I packed up after lunch, a car stopped, and the gentleman asked if I was OK. He expressed amazement there was a trail on his road, as he had never seen another hiker. When I passed Shews Orchard, Pete was on the hill next to the trail watering his cows. We talked together quite a while. He knew about the trail and was interested in me as a hiker. That friendly man wanted to give me water and a place to stay for the night, but their cabin had been rented to a turkey hunter. It was too soon for me to stop, anyway. He told me the other big farm in the area was owned by a guy from Texas who had married a local woman.

That day had lots of up and down and up and down again. After Shews Orchard, it *really* had up and down, over bigger, steeper hills. Put them all together and there was serious elevation gain and loss for the day. The last three miles almost did me in. And some of those roads did not have the preferred slant for my foot.

I stopped halfway up a hill for water and to hydrate my dinner at a cute cabin with a generous owner. Her daughter was an archeologist who had been to Central America, Europe, and, the prior year, Glacier National Park. It was interesting to talk with her, but my water needs were filled, she received a phone call, and I still had miles to go.

I wondered if I was ever going to reach my destination for the day, dragging up that last hill. Yet, in spite of the steepness of the grade, I enjoyed Red Bud trees blossoming purplish pink beside the road.

Old Skid Road was an odd loop drooping south of my main path, though all of it was labeled Buckeye Trial. I bet most hikers skipped it unless they needed a place to camp. Which I did.

I walked almost to the end of the loop and camped right on the trail as everywhere else had little roses, berry plants, or tree seedlings sprouting, which would have poked a hole in my tent floor. I saw a pretty deer, large tail flashing white as it bounded deeper into the woods.

My tent was up with an hour of daylight left. No

other people were on that loop, houses far away, leaving me in privacy in my own little piece of wilderness.

In the morning, I watched the sunrise from my tent and enjoyed the flowers on the trail, completing the loop back to the road. Big white trillium, which are the Ohio State flower, made a flashy show against old brown leaves covering the ground. I had heard a very loud owl in the night, and in the morning, I watched a squirrel run into a knothole. It was a delightful little loop, even if it had not helped me make forward progress.

Suddenly Summer.
Where Was Spring?

The Buckeye Trail wound around all the nooks and crannies at the edge of Burr Oak Lake. That day was suddenly very hot, and I shed my shirt to hike in sports bra. It was necessary to be aware of sunburn possibility though, as trees were not yet leafed out. There was no shade.

I met three older hikers who were talking to a naturalist. They wanted to take my photo, as backpackers were not usual there. Julie, the naturalist, walked with me for a while, so I peppered her with flower questions about the names of spring woods flowers blooming in profusion. Besides trillium and abundant wild blue phlox, there were rue anemone, Jacob's ladder, squirrel's corn, blue-eyed Mary, early saxifrage and others. She also told me the name of a ground cover I had puzzled over since walking Maine on the AT, ground pine.

My foot did well on the trail tread. But there were many ups and downs around the lake. So I was not making good time. I was also not getting enough water. Before Burr Oak Lake, I was confident I could knock on a door and ask for water almost anywhere I went, but there were no houses on that long trail in the State Park. I naively had made a comment to Julie about how I obtained water from houses I passed. She probably thought I was nuts, since she knew the area, and I didn't. I was definitely wrong. There were no more houses giving access for my method of obtaining water for a very long time.

I had three different water treatment methods with me for emergency use if needed. But I was leery of chemical contamination in natural water sources in the East. At any rate, I was running out of water and not drinking enough. The weather had changed dramatically in a day. The morning of the day before, there had been thick frost on grass.

But the day I walked the first half of Burr Oak Lake was 85 degrees with no shade at all. Trail winding in and out around the lake took more time and energy than swinging along on country roads or bicycle trails, even uphill roads. I took an alternate trail to save me seven-tenths of a mile and was very glad to come to a ranger station with potable water.

I walked under my umbrella to make my own shade all afternoon, and was very tired by the time I reached Dock 1. I became aware I might have had an inflated estimation of what I could do when I made my hike plan.

My lodging was a cabin found through Airbnb, a whole house four-tenths of a mile from Dock 1. My re-supply box was there. So I cooked my dinner, washed my clothes in the washing machine on the back porch, had my shower, and reloaded my food bag, all while my feet were killing me. I hobbled room to room and wished I was lying down and had a rest day the next day. I had no rest day scheduled for three more days.

I was whupped. I took a few notes for my journal and fell, exhausted, into bed. The day had been beautiful, if too hot. The flowers had been lovely. Life was good, but I was done.

I slept like the dead but was up early and out the door of the cabin on time. I finished the walk around the lake to the dam and met Mary, Marianne, and Denny once again, the three older day hikers from the day before. Any time you meet someone twice on a trail, they are like old friends.

Mary had made a comment about liking to day hike but not liking to camp. I told her camping was easier than the house that last night. I had been glad for the amenities, getting my re-supply box, shower, and laundry. But everything I did in the house required being on my feet. Plopping down in my tent, I didn't have amenities, but everything was in arm's distance and I was off my feet.

Leaving the day hikers and the lake, I missed an obscure trail sign directly across the road, but fortunately caught my mistake before I went too far. That section of trail was hard for me. It was another 85-degree day, and I never do well in heat. There was also lots of uphill and downhill trail on tread covered by ankle-deep leaves. I could not tell what was under the leaves until I took each step. The trail never seemed to go anywhere, just uphill and down under leafless trees and hot skies as I trudged after the blue blazes of the Buckeye Trail, sweating even under the shade of my umbrella.

I suppose the trail planner had something in mind. But to me, it was just meandering PUDs. (Pointless ups and downs) I knew Ohio would be more difficult than Delaware, Maryland, West Virginia, Illinois, or Indiana, the states I had already done. I found out it was a lot harder, at least that day.

After a horse and rider passed me on the trail, there were hidden horse divots under the thick layers of leaves requiring me to travel even more slowly. I fell way behind schedule. Roads were much easier.

Coming out of the woods, I asked for water at the last house before hitting trail again, and the kind gentleman there loaded me with ice-cold water from his refrigerator. I was very grateful.

Just after entering Trimble Wildlife Area, I encountered a road washout. Not even a four-wheel drive was going to negotiate that road. The culvert was left in the middle, but spring runoff had gouged four-to-five-feet-deep drops on each side and around it. Going upstream a few feet, I found a bank I could manage to get down and crossed the—then hop-across-sized stream.

I was tired. I decided I needed to stop early even though I was three miles short of my scheduled distance for the day. At Mud Fork Road, my waypoint said it was Hunterdorn Road. My way-point on my GPS was where I stood, so even with a different name, I knew where I was.

I walked several yards more, and after crossing a small stream filled with frogs, I put up my tent on grass beside the road. I had been really pushing to get to scheduled stops, lagging in my journal writing, and was feeling rushed and tired. Stopping early by that tiny stream, I was able to clean up the day's sweaty grime with a Ziploc bath and catch up a few days' journals, so my readers wouldn't think I died. I would have to deal with extra miles some way before reaching Logan. I listened to frogs and crickets as I fell asleep.

I woke in the night to take care of nature's needs and appreciated the wilderness around me as I heard a couple screeches in the night that could have been a bobcat. I also heard loud owl hoots. A loud owl hoot is nothing like a soft owl call, but very much an owl hooting, almost a bark.

In the morning, I heard two turkeys talking to themselves from each side of me an hour before a turkey hunter strolled by while I was packing up. The forest shared its normal sounds with me, making me feel at home.

I picked up water in Murray City before houses again became rare. And I made good time, but it was another 85-degree-day. Continuing to hike in sports bra with my umbrella for shade, Ohio was making me stronger, which is another way of saying it kicked my butt. My bad foot was doing well. But the rest of me was hot and tired.

I chose a road walk waymarked for bicycles to avoid a meandering little loop of trail. The T-by-T described a steep climb, winding walk, and steep descent. That loop's beginning required a four-foot straight-down butt slide to cross a creek. The road seemed a better choice. After lunch I took the loop to Shawnee Lake and then walked off trail to the town of Shawnee to find water.

Shawnee was virtually all closed businesses. Walking toward a car and someone talking, I stumbled across the Buckeye Trail Association office, the only place I saw open in the town. There I met Andrew, who graciously gave me water, let me use the restroom, and exchanged contact information with me. He then gave me a ride back to the trail crossing on Road 93. He had a prior engagement and was sorry he could not have hosted me more. But he had filled my need for water, so I was happy. The extra walk into Shawnee made up for two tiny sections of trail skipped, in my mind at least.

The trail from 93 was good trail—wide, not full of leaves. The sky clouded over, and the wind picked up, dropping the temperature. I really should have camped before the next road according to my plan, but it was a pond and swampy area. I startled two deer and discovered blue blazes that went in a circle. They were no help.

Finally, with the help of my GPS, I found the right direction to a road, overgrown and running through pine trees. Pine trees are shallow rooted and were blowing over in the wind. I heard three crash around me as I walked. I did not want to put my tent near any pine trees in a windstorm, though I saw some inviting spots.

The trail then came to a three-to-four-foot-high log jam of fallen trees. It reminded me of McNight Ridge in Colorado on the CDT, a horrid stretch of nearly impassable trail. This stretch of logs was vastly smaller than the mess I had walked through in Colorado. After threading my way around the logs, I ran into guys riding a four-wheel ATV and a motorcycle. I informed them they weren't going any farther unless they had a chain saw. Supposedly they were hunting for mushrooms. They turned around and left the trail, crashing through the underbrush, tearing up the forest floor under their wheels, undergrowth and greenery smashed and flying, making huge tracks of destruction. I had no respect for those who had no respect for the woods.

I continued walking up the trail through thickly flowered banks of blue-eyed Mary and trillium before coming to the road. Confused, even when looking at my GPS, I asked a driver of a passing car the name of the road I was on and we puzzled out together which direction I should walk, eventually reaching a sign that said *Trailhead*.

Just as I was ready to throw down my tent at the edge of a campground, a nice gentleman said the public campground was on the other side of the creek, but he didn't mind if I camped on his property. He wanted to talk, and though I normally love talking with people interested in hikers, I was too exhausted, and was fighting descending darkness to erect my tent. As soon as my tent was up, I crashed inside, caught up with my schedule by mileage and hoped sleep would catch up with my exhaustion.

The next morning, I found the blue blazes on the other side of the creek on a nice bridle trail. Horses don't need bridges, but I would have liked one, as almost immediately, I came to a wide stream I needed to ford. I should have worn my crocs when I left my campsite, since I needed them to ford and had to take the time to change.

On the other side of the stream, the trail looked like a good one. I started to take back all my bad thoughts about the Buckeye Trail since that hot day around Burr Oak Lake. Then the trail, though still a good trail, took me on three long unnecessary loops covering seven miles, just to make less than a mile and a half of forward progress.

Now, I like woods walking, although I like walking to views, lakes or waterfalls more. But these trails were just loops, the last one very meandering. There was a swampy lake and a couple geese, and several black, stagnant looking ponds to see. Nothing terribly exciting, at least not to me that day.

A TRAIL IN PROGRESS

Those random loops of trail made me wonder what the trail philosophy was for the Buckeye Trail. All trails seem to have trail philosophies, not always written. States along the AT pride themselves on difficult trail. If there is an easy way up a mountain, the AT spurns it to take a harder way. The PCT and CDT are generally built to accommodate horses, making certain trail construction decisions work for both hikers and equestrians.

The BT's goal appeared to be to use as much wilderness as could be found in the State of Ohio for as many miles as possible, by twisting and turning, round and round upon itself. If that was the goal, that day the trail successfully achieved it. There is nothing wrong with that goal for those in Ohio wishing to walk in woods to enjoy those patches of wilderness. It was not a bad goal.

But since an ADT hiker was not necessarily trying to see every possible inch of wilderness between the Atlantic and the Pacific, perhaps it would be better to just have one sample loop than take all three. Forest walks were nice, but getting somewhere was nice, too.

The BT had also changed since my three-year-old T-by-T was printed, adding quite a bit of trail farther north of Logan. When I was in Shawnee, Andrew told me more changes were in the offing. The new addition added miles and took the trail some distance from my planned re-supply town and rest day. And the ADT coordinator did not know of the addition when I told him after I reached Cincinnati. I took the older route.

There have been some hiccups in the organization, signage, and maintenance of the American Discovery Trail, only to be expected in such a large endeavor as a trail across the vast width of America. Combining a huge variety of trails large and small, was and is, not an easy task. Trails are not always *finished* things. AT, PCT, and CDT have had changes since I walked them. The ADT, too, is a *trail in progress*.

According to the official website, the route of the ADT was selected through the efforts of citizens working with local, state, and federal land managers in the localities through which the trail passes. In 1990-91 a scouting team mapped the route determined by this citizen effort. There is a volunteer coordinator in each ADT state who leads the ongoing effort to refine the route, incorporate new trails into the route, and promote and sign the trail.

In 1996 Senator Hank Brown of Colorado introduced Senate Bill S. 1725, and Congressman Doug Bereuter of Nebraska introduced House Bill H.R. 3250, but the 104th Congress did not enact these bills.

Since then, many more bills have been introduced, some failing to get out of committee, some never coming to a vote, and some being rejected. In February, 2019, Senate Bill S. 47, which includes legislation authorizing ADT signage on federal lands, passed in the Senate and went to the House. Signage may improve after the signing of that bill.

From walking National Scenic Trails, I know that trails are living things. Re-routes due to changes regarding trail philosophy, acquisition of land, or changes in landscape by natural occurrences like floods or fires are not uncommon.

Legislation authorizing signage is a huge step forward, reflecting many years of dedicated effort by a generation. Putting up the signs will be another daunting task. Communication and coordination of the many organizations involved are administered by the ADT Society. Input from *boots on the ground*, from hikers on this trail, even those who walk the tread and complain a bit, are part of this work.

After the trail became a road again, I stopped at a house and met Nancy, an older woman watching her granddaughter's two-month-old baby who was peacefully sleeping. Nancy invited me in while she filled my water bottles and let me use her bathroom, after which, we chatted.

We talked about age as she had just turned 70. Turning 70 was a milestone that seemed so much more elderly than any number in the 60s. I told her I thought the label *Old Lady* should be a sign of crowning achievement, one to be worn proudly. I had chosen to think so and to proclaim it as a counter-cultural stance. Nancy gave me a nice juicy, Honey Crisp apple which I munched as I walked on up the road.

A little later, on that road, a car pulled up beside me, the man and his son inside talked to me for a little while from the window of his car as I kept hiking. He had hiked some sections on the AT. And I told him about the book I had just written.

One thing I have learned about the book business, is that authors have to publicize their own work. Authors need a *platform* of contacts and publicity even if the author has a publisher or agent. After the conversation with the man in the car, I laughed out loud. The most unusual aspect of my *platform* as an author was that I walk miles and miles across America, talking to locals, telling people about my book. My *platform* included oddly spaced farmhouses across Ohio and random motorists, who slowed to have a conversation with an old lady carrying a backpack. I doubted many other authors had that platform.

Knocking on a door, I asked permission to rest on the porch of a house facing a barn, which dated dating from 1886, Howdyshell Farms. Berdina granted me permission, and her husband said I should come inside, and so I did. As I sat on their couch chatting, a younger couple came in, perhaps family from across the road, supposedly ready to go out to eat, but possibly checking on the stranger who'd gone inside. I told them about trail walking, ate my trail bars, and enjoyed sitting on the couch. They offered me a ride to Logan, but walking is the point of hiking on a trail. My water bottles filled again, I headed out to push down 93.

Howdyshell Farms Barn

Two cars stopped on the highway, one ID-ed me as a Buckeye Trail hiker, the other knew the route I followed was the ADT. Each told me the Buckeye Trail had been re-routed, which I knew then, though I did not get that information in time to change my plans. Each also offered me a ride, but stopping early would just mean miles to make up later. I could still appreciate their offers, friendly gestures that made me smile.

Logan

Reaching Inboden Road, my planned stop for the day, I did need a ride off trail to Logan to my reserved motel. I took off my pack and waved my hat at one car, which sped on by.

On highways, catching a ride is hard, cars go whizzing by too fast to notice someone on foot or to think to help. A stop sign gives a driver time to look a hiker in the eyes, time to decide if they wish to speak a word or give a ride. When a car drove up to the stop sign on the side road, Mark was happy to give me a ride to my motel. I appreciated his kindness and assistance.

Hitch-hiking from the trail is one of those necessary risks that hikers take. I do not hitch-hike in my *real* life, (though sometimes I debate which life is real.) but trails sometimes avoid towns, and towns hold food and lodging even intrepid hikers need, at least occasionally.

Logan was not on the trail, though it was the closest town to the Buckeye Trail before the BT route was changed. I had sent my re-supply to Logan. Although I have hitch-hiked many times to towns on long-distance trails, I have never come to harm. In fact, hitching has often been another opportunity to meet new friends.

As soon as I checked into the motel, the clouds above unleashed buckets of rain. I surely timed that right. After my shower, I walked to Wendy's for a burger, fries, and a frosty. Yum. That low-end motel was near needed food sources, but it had no laundry, nor was any laundromat in town that I could find. I had to wash my clothes in the bathtub by hand.

Logan had the first motel bed I had ever slept in that was too hard. I had to put my air mattress on the bed to have a comfortable night's sleep. But it was quiet and clean, the sheets were clean, the water hot, and there was soap. A variety of food choices were within three blocks. They had held my re-supply box for my arrival. It would do for hiker digs.

Wanting to arrange a slackpack for the next day, at the Family Diner I asked about the possibility of a ride back to the trail. Marvin agreed to ferry me back to my trail and drove me back to Inboden Road in the morning.

The day was cool, the world smelled fresh-washed from rain the night before, and I listened as birds serenaded me. Tiny warblers sing the sweetest calls. Eastern birds are generally more colorful than western birds, though many are simply brown birds. I could not identify the many brown warblers, but even I could recognize cardinals, finches, eastern blue jays and orioles.

Much of the morning was road walking, some on pavement. After the re-route, the official Buckeye Trail now ran north of my chosen route, but the old blue blazes still showed to guide my way, as did my GPS and T-by-T. One section of trail tread went through private property with instructions not to wander off trail. It was not maintained, but still was there, a pleasant walk by a little stream.

Several blowdowns crossed the trail. I was barely able to squat low below them and would not have been able to do so with a full pack. The muddy trail required a slight duck waddle going under blow downs to stay clean. But ADT and BT signage were still clear, which I thought surprising, as it supposedly was no longer the official trail.

After the woods walk, came a road walk to the highway past scattered houses. Barking furiously, a dog burst out of an open door, and headed directly for me. I quickly pointed my poles at the dog, and in my deepest alpha dog voice, told it to go home. The dog stopped just short of me. A woman stuck her head out of a nearby trailer, yelled at the dog and told me the dog wouldn't hurt me. No one thinks their pet could hurt someone, until they do. But I was unscathed that day.

Coming into Enterprise, a small collection of houses, a boy, about eight-or-nine-years-old, wanted to know if I was a hiker? Had I come a long way? Where was I going? Where had I come from? Did I like hiking? He was very cute, but at the same time he was peppering me with eager questions, the family's pit bull was ravening, barking furiously, and trying to pull out the chain holding him between two cars. I surely hoped the chain held. I liked the boy, but not the dog.

Reaching the highway, I pulled out a sign I had made the previous year for Nevada. I had scrawled with a fat, dark pen on a cheap piece of plastic tablecloth, "Hiker needs ride." I used rubber bands and a bit of duct tape to attach it to my hiking poles and also waved my hat at passing cars, quite a trick to manage poles and sign and hat with only two hands. Many vehicles zoomed by, but one big car with two guys, Jehovah Witnesses, Dewy and Gregory, came back and gave me a ride back to Logan and my motel.

The next morning, I walked over to the convenience store to buy some bread and cheese for the trail and a banana and milk to supplement my breakfast. I also needed a ride back to Chieftain Drive, where Dewy and Greg had picked me up.

When hitch-hiking, trying to catch a ride, I feel awkward, somewhat helpless, and a bit like a bum, not feelings most people relish. I don't exactly feel fear, more like nervousness, wondering what will happen, and I worry that maybe this time no one will help me. When a ride is offered, those feelings dissolve, transformed to thankfulness for the ride and enjoyment in meeting a new friend. Before I could be thankful and celebrate a new friend that day, I had to bum a ride.

I needed bread, but that convenience store had no tortillas, flat bread, or even hamburger buns, just plain white bread, which would squish flat inside my pack. I tied the bag of bread to the outside of my pack, put it on, and stood by the door eating my banana, wondering how to ask or who to ask to find a ride to Chieftain Drive. Seeing my pack, one man asked if I was on a hike. He was interested, but he was going the other direction. And then, like magic, John started to talk to me and discovered my need. "I can take you," he said. And I was only halfway through my banana.

John had been a Scout Master, and his son had long-distance hiked and hitch-hiked too. Dropping me off, he even took my banana peel and chocolate milk bottle so I wouldn't have to carry trash. I gave my thanks to John.

Once again on my route, I approached Lake Logan. The marsh at the end of the lake was full of cat tails and many red-winged blackbirds. A little turtle was in the road. I told him to move or he might get squashed. Stomping my feet, I chased him to the roadside, and he reluctantly gave up the heat of the sun-warmed pavement. I hope he lived.

On a beautiful spring day, trees now leafing out, my walk in the woods was shadier than three days before. Tom and Sue, trail maintainers, were out looking for mushrooms in the woods. We talked about the trail and my destination for the day. Tom recommended a campsite, out of sight of the trail, where he once had camped.

Mary E. Davison

A picnic table at Duck Creek appeared for lunch, and a sign on a nearby barn announced, "feel free to dance." A stage or dance floor was constructed at one end of the meadow for dancing or maybe a band. The picnic table in dense evergreen shade kept me deliciously cool as I ate, but I didn't dance.

HOCKING HILLS

Wildcat Hollow Road was a gently even grade, though long uphill. Rock cliffs that made Hocking Hills famous began to show. After startling two deer, I stopped at a house on the Star Route Road, the only house I had seen with a car for quite some time. Most of the buildings I had passed were unoccupied cabins or houses without a sign of life.

Linda, a delightful lady my age, filled my water containers, and we talked of trails and hiking. As I was ready to go, her husband, Jim, came home, and we all talked some more. I regretted leaving those charming people, but hikers need to hike, and Tom the trail maintainer had given me a goal to reach.

Loaded up with water, I went on. Linda had said the *Hemlock Forest* would be beautiful. It was her favorite place to hike. It was indeed a delight, dense shade for late afternoon walking over good trail tread with a little shuffling through leaves dropped from deciduous trees mixed with those Eastern Hemlocks. Early settlers thought the hemlocks were cedars, resulting in *Cedar* place names in that area.

I was a little afraid I would not find the recommended spot to camp. Then what would I do? I found it, though—a big rock overhang, just as described, with benches and a fire ring, too. I went around a little farther to the side to make my cowboy camp under an extended ledge, well out of sight of the trail. I needed no tent, no fire, or even benches, just a place to spread my sleeping bag.

Camping under that huge rock ledge, I hoped there wouldn't be an earthquake. If it would fall, the ledge above would smash me flat. Trees grew their roots over the ledge down many feet to the ground searching for water and dirt. The birds ceased their song as it became dark, and a small nearby waterfall lulled me to sleep.

In the morning, I was careful to leave-no-trace of my presence. Leave-no-trace is the goal of all good hikers. Before leaving, I kicked a few more leaves on the mostly bare ground where I had slept. I had come and gone with no mark upon the land.

There was a bit of road walking on my westbound route, where I met another backpacker going eastbound. What a treat it was to meet another backpacker. Nakedfoot was hiking in flip flops. He had a lightweight pack, and after hiking in Ohio, he planned to thru hike the AT southbound. After talking of trails to walk and walked, we went our separate ways.

At the rock climbing and rappelling site, four horseback riders passed me. My trail skirted the base of some striking sandstone cliffs, then climbed up through a space between those cliffs and traveled along the top of them.

My walk through Hocking Hills State Park was the best hike in Ohio. I had day hiked there once long before, as a young woman. It was just as beautiful as I remembered. I walked through deep gorges cut below cliffs of layered sandstone, the rock weathered by water and wind.

Hocking Hills

Old Man's Cave Gorge was the best: towering sandstone cliffs, waterfalls, streams tending to a beautiful green in deep water, shade from hemlocks and mixed deciduous trees, all in the depths of the gorge. There was much to see. There were also many hikers, walkers, and general tourists. It was a popular attraction, justly so, for its unique beauty. Artists could spend all their lives working on new views of trees, water, and rock, and I passed several working with brush and sketchpad on that day.

Many stairs were cut into steep hills and cliffs. I found those formally forged tourist trails challenging in places. Stairs, more than woodland trail, show up my limitations from knee replacement and arthritis, especially when needing to walk down deeply cut steps. Other folks had some problems, too, especially older folks. But it was all worth the effort and then some.

Old Man's Cave was named for an old guy who had once lived under one of those large overhanging ledges—a modern, historically speaking, cliff dweller. All the caves and overhangs of rock reminded me of cliff dwellings I had seen in the West. Envision western cliffs lacking stone houses built by ancient tribes and add the lush green growth of spring in Ohio, streams, and waterfalls. People in both places used rock overhangs to shelter homes.

After Cedar Falls, I wondered just where the Inn and Spa would be in that convenient space between two sections of the State Park. My re-supply box would be there and a legal place to camp. At the corner of a T-shaped intersection, a van was turning in. I held up my hand to ask if they had passed the Inn on the road they had just driven. The recently homeless couple had all their possessions in the van, yet they *insisted* on giving me a ride to the Inn.

It was a tight fit, as I climbed inside the van, and the woman slid to the middle. I sat with my pack in my lap. Having to hold it for me as I slid in, she was amazed I could carry it. Awaiting my re-supply, it probably only weighed fourteen-to-fifteen pounds at most, with a few extra things past my base weight. But packs are carried on your back, with weight mostly on your hips, a much sturdier body part, not held with one outstretched hand. As backpacks go, mine was quite light, especially waiting re-supply.

The Inn had my box, and after a phone call to Collin, with whom I had talked on the phone months ago, I was allowed to camp on their meadow, out of sight of the road. I added a load of water from the kitchen and trudged up the meadow, carrying much more weight than when I had arrived.

After using some of that heavy water for my dinner and breakfast, I packed up early and walked four-tenths of a mile back to the picnic area and my trail. Gee, my fully loaded pack *was* heavy, even with some water and food now in my belly. But I headed off on good, park trail to Ash Cave.

Ash Cave was the spot I had visited many years before and well worth seeing once again. The Wyandot people lived in my imagination, going about their daily lives under that large overhanging rock. They added to the list of peoples in my thoughts, once come, now gone, the rock remaining. It was an awesome sight early in the morning with only two other hikers viewing its grandeur with me.

As I walked the short walk to the parking area, the daily tourist parade was beginning. The cave would soon be filled. I talked with two guys carrying artist supplies, come to spend the day looking for the perfect picture. Hocking Hills draws a great many people to view its wonders.

After Ash Cave, there was a lot of road walking, some of it quite hot. I walked with my umbrella up much of the time, its silver surface reflecting the sun's rays as well as raindrops. I was wishing for benches to be placed every mile or so, when God provided some nice ledges by the creek on which to sit and eat my chocolate.

Fireflies—Roads—Trails
Good and Bad

The trail maintainers I had met three days before had also recommended staying at the cabin on Pretty Run. The cabin was closed and locked, but the back porch was a nice flat space under a roof for an easy cowboy camp to provide protection from forecast thunderstorms. I had my bath from a Ziploc bag of water and hung my food. I wasn't worried about bears, but an old cabin likely would have mice. Porch posts gave me space for a line to hang a food bag and my daily washing.

As I lay down to sleep, flashing lights in the woods in the general direction of another trail on my map suggested other hikers coming late to camp. No, more and more lights flashed in the woods. They seemed like other-worldly infiltrators popping up with intense flashing lights in the woods all around the cabin.

I wondered if the Earth was being invaded from outer space, deciding this woods cabin was their initial outpost. Then one of those lights flashed right beside me, and I realized I was seeing fireflies, not space invaders. I had seen fireflies years before, but never quite like this or flashes quite so bright. Amazing and beautiful, they were.

A big thunderstorm came by around 4:00 a.m. I was glad to be dry on the porch. The very first feathered alarm clock went off at 5:40. Shortly after, another sat on a branch near the cabin and persistently sang his song almost as loudly as my Washington hiking friend's deafening barking-dog alarm. I guessed it was time to get up.

After four-tenths of a mile on an old soggy road and sometimes creek, I was on asphalt for the rest of the day. I had planned to bypass Tar Hollow to shorten the trip by a day and make my re-supply stops work. There were only so many miles I could walk in a day, and there was only so much food I could carry. I rationalized that I was on the ADT, just the bike route instead of the foot-tread route. I covered ground more quickly on the road than on a trail, though it was harder on the feet. I still had flowers and sights to see, and a red fox ran across the road in front of me.

The saving grace of the day was wind, which helped to keep me cool. When the wind stopped, and clouds did not stand between me and the sun, it was brutally hot. I had always wondered about the line in the song, *Big Rock Candy Mountain*, "on a summer's day, in the month of May, a burly bum came hikin.'" May had never seemed like summer to me. The song writer must have been singing about southern Ohio. May certainly felt like summer there.

When it was lunch time, I stopped at a house with chairs on a porch. Norma let me eat there and later gave me water and shared the use of her bathroom. I stopped at the Dollar Store in Londonderry for cold chocolate milk, which I drank before I reached the cash register to pay for it.

Reaching Lickskillet, I regained the hiker Buckeye Trail and knocked on a door for water. Technically, I wasn't turned down. Someone just closed the curtain on the window of the door when I knocked and didn't answer the door. People in the house next door more hospitably gave me water.

At the end of my day, I wondered where I should ask for a place to tent, finally picking a trailer house on the left side of the road. Don, an older man on oxygen, answered the door. He agreed with my request, and I set up my tent off the lawn at the edge of the woods. Later, his wife, Kathy, came by and introduced herself. She brought a chair over and kept wondering aloud what she could do for me. She offered me cans of Vienna Sausage, which I turned down. Although I appreciated her kindness, I needed to eat my own food and lighten my pack.

Kathy and I had a good conversation about many things, trail talk and otherwise. We shared our mutual nervousness about door knocking: mine knocking on a stranger's door and hers, the nervousness of saying yes to a stranger's request at that same door. Both take a little courage. And we were both glad my door knock, request, and her assent had happened. In our meeting, one tiny microcosm of friendliness existed because we both had fought and conquered the dominant culture of fear in which we lived.

The next day, my trail soon became confusing. I counted three exits from a road, but my directions only mentioned two. I chose correctly looking at the topography, but then there was no mowed path to follow for a trail. Again, I guessed correctly. For a more confident walk in the woods, a splash or two of blue paint at each of those choices would have helped. The short piece of trail to the highway culvert was overgrown and needed love, but it was not difficult to know that it was my trail.

The trail *after* the culvert *really* needed love, the trail reverting to blackberries and poison ivy in the warm and humid climate. At home in Washington, I knew how quickly blackberries could overtake trail, real problem plants, even if they do have tasty fruit.

At my mid-morning snack time, I found a tick on my leg ready to munch on me. At least it had not yet taken a bite. After hang-glider hill, the rocky road and the oppressive heat were really getting to me. Although I had known before that the weather always heats up quickly in the spring in the East, that year it had done so overnight. At the beginning, in West Virginia, moving into Ohio, I had been concerned about a few cold nights. Cold nights had become a distant memory.

I needed a tick-free place in the shade to stop for lunch. Across the very flat and sun-exposed plain on Higby Road, I spied a house in trees. A car beside it indicated someone was at home. Unluckily for me, about half a block before I got there, the lady of the house came out, got in her car, and drove away. I went up to the door and knocked anyway, still wishing for permission to sit on that shaded porch for lunch. There was no answer, only a barking dog inside.

I just couldn't make myself go out into the oven of treeless flat road walking again, and I had my lunch on the porch. No one driving by seemed to care, and I, zombie-like, really needed the break. I wondered if the owner would come back while I was sitting on that porch by two old rifles leaning in a corner. They had not looked like a welcoming sign. I automatically, rather woodenly, chewed my food and left, with my umbrella raised against the beating sun.

I walked on to a gravel company, a spot where I knew another hiker had obtained water, and I was glad to see a porta potty outside, too. The porta potty was an oven absorbing every ray of baking sun. Someone had practiced artwork of a woman's private anatomy on the door in front of my face when I sat down. I ignored the artwork and the heat, appreciating the place to sit.

Deed done, I found nice cold water from the cooler inside the office and talked to the woman at the desk. Her husband had a rare lymphoma, and the prognosis was not good. They were in their 50s, and he was not likely to reach sixty. Tears welled in her eyes as she shared her grief and sorrow, and I listened, promising to keep her and her husband in my prayers. My problems of tiredness, heat, and offensive artwork seemed quite minor inconveniences in comparison to what she shared.

Walking to the edge of the forested hill, I took a few moments to hydrate my dinner and stepped up the hill into welcome forest shade. Looking at my GPS, its tightly bunched contour lines had warned me that stretch would be hard, but I began at a slow and steady pace, not wanting to push too hard in the heat.

I was rewarded by a lovely forest, evenly graded trail, and flowers. There were blooms of May apple, jack in the pulpit, wood sorrel, larkspur, and pretty cinquefoil. My earlier bad attitude disappeared as I enjoyed the flowers. Wild blue iris with a pretty pattern, flowers lemon-yellow, bright-red and pale-blue whose names I did not know, and one glorious lady slipper were treats worth seeing.

The green growth of multiple layers of forest canopy kept the sun at bay, though yes, it was still hot. I had shed shirt to walk in sports bra all day long. But, as long as I kept to slow and strolling steps, my inner-heat level did not rise too high, and that nicely graded trail was do-able. I had a long way to go. But it was all in shaded woods.

I walked until late, completing my planned miles. My tent site was far from ideal, but at least it was not in poison ivy. Between sunscreen early in the day, mosquito repellant, and lots of my own sweat, I felt like a slime ball. Stony Creek provided water for a Ziploc bath as I got naked in the tent at 77 degrees in the dark of night. Fireflies crashed into the tent around me as I, too, crashed, a little cleaner, into welcome sleep.

Packing up, I was glad for the cool of the morning, but it was not cool enough to require more than a sports bra on my torso.

The Buckeye Trail directions said to choose the western trail at the first junction. The trouble was, it was the second junction. I chose the trail, saw a confirming blue blaze and strode along, enjoying the cool morning and flat trail. Soon my trail was marked with different blazes for a Bridle trail. I assumed the Buckeye Trail folks just hadn't put up any more of theirs. Almost a mile from my campsite, after multiple consultations with my GPS, I concluded I was on the wrong trail. And there was no way to meet up with the correct one. I had to go back.

Many bad words! I had wasted, **wasted,** two miles in the cool of the morning. I did not mind the added miles half so much as the wasted coolness. Very disgusted with myself, I walked back and found the blue double blaze indicating a trail change, which I had missed the first time, as it was almost completely covered up by the new growth of green vines.

Immediately, on the correct trail, I had to ford some water. I was in such high dungeon that, not wanting to waste more time changing into crocs, I chose to walk the rest of the way back to the road instead, and I walked that road until Headquarters Bridle Trail. Having, by then, walked out my ire, and needing forest shade, I took to trail once more. Trail and road had gone to the same point.

Almost immediately, after regaining trail, there was a huge blown-down tree with five major trunks spread all over the trail as well as any clear space that had been beside the tread. Negotiating the fallen tree trunks, I went straight uphill for 250 feet. During the day, there were three or four more straight uphill pieces. It totaled about as much uphill as one of my training hills in Washington, Mt Pete. But I hadn't ever gone up Mt Pete in the 80s, in high humidity. Still, most of the walk was shaded, and blessed breezes blew.

Reaching Woods Hollow Road, I stopped at Joe and Karla's house. They gave me ice-cold water, put several ice cubes in each of my bottles, and I drank my fill besides. The kindness of people made the day, even if the weather didn't.

Rejuvenated by all the ice-cold water, on I went. Past the highway, my directions were again unclear. A group of good old boys and one old gal on private property directed me to a driveway and a short climb to the blue blaze-marked trail at the top of the hill. That trail led me through the edge of the woods on private property, a trail involving two or three barbed-wire fences and four dogs. A homeowner controlled the dogs and helped me through a couple fences, though barbed wire nicked me twice, while I was going through.

Before Prussia Road, the trail seemed to direct me across a stream and promptly disappear. I crossed back and forth that same stream twice looking for my desired track. Not finding one, I plotted a route over a meadow liberally laced with poison ivy. Mercifully, a jeep road appeared, which took me back to the trail. The rest of the way was well blazed.

Once on Prussia Road, I held up my *hiker needs a ride* sign, but cars just passed me by, occasionally waving. Ok, I thought, one last try, and maybe I'll have to bribe someone from a nearby house. My one last try was golden.

A somewhat-battered truck with a taped-on side-view mirror stopped. Thank you, God. He would take me to my motel. His name was Kirk (like Star Trek) and in high school, kids called him James T. When I met him, he was nicknamed Bulldog. This gentleman took me to my motel, and along the drive, he told me of his friend named Mary, who had lost two husbands and was a fine woman. I shook his hand, thanked him for the ride, and told him he was a fine gentleman.

As I checked in, the young woman at the desk solved two more looming problems. I would pay her for a ride back to the trail early Monday morning. She would also mail a package for me at the post office so I would not have to wait to leave until after the post office opened. There was absolutely no need to carry cold weather gear any longer. And I was eager to shed a little pack weight by sending it home.

The motel was equally far from fast food in either direction. I chose the Arby's, across from Walmart, for my late dinner. After a gyro and a milkshake, I went to Walmart for tortillas and cheese for the trail and some fruit and a dinner for my rest day. Boy, did I need a rest day.

Finally, on my bed, my feet and legs were screaming. It had been a long day. But I was clean and fed and in air conditioning. Yay!

I woke up after only eight hours. I wanted to sleep more but couldn't manage to do that. I did take a lot of lay-around time that day, but I had to walk to the laundromat. It was already hot at 10:00 a.m. I grabbed a couple snack wraps and a small strawberry shake at McDonald's, since I was on that end of town. Then I asked an older couple there for a ride back to the motel. Walking so much on a rest day was against my religion.

Tough Hiking—
Step by Step

That hike through Ohio was a tough hike. I just didn't do well in heat and high humidity. Of course, I was another year older, and there was unfriendly trail and a lot of up and down. I did some serious thinking, wondering if I should stop this long-distance hiking nonsense after I reached Cincinnati. And was it time to schedule another knee replacement? I could still get planned miles done. But my knee didn't feel reliable on downhills. Pondering, I was hoping to wait *until* fall for a surgery. But I didn't want *to* fall while waiting.

Many wonder why I still hiked long trails, and how I could accomplish them. A long trail is too long, beyond their imagination. Large goals seemed riskier than short ones. Fear was one issue. How to even begin another. Daring to bite off big chunks, though not a thru hiker, simply was my style. By this time, on the ADT, I had been doing so for many years.

Long ago, in a traumatic time in my life, I learned to cut down time into manageable pieces. That helps for walking on long-distance trails as well as getting past an overwhelming future. I have been divorced, twice. Getting divorced at all had never been in my game plan. Sometimes life takes turns we never anticipated.

Counseling was an important lifeline for me back then. A lifeline, as in, I could have died by my own hand without it. I was in deep grief and suicidal. One of many things I learned in conversations with my counselor, was to cut down time into manageable chunks. At that time, the chunks I could manage were quite small. Could I get through the next five minutes?

Yes, I could probably live five minutes more. My counselor encouraged me to make contracts with myself to get through days, five minutes at a time. As time went on, I could lengthen my contracts to an hour at a time and proceed to more from there.

It's a small trick containing a larger truth. We really don't *have* to get through more than five minutes at a time, even though we tend to think we have *forever* in our future. Depending on our life situation, that *forever* may be seen as gift and promise or overwhelming impossibility. Either way, we really only *get* to live one moment at a time. I learned the effectiveness of that life lesson the hard way. And I have learned to apply it in a variety of ways in life.

Applied to a long-distance trail: Although the trail is long, I can only walk it one step at a time, one mile at a time, one day at a time. That is all that is necessary. In fact, that is all that is possible. Concentrating on the short chunks, those short chunks add up to result in distances greater than first thought or imagined possible. Long-distance trails are hiked one short chunk at a time, no more, no less, just step and step and step again. I am not a young hiker. I have never been a super jock. Faster hikers pass me all the time. I just keep walking, step by step, by step, by step. And I still can hike long trails.

Applied to fear: There are thousands of things to fear. The list of possible fears can overwhelm. If I choose to concentrate on one particular fear at a particular moment, I might be able to manage that, maybe even leave that fear behind. I do not have to leave every fear behind at every minute. That would be way too much, and probably not even a good thing to do. But if I concentrate on leaving one fear behind at one moment of time in my life, moment by moment, step by step, fear by fear, I accumulate, if not fearlessness, at least unfear of many things.

If it hadn't been for the heat and humidity, I would have enjoyed Ohio's woods walks more. The forecast for the next day was 90 degrees. I would be hiking with as few clothes on as possible. But I would be hiking, step by step, by step, until my plane's departure from Cincinnati. I might have to focus on small chunks of time and trail, but I had life experience in doing so, having completed other goals. Besides, I was too cheap to buy another ticket for a different flight, and I had to do something with the time remaining until my airplane left the ground.

WHO MINISTERS TO WHOM?

The woman who had checked me into my motel in Waverly, picked me up for an 8:20 start. It took me a tenth of a mile to shed my shirt and settle into the weight of my pack. I was greatly relieved that I had a reasonably cool and shady road walk.

When I passed by his house, an extremely cute little doggie decided I was there to take him for a walk. I thought I had him convinced to go home twice, only to discover half a mile later that he had just gotten sneaky and was walking sedately behind me just out of my sight. I stopped at a house where three men were loading plywood on a forklift and talked to them long enough that the doggie finally disappeared. He was very cute, but I didn't need a dog, and his owner would miss him.

A man sitting with his wife on their porch asked me if I was "going to California?"

"The trail is going there but, I'm just headed to Cincinnati," I answered.

I met and talked with many people that day. The first one after the man on the porch was a United States Postal rural-delivery lady, who stopped as I walked on a country road and asked if I would like a bottle of ice water. Well, sure. I filled my bottle with ice cubes she had carried to cool her lunch and then filled it with water. She told me she and her son hiked, and she took down my journal and book information she was eager to read.

I didn't stop for mid-morning snack at 10:00 but walked until 11:00 and called it first lunch, stopping at Mapleberry Farm, a hiker-friendly place with chairs and table in deep shade next to a swing set. They also refilled my water bottle and provided a restroom.

A little farther on, Cindy stopped to ask if I needed anything. We had quite a long conversation in the middle of the road. She wanted to help me any way she could. She also told me Eden Baptist Church was founded by Thomas Jefferson. The historical marker didn't say that, but it did note the church was from the early 1800s. Ohio State contributed $30,000 a year for its upkeep, according to the historical register.

A mile short of Nipgen, I took a break, sitting on my pack, before heading on. Seeing me sitting there, Rob stopped and asked if I needed anything. He also gave me ice-cold water. He offered his house for my night's lodging, but it was too early in the day for that. I was always cheered when people talked with me. I was a solo hiker, but I didn't feel alone. A few words exchanged, cold water shared, even offers of help I could not use brought smiles to my face and made the miles go by, tendrils of my thoughts connecting people met while steps connected miles.

I asked Debra, who was pruning her roses on the corner in Nipgen, where the C-store was, and we also talked. The little convenience store in Nipgen was an oasis in the afternoon heat. I had a deluxe hamburger made to order, chocolate milk, and an ice cream bar. The ladies in the store took my picture and said they were going to post it on their web site. It was fun to think I was famous, even if very minorly.

So—Who ministers to whom here? All these offers of help and water were wonderful ministries to the old-lady hiker. Yet I also provided ears to hear their stories: the woman who hiked with her son and eagerly wrote down my trail journals information, the woman who had worked as a cook and then had been unemployed, collected rain water for her water supply, and had just been hired by Kroger, the man who was worried about his father's health, and the drug house down the block, the woman who had recently had an accident that totaled her car but caused her no bodily damage. My ministry was listening to people tell their stories. We ministered to each other.

Since it was early, only 5:00, I walked 1.8 miles more than my plan called for. Rick and Gail drove into their driveway as I knocked on their door. They gave me permission to camp behind an old abandoned house. I was further checked on by their neighbor and their nephew. Rick and Gail came over after my tent was up, bringing with them cold bottled water, muffins, chocolate protein drink and V8 Juice. I accepted the liquids and turned down the muffins.

Neurons

I had met so many generous people. Over and over again, complete strangers gave me aid. Each time I asked, or even when I did not ask for anything at all, people who knew nothing about me, other than that I was an old lady walking with a backpack, wanted to help me on my journey, reinforcing my trust in the goodness of others.

A basic principle in neurology applies here. Way back in my college days, learning to be a physical therapist, I learned of neurons, the individual bits of wiring in our bodies, nerves in common parlance. Each neuron makes connections with at least one other, usually many. Immensely simplified, nerves are influenced by how often we use them.

Every time a neuron is stimulated, fired, used, the threshold that must be reached to stimulate it a second time is lowered. Every time it is stimulated, fired, used, it is more likely that it will be stimulated, fired, used again. Neurons that are not used disconnect with other neurons and die. It is a use-it-or-lose-it situation. More than that, it is a use-it-and-it-will-be-used-again situation, neuron by neuron.

Moving our bodies or forming our thoughts requires unimaginable numbers of neurons. I type words on my computer and thousands of neurons are working together inside me, thoughts forming in my mind, fingers causing key strokes, two computers at work, hardware my fingers touch and neurons touching neurons touching neurons, all teaming up to work together, resulting in words written across the screen of my computer.

Of course, there are a myriad of other things that happen in thought and action, complicated chemical reactions and other processes. But one simple basic fact about neurons—a neuron once fired is more easily fired again—has always seemed to me to be the basis of all therapy, physical or psychological, and explains the role of habits in our lives.

Perhaps that simple basic fact helps explain how to leave a fear behind. Each time I meet a stranger, finding friends instead of dangers, I become less fearful in my life. My internal template of who a stranger is has changed. Strangers are those whose lives I have been fortunate enough to share, even for one brief greeting, on a trail or road. Strangers are generous, willing helpers who know me not, but meet my needs. We share that we are human, each of us, separate yet together, sharing words or smiles, encouragement or prayer. With fear in the past tense, we become more than we ever were before. Each time that happens, it becomes more likely to happen again.

Small steps add up to long trails. Small steps at leaving fear behind end up as major changes in life and attitude. Each person I encounter in a positive chance meeting on the ADT leaves me with less fear. It is, in a way, basic neurology.

In my tent behind that old abandoned house, I had new friends who had fortified me with liquids and support. After 8:30, the weather was getting only slightly cooler. But I was off my feet, reasonably clean, at peace, and looked after by those inside the next house over.

HEAT AND BRIARS,
BUT ALWAYS ANGELS

The next morning was very humid. It was so humid I was instantly wet. Of course, I sweat going uphill. But there was condensation when the humid air hit my skin, whether I was moving or not. I walked in a sports bra all day long, no need for a shirt. Settlers from Europe in America called the native Americans naked savages. I think those native Americans had it right for this climate. I wore as little as I could and not get arrested.

The trail had become a strange mix of maintained and unmaintained trail. Blackberry bushes and greenbrier were working overtime to return tread to nature. Yet, there was one lovely spot with a view that had a picnic table and a breeze. I could have stayed there for hours. But much of the time the trail was rough and overgrown. Such trail really slowed me, rough tread covered with blowdowns and briars. Just before Pike Lake there was another behemoth downed tree to thread over and under trunks and branches.

Though I was late getting to the lake, I hydrated my dinner, loaded with water, and looked at my paper map, T-by-T directions, and my GPS. Then I had two scoops of hand-dipped ice cream from the little store.

I needed to get in a few more miles as I was again falling behind schedule. The next section was even more horrible. I needed a machete, Pulaski, and a chain saw. Didn't have them.

A question: If there is no maintenance, is there really a trail? I had the feeling that there had been no maintenance in that section for a long time. And it doesn't take that long in southern Ohio for trails to be overgrown. That short stretch was one of the worst. I was all scratched up from pushing aside blackberry bushes and greenbrier. Trail tread was often non-existent. I thought if the trail was closed, it should have had a sign. I followed blue blazes through the mess but wondered why it could be called a trail.

I know maintenance is by volunteers, and maybe there just were no volunteers and therefore no maintenance. In some places the trail was disappearing except for blue blazes on tree trunks, some standing, others blown down on the ground. A sign on one section of trail named it in memory of a volunteer who had worked to maintain the trail. It seemed rather sad to name a trail after someone who worked so hard and then let the trail named in their honor go to pot.

At Greenbrier Road, I left the trail in disgust and took the road, or I would never have made the day's mileage. As it was, I walked onto the main road quite late, in dusk fading fast to darkness. All the houses I could see were trailers. Two people on an old porch suggested I should ask permission to camp at the second trailer, the owner of the others in the neighborhood. The guy came to the door and told me to put my tent anywhere

I wanted in their big back yard. Gratefully, I did. It had been a long day in time and effort, if not miles.

It rained in the night, softly but steadily falling on my tent, conveniently stopping at 6:00 a.m. I met Lana at the trailer door in the morning and asked to use the restroom. Digging cat holes in someone's lawn would not have been a good idea. That issue taken care of, I walked my road to Green Ridge Road and then tried trail again.

One-and-a-half miles in, I was met with a wall of blackberries. The last blue blazes seen seemed to lead straight into the blackberries. I looked all around in each direction for more blue blazes, even pushing part way through the blackberries to no avail. The blackberries extended as far as a football field—or two. I retraced my steps. Returning to the road, that three miles was for nothing in the way of forward movement.

I was becoming pretty discouraged about the trails on that section of the ADT through Ohio. I was pretty tough for an old lady. I had completed the three scenic long-distance trails in the United States, even if I had done them as a section hiker, not a thru hiker. I had hiked desert, high altitude, forest, and rock scrambles. I had learned how to be independent in the wilderness. On the ADT, I had learned how to ask for and accept what help I needed on the trail. I enjoyed the somewhat masochistic challenges of long-distance hiking. But I did not enjoy trying to get through walls of blackberries and greenbrier on unmaintained trails.

I still wanted to walk across Ohio. I wanted to stick as close to the ADT as possible, but there was a bike route, too, as well as a foot-trail route. I could see the broader area on both my paper map and GPS. I could see the bike-alternate waypoints. I took the bike path marked on the roads. It was still the ADT, just not the foot trail part of the ADT. Close enough, if the trails were going back to nature. Stopping in Latham for late lunch, people in the convenience store were very nice. The *people* were wonderful, the trail considerably less so.

I tried the foot trail again past the fish hatchery for a tenth of a mile. It was again crappy trail. If I had to fight my way through overgrown trail looking for safe foot placement and searching for blue blazes, it would have taken me three times as long to get across Ohio. I did not have three times as many days in my plan before my airplane left Cincinnati. I went back to the road, looked to see how I could once again connect with the ADT, and took the highway until Bell Hollow Road.

There was a *huge* RV campground on Bell Hollow Road. A *ba-zillion* big rigs covered hill after hill. There were group sites, too. The campground the road cut through went on for at least three-quarters of a mile. Signs called it a family resort. There was nothing wrong with that kind of camping, but I needed no hookups and did not think I would fit in. Somewhat intimidated by all the big rigs, I walked on, looking for something appropriate for just my solo tent.

Cave Lake suited me to a T. Only, the office was closed, and the sparsely spaced trailers had no people. The restrooms were prominent. Using them, I noted there were showers. At that point, I was dying for a shower.

I finally found a trailer with a car present and a man on the porch. Don and Virginia, one year older than I was, invited me to stay next to them or under their awning, and began scurrying around to clear the area. I told them they did not need to do that as my tent stakes would not have penetrated their pad and needed the edge of the lawn.

Camping with Don and Virginia at Cave Lake

Don was a retired farmer, Virginia a retired school cook. I put up my tent and ate dinner on their picnic table. I had a pleasant evening with a shower and congenial company. They served me ice cream and cookies as we enjoyed getting to know each other. The day had certainly had its ups and downs, but the evening with Don and Virginia was perfect. They came out and took my picture before I left in the morning.

Quite stung by the bad trail I had encountered, I came to a bike bypass. Succumbing to temptation, I took it. It was still the Buckeye Trail, and it cut off miles as well as possible problems. It just didn't make sense in my mind to choose trail and more hideous fights with overtaking greenery. My feet, knees, and shoulders thanked me. My short cut meant I reached Sinking Springs early and was then ahead of schedule. I liked thinking I was ahead as opposed to the pressure of pushing hard to make scheduled miles.

Serpent Mound was quite interesting, and I took the time to read interpretive signs and to climb halfway up the tower for a picture. Serpent Mound is an earthwork effigy in the form of a snake, made by the ancestors of the Woodland Native Americans. Two ancient peoples, Fort Ancient dating back to 1000 AD and Adena dating back to 800 BC, left evidence of amazing cultures. Some of the artifacts found looked similar to me to designs of Aztecs, tantalizing my imagination with thoughts of ancient peoples communicating over vast distances long before Europeans ever trod these lands.

After turning on Louden Road, I knocked on a door, searching for a tenting spot. A young couple,

Vince and Korina, knew nothing about the trail and were amazed at what I told them. They gave me permission to camp, and I was very grateful to have a place to be.

Then I spilled a whole bottle of water in my tent. In the ensuing comedy of saving sleeping bag and other gear, I discovered I could stand up in my tiny tent. Really. In a *bend over and touch your toes manner*, straddling a large puddle, with my butt touching the highest part of the tent roof, I frantically moved to save my sleeping bag and sopped up water with bandanas and camp towel. Once my sleeping bag was safe, I thought the episode slap-stick funny. Who knew you could stand in such a tiny one-person tent, well, not straight up, but on my feet with straight legs even though the rest of me was bent.

Spreading wet maps and foam pads in the shelter of an outbuilding that housed a big mower, I hoped my things would dry by morning, and I cleaned myself with my water-soaked bandanas. A whole bottle of water is a lot of water in a confined space, but it did not go to waste. I had my bath without the step of putting water in a Ziploc bag and dipping my bandana in the bag of water. My sleeping bag stayed dry. The comedy and drama over, it was time for sleep.

Vince and Korina looked me up online before morning and were eager to help in any way possible. They helped tremendously. Besides morning bathroom privileges and water, they gave me most of the day as a slackpack, and Korina washed and dried a couple pair of my socks, my underwear, a bra, and my headband which all had been victims of the water debacle of the night before.

I scurried to organize my gear to carry only pack brain (A pack's brain is the top detachable pouch on some packs.) and water holsters. (Holsters are little bags carrying my water bottles that attach to my pack's shoulder straps but can also attach to a belt.) Lunch, drinks, first-aid kit, bathroom necessities, camera, hat, umbrella, and I was set. It was very worth the late start to leave the rest of my gear and walk on to the town of Peebles. Walking with just a slack pack was so nice.

Ohio was very green, with forests, pastures, and lawns. It was expected to rain and be cloudy. I loved the clouds, enabling me to wear a shirt comfortably. I didn't really walk much faster without a pack, but it was easier on my body and my joints. My usual pace was somewhere between a saunter and a trudge. Although it rained quite hard, I was comfortable under my umbrella. Only my feet got wet.

By the time I reached Peebles, those feet hurt. That's what happens when it continues to spit rain all day; it makes everything wet so there is no place to sit down, and you walk five hours straight.

I called Korina and Vince, and they brought my gear to me (including dry socks and underwear) as I sat in Subway for a long rest. I charged my GPS, ate a late lunch, and hydrated my dinner. What a sweet young couple to be so kind to me.

Oldest Barn in Adams County

After walking without it most of the day, when I first put my pack on, it felt heavy. But I quickly got in the groove, and the next few miles disappeared on somewhat rested feet. The sky was darkening and ready to let loose with rain again when I knocked on a door and asked for a place to put my tent or, better yet, a place to be under shelter.

The man at the door suggested the barn and took me across the street to the oldest barn in Adams County. From the street, it looked like the remnants of a bombed-out house. The sound part of the barn was hidden from the road by drooping trees and three-foot-tall grass and bushes. That night, I slept in that very old barn. If Jesus could be born in a barn, (stable in most translations of the Bible) I could certainly sleep in one—and be glad for my shelter from the rain.

There was lots of straw and hay, though the barn was also a storage area for cast-off furniture and junk. My host said I could use one of the old chairs tossed in a pile on one section of hay. After dusting it off, I did so. It was quite a nice old-style chair that I think would have been worth some money in an antique store.

A night in the oldest barn in Adams County

I didn't have to put up a tent. I spread my now *three* garbage bags, making just enough room for my little nest of bed and gear. (I had sent a garbage bag in a couple re-supply boxes to replace my original if it was torn. I decided to keep them all for times like this.) Three garbage bags laid end-to-end make a luxurious amount of clean room on which to put my sleeping bag and gear— at least luxurious room for a hiker. (I carefully fold them dirty side in when packing up in the morning to use again some other night.)

In the privacy of the barn, I had dinner and a good Ziploc-bag wash. For fear an old barn would have mice or rats, I hung my food between the ladders to the second-story loft. My strung line also provided space for that night's wash of bandanas, socks, and undies. (I only take three sets so one is on, one ready for the next day, and the third set gets washed each day if circumstances allow. I was dry and snug, as rain poured hard for hours. A few leaks in the old barn roof necessitated a slight move sideways for my nest, easily done. I slept with the comforting scent of dry hay in my nose while I listened to a few drips not far away.

The next day presented another trail challenge. The descriptions in my Buckeye Trail map folder warned me there would be no blue blazes to follow for a shortish stretch over a small range of thickly wooded hills. On my GPS, I could see a trail that seemed about where I needed one to be, and I hoped it would get me to Beaver Dam Road by mid-morning snack. The last blue blazes that I saw took me beside a trailer on an ATV track that went steeply up a ridge as described in the T-by-T. The track disintegrated into an eroded gully, but I looked at the trail on the GPS, and it seemed to be paralleling the gully. I could see where I would hit the ridgetop skid road, which I shortly found.

The ridge top was nice, as was the skid road. Too bad it didn't last longer. Though I had no blazes to guide me, I thought I chose the right track off the ridge, but there might have been a better one farther on. My choice went steeply down, which I needed to take very slowly, caring for my decrepit right knee. Eventually, I reached a creek valley, but the steep road/trail became the creek bed or tall wet grass. It took quite a while, but I finally hit a better road, perhaps the one I should have taken from the ridge. That road dumped me out on my objective, Beaver Dam Road.

Sitting in the tiny shelter at Davis Memorial, I wrung out my socks and contemplated my next move. There was a trail, probably maintained, through Davis Memorial, or there was a road, which was probably faster. I had also been wondering, since I was a few miles ahead of schedule, about taking bike routes, instead of the sometimes miserable trails, in order to get to Shawnee Lodge one day earlier than planned. That would take a big push the rest of that day and the next, but would grant me a rest day at Mount Orab, a few days later on when I would need it.

Could I change my reservation at the lodge? Did I have a cell signal? I had one bar. Normally, one bar is not enough to make a call, but my call went through perfectly. The reservation was changed easily. The die was cast. Now I just had to get there by the next day's night. I missed looking at some dolomite rock and some sink holes, but I would get a day off at Mount Orab.

When I reached the top of Peach Mountain, there was another of those circular road walks with no reason given. I took the shorter way. But first, I looked for a house with a porch and people so I could eat and rest.

A dog came barking at me, its owner calling it Lacie. I called it Lacie, too, and the dog decided I was a friend. I asked the dog's owner if I could eat sitting somewhere in the shade on the porch. Tom called his wife out to meet me, and they invited me in. Tom and Maggie were wonderful. They did not know about long-distance hiking but had a son who was into other adventure activities. They served me milk with lunch and offered me a place to stay for the night. Unfortunately, I had many more miles to walk before the day was over. Tom and Maggie were such gracious people, I was sorry to leave. They looked at my map, agreed on my choice of road, and off I went downhill.

Snake Charmer and Trail Magick

About a mile later, a red truck drove by, stopped, then backed up and stopped again to wait for me to catch it. ADT Trail Magic was written on the side of the truck and it contained another hiker, Snake Charmer, (PCT, 2015) and her mother, Trail Magick. What a delight! They were camped at Ironton. Snake Charmer was also hiking the ADT in Ohio, and her mother was playing trail angel. Yes, she had hiked the PCT. Would I like to camp with them? They would wait for me in Wamsley and bring me back in the morning. They could take my pack.

Snake Charmer and Trail Magick

In fewer than five minutes, I had made new friends, given them my pack, popped two water bottles into my pack brain tied around my waist, and took my poles as my new-found friends and trail angels drove away. I slackpacked the remaining five miles of my goal.

Even then, I was not yet through meeting charming people for the day. John stopped on the road a bit farther on to talk to me. John was an 80+ year-old member of a local hiking club, who told me of the heyday of Mineral Springs and its two big hotels. Now, a restored schoolhouse and Ohio Historical marker mark the spot. I also chatted with Jerry, a retired disabled vet out with his dog. Yes, the people on this trail make the trail, even when trails are less pleasant than desired.

For the previous two days, I had been thinking my hike would be a lot nicer in that hot weather if I could get slackpacks and showers. And what did I get? A slackpack and a shower.

In Wamsley, I climbed in the truck with Snake Charmer and Trail Magick, and we drove to their campground in Ironton, more than an hour away. Snake Charmer even had a two-man tent set up as a site holder in the campground, though they slept in the truck. I ate, moved my gear into their tent and enjoyed the campground shower. Snake Charmer and Trail Magick also offered to slack-pack me the next day, delivering my pack to the Shawnee Lodge, my day's destination.

We were up early to drive back to Wamsley. I was

set to go with my slackpacking bags tied around my waist. They were usually up even earlier, but they put me on the trail by 7:30, which was perfect as far as I was concerned.

The day soon heated up, no clouds at all in the morning. I was glad for my umbrella to hold off the sun's direct rays. For my mid-morning snack, I had trail bars and a rest, sitting in a chair in a house under construction, as the owner, Scott, stood outside on a ladder, staining siding.

On the American Discovery Trail there truly was no way I ever could have imagined all the various places I saw and the people I encountered. About lunch time, I knocked on a door for water and was told to come in so the flies wouldn't. I followed the gentleman who had told me to enter down the hallway to the kitchen. He was down-home friendly, and I asked if I could eat at the corner of his kitchen table in his nice cool house.

"Sure," Mike said, and cleared a little more space for me. I was probably being pushy when I asked to take off my shoes, but my feet so needed to be free while I ate lunch.

As I ate and we chatted, his wife came home from church in West Union, where her son was preaching, and she had led the children's church. Mike had gone to the little church I had passed earlier in the day. "How did *she* get here?" Kathy asked, perplexed to find a strange lady sitting in her kitchen and no car outside. That required explanations, and I talked of trail to catch her up to date with my presence.

Mike's hobby was hunting dogs. I had passed a sign about a fox-hunting club, a big deal in those parts. Their dog had just produced puppies, early arrivals that very morning. Mike and Kathy were concerned about them, hoping mommy and pups were now quietly settled down. I didn't get to see the puppies. Mommy and babies needed rest and privacy.

Lunch and rest time over, I said good-bye to my latest new friends and headed down the road again. I saw an older gent sitting on an ATV looking up the road as I walked toward him.

"How long did it take you to figure out that umbrella arrangement?" he asked as I came closer.

"I figured that out several years ago," I answered, and we started talking about the trails I had walked. He was impressed I had walked the AT, PCT, and CDT. Then we talked of old-age topics like arthritis. His wife drove up, and he blocked the driveway with his wheels so she would stop, and I could tell her how I managed my arthritis. Topping off our chat, they filled my water bottle with refrigerated water. I had made two more friends before I walked on.

After passing a field, blue with wildflowers, I found the trailhead I was looking for about 250 feet before the waymark on my GPS. I was happy and relieved to see it was real trail, not overgrown trail, marked with red blotches since it was in the state park, instead of Buckeye Trail's blue blazes. Unfortunately, it was built like most Eastern trails, straight up and straight down, over and over again.

My knee did not do that well or quickly. It took a long time for me to go two-and-a-half miles. It was even longer as my umbrella, stored while under the shade of trees by shoving in my belt like a sword, had somehow fallen to the trail without my notice. I had to backtrack quite a way to find it. After retrieving my umbrella and walking on, the seemingly interminable series of ups and downs finally put me on a road, and I discovered it was a long way yet to the lodge.

I was bushed, tired, and weary. There was a shorter trail steeply up, but my knee was done with steep trail for the day. I walked to the double-back turn before the lodge and waved down a car headed in that direction for a lift. I would be walking out that way anyway, so I didn't feel it was cheating. And if I had taken the steep trail up the distance would have been shorter than the way I walked.

I checked in, got my shower, food, and had two long conversations with the girl at the desk and a waitress. Their large indoor pool was their major attraction, and it was being fixed so there were not many people staying there. They were happy to have a trail-worn hiker who had booked a room. I was happy my impromptu plan change had succeeded.

More immediately, I had a needed rest day at the

lodge. Although not overfull with people, there were others there besides myself. I met the Jacksons at breakfast. The dad had hiked some of the AT, and their two sons had completed the AT in the 90s. Walking trails gave us lots to talk about.

Besides the regular chores and resting of a rest day, I perused the state park map and was in contact with Snake Charmer and Trail Magick. A few more changes were made to my plans. Although I plan my hikes in quite a bit of detail long before setting foot on a trail, flexibility is a virtue when presented with new opportunities for vista for the eyes or respite for the body. Snake Charmer and Trail Magick would provide me with another food drop, so I wouldn't have to carry six days' worth of food. Deal.

Then plans were altered once again. Snake Charmer and I could hike together for a few days. That meant slackpacking and company, which sounded wonderful to me. Snake Charmer would slow down a bit to match my pace.

I discovered alternate roads for the next day that would cut off a few more miles of difficult trail. It wasn't exactly that I couldn't do the trail. But it was clear, walking on steep trail with my bad knee would take longer than planned. I had hiked more than 10,000 trail miles since I'd turned sixty, and I just didn't feel I had to get every foot of this trail completed as listed. I didn't need to kill myself to accumulate more trail cred. I still would have continuous footsteps across Ohio, in roughly the same area as the trail. I decided that was close enough.

Snake Charmer and I would walk an old road made into a bridle trail connecting with other forest roads. It would save time and wear and tear on my body. It was a good choice for me. It turned out to be a good choice for Snake Charmer, too, and her last day on the trail in Ohio.

Snake Charmer and Trail Magick showed up at the lodge at 7:00 as I checked out. We drove down to the service road and headed out. I had gratefully chosen to walk roads instead of trails, but I also had the enjoyment of a hiking companion and the good luck of a slackpack.

Snake Charmer and I chattered as we walked, getting to know each other as the miles slipped by in good order. Trail Magick met us in the truck at a designated spot crossing a forest road for mid-morning snack as we sat on the tailgate. Again, similarly, we joined her for lunch, and I sprawled comfortably in the back of the truck. What luxury.

But Snake Charmer had some nasty blisters. She was younger and a faster hiker than I was, but she had also been recovering from serious surgeries following a bad accident. We were doing well until we missed a turn and added six-tenths of a mile in the wrong direction, which then meant another six-tenths of a mile getting back to our correct route.

Then heat and humidity got to Snake Charmer. Fairly abruptly, she got nauseous and suffered heat exhaustion. She had also sprouted new blisters over old, which we treated. But rest and blister treatment were not enough. Her old blisters were infected. We needed Trail Magick to come to the rescue. It was fortunate we were on roads. As I walked ahead toward the agreed meeting waypoint, I met Trail Magick in her red truck. She was searching for us and concerned that we were late. We picked up Snake Charmer, and she slowly recovered a little in the truck as we drove back toward the campground.

Back there, Snake Charmer had the first shower as I organized for the next day. She discovered a very hot rash high on her leg, and we were worried about the spread of infection from her blistered toes. Possible complications from a previous accident were also a worry. Trail Magick took her to the Emergency Room while I stayed, had my shower, and accomplished my camp chores. A call to my cell phone said Snake Charmer was being admitted to the hospital. I prayed she would receive the care she needed. Our bodies are strong and resilient, but at the same time they are quite fragile.

Trail Magick was still intent on supporting me another day. At the same time, she was quite concerned about Snake Charmer. She delivered me to the trail at 8:30 and drove back to the hospital. I walked on, observing flowers and green Ohio countryside, concern about my hiking buddy tucked in the corner of my mind.

Tulip tree petals had fallen on the road. Daisies, red columbine, honeysuckle and a scattering of other flowers were seen, but the flower of the day was wild white rose, a weed rose that farmers dislike, but one whose perfume I loved, wafting over all on a hot day. A box turtle, a turkey gobbling in the woods, and a brown fox were my wildlife viewings.

I stopped for a late lunch and met Scott, an older gentleman who told me—with a very pronounced drawl—that he was retired. He and I sat chatting on his porch as I ate. He fetched a bottle of cold water from his refrigerator for me and put ice in my water bottles, too. He offered the restroom before I had a chance to ask. I meet kind and thoughtful people everywhere. Scott had worked in construction in every state in the union except Hawaii before he retired.

In the afternoon, after talking with a beekeeper who was tending thirty hives, Trail Magick was waiting for me at my ending waypoint. I was glad to hear that Snake Charmer was much better. She was still in the hospital, and her infected blisters were being cultured. Infected blisters are not a minor problem. Infection from broken skin can turn to sepsis and kill you if not treated in time. I was so glad she had gone in for medical care.

I may never see her again in my travels, but I enjoyed hiking with her, getting to know her even for a short time. Trail Magick, only three years older than me, had also been fun to meet, and they had certainly blessed me with trail magic.

Back at Ironton, I organized my gear and food to be ready to hike with full pack the next day. Snake Charmer would have one more night in the hospital, and they would head to Wisconsin, our paths having crossed, combined, and diverged in a matter of just a few days.

Brief contacts do not grant me an in-depth understanding of the many people I meet. Yet each one is like a sparkling gem in my memory, etched more firmly just for mentioning them, whether we met to chat about bees, get a bottle of cold water, talk about mutual problems, or walk a day sharing excerpts of our lives before our paths diverge. Meeting them, seeing them, chatting long or briefly, caring for each other, I treasured each one. And with each contact, fear of unknown people receded even more from my repertoire of ready responses.

That night the temperature dropped to the deliciously cool high 50s. I packed up my gear, helped Trail Magick with the tent, and we loaded into the truck for the drive to the trail. After dropping me off, hopefully Snake Charmer would be discharged. They would leave for Wisconsin and hike again some other day or other year.

I hiked up a bunch of uphill roads as well as over

rolling hills, at least 1400 feet combined-elevation gain. Now, that's not huge, but in 80-degree heat it surely seemed like a lot to me. I had a hard time finding people present in their homes to ask for a lunch spot and water. I finally found two ladies who let me use their porch and restroom, but they were not interested in chatting. I tried especially hard to be polite and cheerful, hoping that would help the next hiker who might stop in need. The end of the day had no shade, as I walked directly into setting sun.

Wearily looking for a place to stop, I turned in a driveway to knock on the door at Ranly Farm. Jackpot. Not only did I get a place to pitch my tent, I was offered a shower. Golden. Clean again and resting, I watched cardinals, white pigeons and mourning doves while Mike and his son went to town. When he returned, Mike was a talkative fellow who proudly showed me his woodworking skills. He was making a walnut bookshelf, very unique and beautiful woodworking. He had been thinking of doing something to help hikers on the Buckeye Trail. I gave him the number for Andrew of the Buckeye Trail Association.

Besides making beautiful woodwork, he had been employed by the electric company in a coal-fired plant until it was sold, and the plant shut down. His wife, Sherry, came home late, and I would see her in the morning. Tucked into my tent, fireflies sparked in the darkness, and I listened to crickets and frogs. I was so glad the night was cool, as was the morning.

I even wore my long-sleeve shirt for the first mile of the day, and I hiked beside a creek as it merrily burbled over layered ledges making small waterfalls, cool and shaded walking. But the coolness didn't last for long.

I stopped for water, mid-morning snack, and a shaded chair on a porch, where I met Marlena and Scott who were getting ready to move to Florida. Marlena suggested I fill my bottle first with ice and then add water. I didn't put the icy water bottle in its usual pack holster. I put it in my cleavage on my chest for air conditioning.

After turning on Mt Aire Road, there was no real trail shade for most of the afternoon. I had one last break for lunch in the deep shade of evergreens on a mowed lawn. Then, the shadeless road just had to be endured. I have always been better at endurance than short runs. But, oh, there is a lot of enduring in the word endurance. Still, there were things to catch my eye. Yellow Creeping Jenny grew along the side of a farmer's field. Besides pastures being cut for hay, I also saw wheat, some ready for harvest but most still green. The barn and outbuildings at one of the more prosperous looking farms had fresh coats of bright-red paint, the reddest barn I ever saw.

A mile before Russellville, I stopped again for water and met Gail, a young grandma babysitting her grandchildren. She was so nice, calling her grandkids to gather near so I could have a show-and-tell about my hike. They prayed for me before I left. If they had been on the other side of

Russellville, I would have stayed, but it was too early, and my daily goal called for more miles to be completed.

The gas station in Russellville was small and cramped, but I did find an ice-cream sandwich there for a last snack of the day. North of town more than a mile, I stopped at a house and met Lisa, Chad, and their children. Lisa gave me ice water and suggested I tent near their pond. She had read a book about people walking across the country. I had never heard of the book, but she was entranced with the idea and happy to help a hiker.

I put my tent up near the pond, a secluded and peaceful setting. But then I checked the weather. Probable rain at 5:00 a.m. Oh, Heck. I asked Lisa and Chad if I could change places to sleep and move to their big arched outbuilding that held tractors. It wasn't nearly as scenic as by the pond, but I didn't want to pack a wet tent in the morning if I could avoid it.

In the outbuilding, a giant spider jumped over my pillow, then considerately remained motionless as I dispatched him with a crock. Spiders aren't all bad, but they are not allowed to sleep with me.

As I started out in the morning, Lisa called to me. She wanted to give me a cup of coffee and gave me a sweet note from her, the kids, and Chad. She so wanted to do something special for me. I hoped other hikers would stop there, too, to receive her kindness, help, and know her sweet spirit.

Ohio was not devoid of wildlife. I saw four or five deer, several hawks, two eagles, and a few turkey vultures on that day. I stopped for a late lunch in West Fork and met Duwayne, he and his family just back home from a vacation the hour before I knocked. Even so, he sat and chatted with me as I ate.

Shortly after I left his house, the first thunderstorm struck. It didn't just rain in southern Ohio. It poured buckets, with force. It was best to just wait out the storm. But where could I find shelter to do that? First, I tried someone's porch, but they were not home, and the porch was too small to shelter well. A block or so farther, I found an abandoned little barn. Its roof and sides were mostly whole, and it even had a chair inside. I stayed there while rain fiercely pounded all around.

MOUNT ORAB

More miles later, I should have stopped but didn't because it was still early. Then, when I was ready to call it quits, houses with people in them were not nearby.

My directions led to some odd jumping around. Roads were poorly signed, my unclear instructions said something about climbing embankments, and what appeared to be my path was filled with three-foot-tall grass that no one had walked on or mowed in quite some time.

I was trying to figure out where I was and where I should be, when I was blasted by another huge thunderstorm. My head stayed dry under the umbrella, and my pack was dry under pack cover. But my shoes and shorts were quickly soaked, and the wind tried mightily to blow all the wet it could under my umbrella to the rest of me. Fast-moving traffic on Highway 68 sprayed me and completed my dousing, and lightning flashed less than a half mile away by my slow count until the thunder pealed.

OK, I was done. Soaked even under my umbrella in the pouring rain and car spray, I called to see if there was a room in my motel one night early. I thought he said *yes,* though it was hard to hear along with thundering rain. Somewhat desperate at this point, beginning to chill in the wind, I wondered if it was possible to get hypothermia in a state that recently had been so hot? It wasn't that cold, but I was fatigued and miserable. I paid $10.00 to a kind guy named Eric, whom I accosted at a stop sign to drive me fewer than four miles to my motel.

The Green Crest Motel was less than classy. It was the first motel I had ever stayed at that didn't even have soap. But the rough washcloth scratched my itchy back as I washed with my own shampoo. The bed was a good one, and I was glad to have it. The sheets were clean. Life was good, at least better than it was when I was being drowned in the thunderstorm.

My rest day had come one day early. No laundry was available. I washed my clothes in the tiny corner sink and hung them on a little line I strung from shower bar to towel bar. That done, I went back to bed 'til noon. My pretty light-blue shirt would never be stainless again, but it was cleaner. Being horizontal all morning improved the rest of me.

That was a rather strange motel, not a tourist motel, more a place for country tenants. The person I dealt with was Robert, who lived there. I think he may possibly have cleaned rooms for his rent and was the English-speaking contact between tenants and the owners, who I believe were from central Asian background.

My room was newly repainted and refloored. It had a nice TV; the air conditioning worked, and the bed was good. The biggest problem was a lack of food, short of a mile away. I wasn't going to walk that far for miles that did not count as trail miles. Hikers hate town miles. I had extra food I was carrying, and I picked up a re-supply box, which I had sent there. I ordered pizza delivery. I wouldn't starve, but I would have no ice cream. Sadness.

After consulting by phone with Don, the Ohio ADT Coordinator, and looking at maps and my GPS, I decided to take the old bike route from Williamsburg to Batavia, which would put me fairly near a motel on the second day from where I was. It would also save me miles and, no doubt, grief from muddy unmaintained trail. I would just pretend I was a rather slow bicycle. Hikers usually prefer trail to roads, but I was getting an accumu-lated deep tiredness in my bones, and I preferred the road.

I was glad I was getting close to the end of my hike that year. Much of Ohio had been challeng-ing and I another year older than the last one. I had enjoyed the people I had met and starting out each morning I was in good spirits, loving the trail.

But by 2:00 in the afternoon, in stifling humid heat, I wondered why I was doing this. Ohio seemed to be trying to cure my long-distance-hik-ing addiction. Well, that statement wasn't fair. Ohio wasn't doing anything but being there. But I was wondering if I wanted to continue long-dis-tance hiking. Then again, hikers have selective memory. I would probably remember the morn-ings and the people I had met, more than the enervating heat, bad trail, and my fatigue.

Robert was not able to find me a ride back to the Covered Bridge, where I had stopped in the rainstorm, so I walked the route with just my fanny pack of pack brain and water bottles. I saw both Brown and New Hope covered bridges, farms, and fields. After studying my maps and GPS while not being pelted by rain and wind, it was much easier to figure out where I was.

I left my room before 7:00 and was back at the crossroad by 10:30, completing the section I had missed. Then, I stuck my thumb out and watched the cars go by for five minutes. A nice young couple with a little one in the back seat stopped and drove me back to my motel (only three miles then, by highway, which I had walked on my way back to the covered bridge). I was in air-conditioned comfort by 11:00 and eating left-over pizza.

The rest of the day, I dozed some, watched TV, and kept cool. Only four days left. Heat and thunderstorms and miles to go, but the end was in sight.

Since I had altered my route, I had more time than necessary. I wished I could hike in the morning only and hide out in air conditioning for the hotter part of the day. I only needed to cover what could be done in two longish days, but I had four days in which to accomplish those miles. I didn't want to impose on Don's hospitality in Cincinnati by being a two-day house guest.

Even though I had extra time, I left early, at 6:30,

to hike in the cool of the morning. Yet, even in the coolness of the morning, there was high humidity. I wiped accumulating moisture from my face with a bandana and then turned that bandana into a sweat band for my forehead. By the time the bandana was a sweat band, I needed to wipe the moisture from my face again. And so it went.

The air could not carry the weight of so much humidity for long, and it turned to rain. With pack cover and umbrella, I was dry except for my feet, which caught rain and drips from the leading edge of my umbrella. It rained more than an hour. I decided I preferred my humidity as rain instead of just condensing on my skin.

Stopping at a door, I met John, who filled a water bottle and let me eat trail bars on his porch and use his restroom. I watched purple martins get excited as I was sitting near their nest. They calmed down after I took the second chair, farther away from their nest in the eaves.

About 11:00, as I was passing a nice farm, I met Steve, who was walking to his barn, and we struck up a conversation. He offered a nice new deck overlooking a pond as a place for me to have early lunch, but it was in direct, hot sun. Then he offered the chairs and table in the shade by the house. Perfect!

He went back to working on his barn, preparing it for the wedding reception of his daughter the next week, and I ate my lunch early with the comfort of chairs and table. Later, he let me use the restroom and get water, opening up his house to me, no longer a stranger but a now known person who had eaten on his patio.

After more hot walking, a young woman at another house filled one of my bottles with ice and water, which I again carried in my cleavage. In five minutes, most of the ice had melted. The water tasted so good it did not last too long either.

Cops

Reaching Williamsburg, I stopped at the gas station, finally finding one with a place to sit. I ate two scoops of ice cream and consulted my GPS. I was only seven miles from the motel I wasn't supposed to reach for another day. People in the gas station were watching me and probably didn't want me sitting there all afternoon, so I wandered on, wondering what to do with myself.

Then I passed the closed donut shop and found a Subway. Perfect. I sat in Subway's air conditioning and wrote my journal and chatted with the Subway guy working there. Eventually, I bought a sandwich. I walked through the rest of Williamsburg using old waypoints of the Buckeye Bike Trail.

Just past the big school, I started looking for a place for the night. I knocked on a door, and a grandma invited me in. But she said her son or daughter-in-law would have to give the OK to stay. She thought her daughter-in-law would be home soon. *Soon* sounded like I should wait to find out an answer. So, I waited, and we shared pleasantries and a bit about ourselves.

More than an hour later, her daughter-in-law arrived but said she couldn't tell me if it was OK for me to stay in their yard; her husband was the one who needed to give permission. No one knew when he might be home. I was getting pretty concerned by that time. Maybe waiting had not been such a good idea. If I was not staying there, I needed to find somewhere else to stay. And I needed to find a place before darkness settled in.

Eventually the woman made a phone call to her husband, and he turned down the idea. OK, I packed up and left as politely as I could, though I was not at all happy to have been sitting there for a couple hours with no positive results. It simply was a door I should not have knocked on. I had made a bad choice.

There appeared to be only two more houses before the road went on between farm fields. I calmed myself as I walked by the first house and into the driveway of the second. A woman approached me walking from the first house and asked if I needed anything. I went through my door-knocking spiel, and she said it would be better that I did not knock on the door of that last house. Her mother lived there, she said. And she was afraid of everything.

Pat sized me up as we walked through her yard to her house. By the time we were looking at her garage as a place for me to shelter from the weather, I was invited in for a shower and to stay in her guest room. Pat and I hit it off and were quickly talking together like old friends. I unloaded my gear in the guest room and headed for the shower.

While I was in the shower, her twin sister came to the door. She had been visiting her mother in the house on whose door I had not knocked. She and her mother had seen me go inside, and they were certain I was a vagrant with ill intentions.

The sister furiously berated my benefactress, Pat. Her sister said I could not possibly be a pastor. (I had already shared my trail name with Pat.) "If she was a pastor, she would be staying in pastors' houses, not knocking on doors." She said.

After getting out of the shower and learning of this conversation, I incredulously, with humor, wondered where this list of all America's pastors was for all the towns through which I had gone. Planning my hikes would be so much easier if there were such a list of every pastor in every town.

I offered to go on walking farther if my staying was causing such a problem for her with her mother and sister.

"No." Pat firmly said. She told me she had long-standing problems with her twin, who always thought any decision she made was a bad one. She had invited me in, and she insisted that I stay. Pat suggested, since I was then presentable, and not all sweaty, that we walk over to her mother's house, so she could meet me and see I looked rather normal and non-threatening.

She called her mother, and as we walked toward that house, her mother walked toward us. I put on as much charm as I could muster. We shook hands, and I pulled out my cell phone to show pictures of my grandchildren. I was, and am, after all, just an old grandma who likes to hike.

That seemed to help, though she sharply addressed me, questioning, "Don't you understand it from my point of view?" Letting a stranger into your house was such a dangerous thing to her. Pat's mother returned to her house, and Pat and I to Pat's, where we learned a lot more about each other in a long and pleasant conversation.

Pat had never heard of the Buckeye Trail, whose old bike route was in front of her house. But as we talked, she realized she had seen both hikers and bikers go by her house before.

When we were about to end our conversation and turn in for the night, the doorbell rang. A young policeman was at the door. Pat's twin sister had called the cops to check out the situation, still sure I was up to no good and was certain to be an ax murderer who would then leave with anything of value in the middle of the night. (I wondered how an old lady was supposed to run faster than a car in pursuit, or how I was supposed to carry anything more than my pack in my get-away.)

Pat and I explained the situation to the young cop, who had also never heard of long-distance hiking or the Buckeye Trail. After checking my ID and seeing my professionally printed map of that section of the Buckeye Trail, he decided I was harmless. I had never had the cops called on me before, and I hope that does not ever happen again.

But if I needed a prime example of the culture of fear in which we live, this was it. I was a stranger. There was, therefore, fear. I must be dangerous. Don't talk to strangers. Don't let them in your house. They are thieves, murderers, and ne'er-do-wells.

No, my travels have taught me that is **not** the dominant culture. I have been graciously received and assisted way too many times to count, yet a parallel culture of fear also exists. And, I admit, there are just enough scary instances of truth to feed that culture. I could see how it controlled some of the lives in Pat's family. I was glad it had not controlled Pat's life, and I had met another friend.

I have heard the Lakota Sioux Chief, Sitting Bull, once said, "Inside of me there are two dogs. One is mean and evil, and the other is good and they fight each other all the time. When asked which one wins, I answer, the one I feed the most."

Fear and unfear are similar dogs. There are fears that are valid. Fear can keep us safe. Fear can also control our lives and our decisions, keeping out those whom we deem *the other*. I choose to look for ways my experiences feed unfear. There are also those who choose to feed their fears. Different experiences take us to different choices in differing circumstances. But there are times we have a choice which dog to feed, which path to take, and whether our primary stance is to fear others or meet face to face, and to be open to knowing each other.

In the morning, I said good-by to Pat. What a dear person. How I appreciated her for not being part of the culture of fear, for standing up to her sister and mother, for her generosity and hospitality, and for her sense of humor. How lucky I was that she had walked out on her mother's driveway to meet me.

I walked down Old 32 to Brunk Road, turned right on Bauer, and had snack wraps and a shake at McDonald's. There, I also received directions to my motel, on the corner I had already passed. By noon, I was checked in, took my shower and washed my clothes in the sink. I did not hike in the heat of that day.

After one more long day of real hiking, I could get to Milford. But then I would be there too soon by a day. Unfortunately, the temperature would still be hot. The afternoon I rested in the motel it had been 90 degrees before it rained, the *feels like* at least five-degrees higher. The forecast for the next day was for the same. Unless someone dropped out of the sky or sprang out of the bushes at my noon break to invite me to stay all afternoon and evening, the next day would have a miserable afternoon.

I wanted to be done with Ohio. It would have been a much more pleasant hike with lower temperatures and less humidity. For much of southern Ohio, it had seemed like I was walking in a thorny jungle while carrying my pack.

Then, I discovered the TV in my room didn't work. For an hour or so, various people traipsed in from the front desk as I sat in my underwear and last clean, dry shirt while my wet shorts and bras were hung to dry. Eventually, the TV worked. My mood was resigned but not eager for the next day. That night I felt like my hike was ending with a whimper.

Leaving my motel in the morning, I dropped back to Old 32 and walked into Batavia, where I stopped to take a picture of the town sign. An African-American woman on a porch across the street smiled at me, said "Hello," and asked where I was headed. I crossed the street to talk with her. She knew there was such a thing as long-distance hiking, and she even knew someone who had done some.

We chatted about people-helping-people, and I told her how I had enjoyed her smile from across the street. I told her she reminded me of my mother in Denver so many years ago. My mother would smile at everyone she passed on the street, trying to get them to smile back at her, a kind of game and challenge. She usually won, and they smiled back. And before I went on, that woman opened her screen door, and came off the porch to give me a hug. The meeting, the conversation, and the hug lifted my spirits and reminded me of my mother and of my extended African-American family in Denver.

Moving onward, I stopped at a house with a porch for my mid-morning snack. The woman graciously filled my water bottle, and I talked with her daughter, a young twenty-something, about trails before they left for town, and I walked on.

God Laughing

The humidity by then was 80 percent and I was constantly mopping my face—*feels like* temperature ninety-one according to the information on my cell phone. The heat was getting to me. And I was just plain tired of having to knock on doors, in spite of all the wonderful people I had met doing so.

Somewhat disgruntled, I said out loud, I would just walk all the way to Milford and stay under the tiny shelter where I had begun my American Discovery Trail hiking in 2015. I would just sit there all the next day and wait for Don. I was sliding into a funk of discouragement amplified by heat. I wouldn't stop early unless someone just popped out of the bushes and asked me in. And then, exactly halfway to Milford, someone did.

I was walking up the road and saw a house to my left past a big lawn and nice landscaping. A man and woman were getting out of their car, unloading groceries. When the woman looked up and saw me, she walked across that large midwestern lawn to the road and asked if I was walking the American Discovery Trail.

She *knew what it was*. To my amazement, she said they had hosted other hikers before. What could they do for me?

I stammered that it was really hot, and I wished for some shade to eat my lunch. Of course, she said. Come on over to our house. We have a nice covered porch. What would you like to drink with your lunch? Why don't you just come inside? We have air conditioning.

One thing led to another, and I was offered a shower, dinner, and a bed. They wouldn't let me use my sleeping bag on the pull-down bed in their spare room but insisted on putting on nice clean sheets for me. And if there was any doubt that my arranged pickup in Milford couldn't come when I got there, they would be happy to pick me up. I could stay another night, and they could drive me to the Cincinnati airport to catch my flight. Oh, and did I like ice cream? She sent her husband to the store to get their favorite brand of ice cream for me. And I hadn't really asked for a thing or even knocked on a door.

In my amazement at all of this, I swear I could hear God laughing at me, saying, "It's what you said you needed. Didn't you think I could provide it?"

Kay said she had felt a call to go out to talk to me. I could not argue with what she said she had felt. I had felt it, too. So, my last night on the trail was not a whimper, but a joyous meeting with simpatico and extremely gracious trail angels sent by God. Absolutely perfect. And it was all a gift.

Tom and Kay asked me many questions and kept me telling trail and life stories. They fed me a most delicious dinner, best on whole trail, with a taste of fresh kale and garlic from her garden.

After ice cream, we capped the evening with a cup of herbal tea. And I sang Holden Evening Prayer for them.

Kay and Tom

In the morning, Kay, Tom, and I took each other's pictures and exchanged contact information. We also prayed for each other, and I set out into the rain. The rain was just rain, falling straight down and not sideways. With pack cover on and umbrella up, I walked in my own little circle of dryness.

The miles went by smoothly. In Milford, I found the same tiny shelter with three picnic tables from which I had begun my hike to Moline and the Mississippi River four years before. Not long after that, Don arrived. He told me the news had said Cincinnati was experiencing the hottest May on record. It was not a huge surprise to me. I had been walking in that heat.

Don took me to the airport; and I flew home, reflecting on that spring hike. Again in 2018, so many people had helped me along the trail. I often had cause to think how glad I was that I had been able to step past my fears. Without doing so, I would never have met all those people or had all these stories to remember and to tell.

Ohio had been the most difficult part of the ADT thus far, and the weather had been far from perfect. On April 30th there had been heavy frost on the grass. On May 1st it had been 85 degrees. It was never cold, and rarely cool after that. Winter had changed to summer, and spring was only seen in a few spring flowers. It became summer by temperature before trees could leaf out.

Ohio did not have high mountains like the Sierra, Rockies, or Cascades, which I had also walked. But uphill and downhill always works the same, and I do not do so well in heat. As each year passed, I was another year older, and problems with my foot and knee had slowed me down, even on good trail. The ADT in Ohio had not always been experienced as good.

But the charm of the ADT continued to be the people I met along the way. After a section of the ADT in Colorado's high country and a knee replacement in the winter, I anticipated being back on the trail again in the spring, heading from the Mississippi River to the Missouri River. I would not be afraid to again walk and knock on doors.

The 23rd Psalm is probably the most well-known passage in the Bible, if only because it is so often read at funerals.

"The Lord is my shepherd, I shall not want; he makes me lie down in green pastures. He leads me beside still waters; He restores my soul. He leads me in paths of righteousness for his name's sake. Even though I walk through the valley of the shadow of death, I fear no evil; for thou art with me; thy rod and thy staff, they comfort me. Thou preparest a table before me in the presence of my enemies; thou anointest my head with oil, my cup overflows. Surely goodness and mercy will follow me all the days of my life; and I shall dwell in the house of the Lord forever."

Is that Psalm only for our life's end? Our funerals? Or is it for our living?

The center verse of that Psalm, *"Even though I walk through the valley of the shadow of death, I fear no evil; for thou art with me..."* is a very big claim. Living this verse is a very big life challenge.

I get practice doing so by taking long-distance hikes.

There might be heat. There might be cold. I might fall. Someone might call the cops on me. I might be injured. I might die. I will not be alone, though solo hiking. I will have many opportunities to leave my fears behind, to live the Psalm. Hiking on long-distance trails, knocking on strangers' doors is not the only way to live this Psalm. But it *is* a way for *me* to do so.

2019

American Discovery Trail

RECOVERY

Some people expressed surprise at my planning a spring hike so soon after my second knee replacement.

Once upon a time, I heard a Doc say it was impossible to tell the length of time necessary to recover from a total knee replacement; perhaps someone could recover in two months. I thought then, well, that someone should be me. Nope. It takes more time than two months. I gave it four and a half. But I always have been the eternal optimist.

Rehabbing a knee runs contrary to popular wisdom. Sometimes people think one should rest for recovery. Sitting and standing still are the worst things for recovering from a knee replacement. My knee wanted to keep moving or it stiffened up and hurt. Repetitive motion was the key, working to retrain muscles and nerves. They don't just heal up and work as before. A knee replacement is a lot of trauma and cells don't *remember* their function automatically. Retraining is not just a matter of time. It is also a matter of work and repetition.

Of course, one can overdo it. Too much work at any given stage could set the knee back in recovery. There was a fine line to find to do the maximum work for optimum recovery in the shortest time, without doing too much and setting recovery back. I hoped I was finding that fine line.

While visiting my daughter's family with her eight children, my grandchildren, I kept an eye on the weather in Iowa. It was not good news.

Iowa is bracketed by major rivers: the Mississippi River on the east and the Missouri River on the west. In 2019 there were huge spring floods. A blizzard was happening in northern Iowa and the flooding wasn't over. Re-routing was needed before I even began.

Figuring out the re-route was a bit of a challenge in an RV with eight grandchildren ages thirteen-to-two. Quiet moments were hard to find. Snuggles in the morning made up for the chaos. Each morning of my visit, two-to-four small bodies piled under my sleeping bag, which I was using for a quilt, getting and giving snuggles in the morning. And I did find time to figure out my re-route.

Iowa

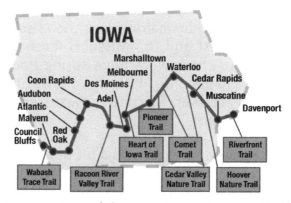

Iowa portion of the American Discovery Trail

Saying good-bye to my family, I took a flight to Moline. Debbie and Parker, who had put me on an airplane at the end of my first ADT hike in 2015, met me at that same airport once again. The next morning, Parker took me to Davenport, within half a block from the spot RockStar and I had stopped four years before. The road was closed off below that for the flood.

Debbie and Parker

My re-route to avoid the flooded American Discovery Trail was all on roads. I took my time, concerned first about my knee and also the lack of proper conditioning for the rest of my body. My knee did pretty well. But the rest of me was extremely tired after that first twelve-mile day.

While walking on my re-route, I stopped for a snack on the steps of an abandoned school, which was plastered with signs saying I should smile because cameras were watching me. I smiled. Lunch was in the shade of fir trees in front of Hillcrest Church. A laundromat, gas stations, a Casey's General Store, and Subway provided bathroom breaks; two cute bunnies by an 1830s barn served as entertainment and wildlife.

The year 2019 was my fourth year doing this kind

of hiking. I was now experienced at knocking on doors. I stopped at the VanNice farm, and they suggested I tent between two barns. They also gave me water. I had expected rain and thunderstorms all day, but they did not come until 8:00, when I was all tucked in. I felt like I lived a charmed life. The friendly cat seemed to think I was nuts, staying in my tent in the thunderstorm. From the barn, it meowed, piteously or indignantly. But my tent worked fine. I was dry. I had made my miles. My hike had begun. Life was good.

The verdict on my knee, at least for the first night, wasn't too good. It did not totally recover overnight. I had lost a bit of range of motion. While on my back in the tent with my leg extended straight up by the hiking pole that held up the tent, I did many repetitions of bend and straighten, convincing it to move well enough to proceed. I packed up and walked onward past Wildcat Den State Park through rolling green hills. By early afternoon, I was struggling and tired, and my legs no longer wanted to move. After some Vitamin T (Tylenol), I continued on, hoping that T would take the edge off pain and somehow manufacture energy.

That second day was very windy, the first time I learned how windy Iowa could be. The first day had been shorts-and-sunburn weather. That second day was cold, threatening clouds, and a strong, biting wind. I wore my down jacket the first half of the day and switched to frogg toggs (rain gear) for better protection against the wind in the afternoon.

Late in the afternoon, seeing a farmer looking at the edge of his wet field, I asked if I might tent in his yard, a little protected from the wind.

When my tent was up and gear was stowed, I met Ken's wife, Judy, at their door, as I asked for water. Judy was very interested in my hike. They gave me a chicken breast and some delicious banana bread to supplement my dinner. I had taken a route created in short order due to floods, not even on the ADT. Yet, I had again found gracious-and-hospitable people.

In the next morning, my knee was swollen more than the morning before. That was not good news. I did 150 vertical bend and straightens and then another 100 with resistance from an elastic band I had brought with me. After all of that, my knee bent better. Best I could do. I wondered if the stiffness of my knee was going to be cumulative. Was I really going to be able to do this hike? The jury was still out. But I decided I could probably do that day.

Before I left, Judy gave me a postcard of the bridge at Muscatine and wrote down my Trailjounals. com address so she could follow my hike.

New Source of Friends and Angels

In three years of hiking on the ADT in the East, I had learned that strangers were just friends not yet met. Day after day in those three years, I had practiced going past my nervousness to knock on strangers' doors to meet my needs.

That my first two nights in Iowa were on a re-route, not the waymarked ADT, made no difference. I still knocked on doors, and I still met charming people who helped me. But in Iowa, a new dynamic occurred. I would have fans, not just friends from life experiences, friends met while hiking National Scenic Trails, or friends made because I'd knocked on doors.

I had written my online journal for a number of years, and some people had followed me on Trail-journals.com and occasionally reached out to me. Winkle read my journal and then hiked a couple days with me on the AT. Friends from Washington, my cousin from San Diego, hiker friends from California and Wyoming had supported me. In the last three years on the ADT, I had made friends from strangers when asking for their aid. But this was different.

My first book, *Old Lady on the Trail*, had been out just six months. Far more people than my *Trail-journals* fans had read my book and found it interesting. Some, I discovered, lived in Iowa. Some knew I had a journal on Trailjournals.com and were following me there.

To publicize my book, I had joined hiking groups on Facebook. Word spread. I wasn't exactly famous, but I was more widely known. My hike planning had been done incorporating new sources from social media.

And when I needed help, other fans appeared like magic. People met from doors on which I knocked, people learning of my trip on social media, and an old neighbor from Washington, worked together to support my journey, making Iowa a special joy to hike. It wasn't that everything went perfectly. After all, I started with the trail flooded. Yet I had new and old friends and fans.

My first new friend from added social media was Jessica. I met Jessica on the Facebook hiking group, *Hike Like A Woman*. She was especially involved with the *HLAW Book Club*, which had chosen my book as a pick for one of their monthly reads. We had arranged to meet for lunch on my third day of hiking in Iowa.

As I set out that morning into Muscatine, I was soon on a bicycle trail which went to Weed Park, a pretty park with geese serenely floating on a lake. Shortly after the park, the trail passed Highway 22, and I could tell that I would soon be swimming in floodwater if I stayed on the trail.

I emailed Jessica, and she picked me up after I walked up the hill on 22 away from the water in the lower valley.

Jessica drove me on the roads I would need to walk for a detour around the flooded areas. With that knowledge then recorded in my brain and on my GPS track, we went to lunch. She even bought my lunch.

Riding around in a car and eating lunch in a restaurant was a nice interlude from hiking for my knee and the rest of me, too. It was always fun to talk about trails with another hiker. After lunch, Jessica took me back where she had picked me up, and I resumed the detour track then showing on my GPS. When I sat down on my pack for a snack in the afternoon, I took some time to lie down on my back in someone's lawn with my leg straight up in the air and did 100 bend and straightens to keep my knee limbered up.

A little way past Muscatine, needing water to mix my dinner, I saw a sign for a Lutheran care center for aging adults. That sounded like a good place for an aging Lutheran pastor to ask for water. I started up a significant hill, but, seeing the switch-backing road went farther up than I desired to go, I detoured to some duplex apartments of the complex where I met Lisa, who was visiting her mother, Mary Elizabeth, (my name, too) who was just recovering from surgery.

Yes, I could have water and mix my dinner was the answer to my request. I did so as Lisa peppered me with questions about hiking trails. Then I sat down, and we talked more. This conversation led to an offer of a place to stay for the night. Lisa would pick me up after I walked two more miles *without* my pack, completing my scheduled miles for the day.

Not only did I get a bed, I had a shower, and then accompanied Lisa and her husband, Bob, to their Good Friday service. I had made another friend. It seemed another of those God-arranged moments with which I had so frequently been blessed on the ADT.

Lisa and Bob lived in Fruitland, not on the trail. Fruitland just happened to be where Jessica used to live, and they knew her, verified with my photo, as someone who used to live one block over. The trail was always giving me surprise connections.

The trail also kept providing me with bits of information about the people of America. Folks with Czech heritage had settled those parts. Bob was of Czech heritage, and I learned Czech names often leave out vowels in their spelling. Mary Elizabeth, Bob, Lisa, and Jessica were my surprise connections, sharing their lives with me and teaching me new things for the day.

Amazingly, my knee responded to the comfort of a bed by nearly complete recovery the next morning. Glory be to God. Maybe I could pull off my spring hike, after all.

Even though Bob and Lisa were leaving in the

morning for Minnesota for the weekend, Lisa cooked me eggs with bacon for breakfast and packed extra bacon and peanut butter cookies for me to take. She dropped me off where she had picked me up the day before, and I started my walking day listening to birds cheerily singing, watching a turkey vulture soaring overhead, and hearing a turkey gobbling in the woods beside the road. A large part of the day was walking on Highway 28—a long way in a straight line.

After a few miles down that road, I was feeling the need for a restroom. As I approached a farmhouse, a young man came down the driveway to the road to meet me, carrying two bottles of water. He had simply seen me walking from his window and wondered if I needed water. This same thing had happened once before in Maryland in 2016. I wondered what had spurred him to glance out his window right that moment and decide I needed water? I told him what I needed even more was a bathroom.

After that need was taken care of, I talked about my hike, hiking in general, and the book I had written. Sy asked to walk with me as far as his mother's farm, and we chatted along the way. Sometimes you don't even have to knock on a door to have needs met and meet new friends.

Encountering Sy brought me smiles as I walked that long stretch of highway. I needed the smiles as the stretch was long, was highway, and I wearied of both length and pavement.

On the way into Muscatine, and then on Highway 28, my eyes were often on the side of the road, looking where I put my feet, along the painted white line that marked the edge of pavement. Wear and tear had chipped off the white line in places, leaving black pavement showing through white paint in odd shapes resembling Rorschach ink blots.

I passed the time identifying dragons, rampant eagles, ducks in a row, four-hump camels, and other oddities which appeared to me, my mind insisting on recognizing forms from random blotches in the paint. Salty bacon and peanut butter cookies along with cheese and crackers made a tasty first lunch under shade at the edge of a farmer's lawn. A woman driving down the driveway asked if I was OK. I enjoyed the people of Iowa and friendly waves from passing cars.

Reaching a farm and nursery that grew produce for Hy-Vee, a grocery chain in Iowa, a woman prepping a wall for painting gave me permission to use the facilities and fill my water bottles. Sitting down was a nice break from walking. Afterward, we talked a bit. She had seen my book title on Amazon. She said she might buy it now that she had met the author. Though she did hard labor in farm work, rode tractors, and liked being outside, she thought carrying a pack and walking a highway would be more difficult.

She recommended I sit and rest after crossing the Cedar River, and when I crossed the river, I followed her advice, though I probably found a different spot to sit than the one she had in mind.

I was on sand, tucked under the shade of a fat tree trunk, covered by mostly bare branches just beginning to bud out leaves. I had a second lunch there and watched people fish from the iron bridge. One caught a two-foot catfish and yelled excitedly at his first catch of the season.

The highway took me past large swampy areas to the start of the Hoover Nature Trail. It was not an auspicious start on the edge of a barren farm field. But past the field, my path was walled by thickets and trees, which made pleasant seclusion.

At a farmhouse emerging from a break in the undergrowth, I roused the guy inside to ask for water. He mowed the trail in that section but said he had never seen anyone walking on it. I thanked him for mowing and pointed out he would not have known I was walking by if I hadn't knocked repeatedly.

Walking beyond the house about a mile, I put my tent up beside the trail. I really liked this section of the Hoover Trail, a nice break from road walking. After I unloaded the contents of my pack into the tent, I heard sounds of snap, crackle, and pop. I looked in the thickets beside me to see what could be making the noise and saw nothing.

Then I looked farther, beyond the twenty feet of shrubs lining the trail. On the other side of the thicket was a road, and on the other side of the road was fire. Intentional fire.

Farmers were burning corn stubble, which seemed quite odd to me. The whole field, as far as I could see in either direction, was being set on fire. I hoped they knew what they were doing, and the fire wouldn't cross the road to burn my temporary home. I stood on tired feet, longer than I wanted, watching the nearby fire die away and other flashes flare as more swaths of land were ignited, burned and turned to ash. The smell of smoke was strong, but I was tired and needed sleep.

In the morning, I woke surrounded by cheerful birdsong under blue skies, a nice way to wake up. After 150 vertical bends and straightens, my knee was still a little stiff, but it would do.

Since it was Easter Sunday, I sang Easter hymns as I headed north. Yes, north. I had been somewhat out of sorts about the ADT across Iowa ever since I first looked at the overview map four years ago. All trails tend to wander. Iowa's ADT goes to extremes. Iowa is 300 miles straight across, but the ADT takes extreme zig zags to make the *trail* crossing Iowa 512 miles. Oh well, that's the trail, somewhat annoying, though.

My directions said the Hoover Trail ended, but I thought it looked like it went on, so I did, too. Mistake. Soon I was on a matted grassy berm on a levy looking straight down fifteen-to-twenty feet at a stream, and I had to go back to the highway, anyway. I laughingly wondered if that grassy berm counted as wilderness in Iowa. Maybe I should have just followed directions.

Walking through Nichols, I came to Nichols Methodist Church. I had been hoping to catch a bit of an Easter service. A bit was all I caught; I got there only for the last hymn. And they certainly knew I had come in, as they were all very quiet, and I sang out. I was welcomed, even if I had missed most of the service. The pastor and his wife left to go to the next church a town over, part of their three-point parish, but not before they talked to me. There was a pastor shortage in the Midwest. They were soon to have four churches under their care and leadership.

An Easter breakfast followed the service, and I was invited to join in to eat. The parishioners were interested in my hiking. One woman was amazed I had slept outside the night before, sure rattlesnakes could have gotten me. Another of the women looked on her cell phone and ordered my book on the spot.

I learned from these locals that the fires last night were not simply about burning corn stubble. Fires were to encourage the native grassland to grow, mimicking the lightning strikes which burned the prairies when buffalo roamed this land before the time of farms. Such burning was sponsored by the Conservation Bureau Program in Iowa. Evenings, when the wind died down, were chosen for better fire control, as the burning embers could be better seen as darkness descended.

After Nichols, I continued on the Hoover Trail, but no thickets or trees sheltered that part of the trail from the 85-degree heat of the afternoon.

I felt like I was in the Southern California desert. Well, Ok, maybe it wasn't quite *that* hot. But then, it was only April.

The Hoover Trail came to an end, and I walked on non-highway roads, freshly covered with gray/white dusty gravel, the dust blowing in a twenty-mile-an-hour wind. When I heard vehicles coming, I moved to the upwind side of the road, but still, I was covered with white dust.

Back on a paved road once again, I stopped at a farmhouse and was met at the door by Marla. Yes, she said, I could have water to mix my dinner and have a rest. That led to conversation with Marla and her husband, Tom. Trail talk then led to an invitation to stay, complete with a two-mile slackpack, pick up that night and tomorrow morning drop off. Golden hospitality. Leaving my pack with them, I was armed with their phone number, my umbrella to shade me from the sun, a water bottle, and one hiking pole. I walked into the sun and wind to conquer the last two miles.

After they picked me up at the end of my day's walk, I enjoyed a needed shower, ate the dinner I had earlier mixed, plus a hamburger and corn, which they offered. Iowa is famous for corn. That Iowa corn, preserved from the previous year, was better even than the corn I grew myself. At the rate people were feeding me, I was in danger of gaining weight, even on a long-distance hike.

Marla and Tom learned about long-distance hiking, and I learned about them. Marla was a substitute teacher, and Tom was a farmers' consultant, doing such things as checking soil samples for nutrients. He said he farmed farmers. As the evening ended, I climbed the stairs to an upstairs bedroom and enjoyed the comfort of a bed. I was blessed. Indiana, Illinois, Delaware, Maryland, Washington DC, West Virginia, Ohio, and now Iowa, wherever the ADT led me, I met such gracious people.

The next day, I had a pleasant walk in the coolness of clouds, the first day since I had begun at Davenport that I felt like a hiker instead of a struggling old lady. My body was slowly but definitely getting in shape. Of course, my food bag was empty, which also lightened my pack. Still, I walked better, more steadily, and I wasn't always searching for excuses to take sit-down breaks.

The gas station at I-80 provided my lunch, topped off with an ice-cream sandwich, before I walked to the next road and then to West Branch. West Branch was the home of Herbert Hoover.

I had not known the National Park System included his home, but I was more interested in reaching my motel, seven-tenths of a mile south of my trail. My re-supply box was at the motel, and my dinner was at a Casey's across the street. Unfortunately, that motel had no laundry facilities. Hand wash was a pain, but you *do what you gotta do*. After seven days walking, I was ready for a rest day. After my laundry, it felt good to not do much of anything requiring work.

While I rested on my zero day, unexpectedly, I met another fan. Michelle, who had read many of my trail journals, contacted me and wanted to meet me and to help. She lived five miles west of Solon. An AT *wanna-be*, she bargained time with me to pick my brain in exchange for lodging and slackpacking. What a wonderful arrangement. We would aid each other.

Mary and Michelle

Hikers learn from other hikers. I learned camping and hiking skills as a Girl Scout and a Mountaineer. Friends I have hiked with taught me more. I did not start solo hiking by myself, strange as that statement sounds. I first had observed other solo hikers hiking and learned from them. The most common forum for sharing hiking skills these days is social media.

I was a late comer to Facebook. I had a journal on Trailjournals.com before I knew of Facebook. Trailjournals.com was my social media site for learning and for sharing for many years. I had always figured that was plenty, and I saw no need to add something else. Facebook would just be more work.

But as I was learning how to publicize my book so others might consider buying it, a friend at church put me in contact with a successful self-published author. He told me to get on Facebook and join every hiking group I could find to post news of what I had written. And I did. And, principally, that is why my book sold, well more than 8,000 copies so far. So, while walking across Iowa, I was on Facebook, and yes, it was added work to read what kept popping up from all those hiking groups.

But it was enlightening to me, too. I discovered a whole new world of friends discussing hiking topics, including discussions about fear. Fear of going solo was a frequent topic raised by a multitude of women who wanted to hike or camp solo and to leave fear behind.

From my observation, almost every women's hiking group can count on several posts a year from someone asking how to move past their fears, wanting to know from other women how they did so, and how they could do it, too. On Facebook groups they helped each other. In lively discussions, suggestions were shared, encouragement given, and women, empowered, moved past their fears.

On September 12, 2019, I read a thank you from Annie to the group, *All Women, All Trails*. (I asked her for permission to share from her post.) She said, "You gave me all the best advice, and I tried it all ... meditating, breathing, putting myself in a place of fear to get used to it ... I did it all, and it worked. My mantra now is 'I'm not trying to not be afraid, I'm not letting my fear be my focus.' And It's working - for all kinds of things."

Fears *can* be left behind, or at least, *out of focus*. And we can help each other in that process. I am not saying that everyone wants to, needs to, or must leave fear behind, but I do suggest that, just as I have learned lessons about fear in my life, sometimes, from friends or strangers, leaving fear behind can be a learned behavior for those who wish to follow a more fearless path.

Leaving my motel, I walked to McDonald's for breakfast. I smiled to see an Iowa old-boys' club at one long table. It was a thing in Iowa just as in Indiana and Illinois. One of the men talked to me, as an old lady carrying a backpack was unusual. It was nice to be noticed.

On my waymarked trail again, a construction worker showed me a way across a creek where a bridge was out, a new one under construction. I proceeded out of town on the Hoover Trail, which had materialized again.

At a playfield outside of the next town, there were big *trail closed* signs. As I pondered what to do, it began to rain. So, I took advantage of a picnic shelter to dig out my raingear and used the near-by porta potty. I dithered around long enough that a workman came by and told me the sign referred to a bridge, but it was passable, though he wasn't supposed to say so. I was glad I didn't have to invent a detour on roads and thankful for his information shared with me, glad he stuck his neck out with his statement to a hiker. The bridge was new and just didn't have the approaches finished. It wasn't too hard to negotiate.

After the first lovely stretch of trail that day, came one that had not been maintained for quite some time. More slowly, I walked through tall grass, weeds, pokey stalks of all kinds, and sumac. I quickly took off my rain pants before they'd be ruined by stiff pointy things.

Another section of trail was semi-maintained. It had been mowed sometime, just not recently. Another section had been recently sold and was fenced, gated, and locked. I road-walked around it and added at least half a mile to my day. Oh, well. Road walking was a relief from the unmaintained sections.

My knee did well, only a little stiffened at the end of the day. My left foot hurt, off and on all afternoon, sore at the site of a stress fracture sustained a few years before. I was already an old lady when I wrote my first book. An alternate title for this one could have been Old Lady II. Some body part was always complaining. But I looked forward to a treat at the end of the day, a bed not originally planned. After reaching my mileage goal, I called Michelle, and she picked me up. She would slackpack me the next day, too. What luxury for a hiker. A blessing from a previously unknown fan.

I had a shower. We ate and talked. Michelle reminded me of what I had said in my journal about fear and guns to someone on the ADT below Chicago in 2015. I was astonished that my words were valuable to her. She had used them to persuade her husband to her side to plan her own coming hike on the AT. Hikers learn from hikers, learn not to be controlled by fear. Perhaps my thoughts and words could be valuable to others as well.

In the morning, Michelle drove me back to Turner Road for a slackpacking day. My knee, and the rest of me, too, appreciated leaving the pack behind. I enjoyed my walk, with water, rain gear, a few Band-Aids, and trail bars.

As I walked along, I found an open knife on the ground at the edge of the road. It had a good blade, but the housing had been run over a few times. I stood on the road for several long minutes fiddling with it, trying to close it, finally getting it three-quarters closed. On the next street over, I found an old beer can at the side of the road and fashioned a sheath from the bottom of the beer can, to transport the knife which I put in my pouch. Maybe Michelle could use it, as she was assembling gear for backpacking.

Road walking meant I became intimately acquainted with the flotsam and jetsam people lost or tossed from their cars. Earlier, after Nichols, I had found a perfectly good screwdriver in the tall grass along the side of the road, which I had donated to Tom's workshop. I hated seeing something still useful not being used.

Walking into Solon, I stopped at the Casey's to find something for lunch. Unfortunately, there were no chairs or tables to use to eat the club sandwich and donut I'd bought. I tied the bag on my belt and went looking for a place to eat.

Approaching the parking lot to McBride Park, I met another woman using trekking poles. As we walked together, she told me her grandfather had owned the land that had become that big open park. She considered the park hers, as the land had been owned by her family in years gone by. She pointed out her grandfather's house at the edge of the park. She also pointed out the round barn replica a man had donated that could be rented for parties.

I liked having a local guide tell me stories as I walked. She had also been excited about the new-ly paved bike trail, which would someday reach clear to Minneapolis. My local guide continued to circle the park on her walk as I left her, taking the bike trail, finding a rock to sit on while I ate my sandwich and donut.

I followed the paved bike route past a finger of the lake, an area thick with spent cattail stalks and cheerily blooming marsh marigolds, the first striking wildflowers I had seen that spring. The bike route and my T-by-T did not entirely agree, but I matched up one of the waypoints on my GPS and headed north to Ely.

All trails and waypoints change over time. The American Discovery Trail covers vast distances to cross the whole United States, and printed direc-tions sometimes take a while to catch up with changes on the ground. Eventually, I saw a newly paved bike trail coming into my road from the east, part of that newly constructed section that would someday go to Minneapolis.

Arriving at Ely, I called Michelle for a pickup. That night I told more tails of my travels as she, her husband, Steve, and I ate dinner together. I gave the knife I had picked up along the road to Steve. He got the blade moving, but the housing was pretty battered, perhaps beyond repair. He thought the knife was a cheap $5 knife, but I said it was a better blade than that. He looked it up on the internet and discovered it was a $60 knife. Maybe he could figure out a housing for it, and Michelle would have a nice knife to add to her gear.

In the morning, I was all packed and ready to go, but Michelle surprised me by suggesting I slack-pack again. She would bring my gear to me in Cedar Rapids. Well, OK then. I never turn down an opportunity to slackpack.

Cedar Rapids

Without my pack, I headed north from Ely on a bike path, enjoying trees and bushes leafing out in pleasant, warm, spring weather. Nearing Cedar Rapids, I walked along the river. At the Lion Bridge, I used the restroom at an outdoor equipment store and found the SyKora Bakery in Czech town. From interpretive signs, I learned 20 percent of the population of Cedar Rapids were of Czech ancestry.

Bridge at Czech Town

The carvings of lions on the bridge and the Catholic Church with bells that chimed the half hour reminded me of the Camino de Santiago in Spain and other European towns I had visited in years past. I walked by the African American Museum on the north side of the river and by the art museum, too, a meeting of cultures in the space of a few blocks.

At my destination in Cedar Rapids, Michelle met me with my pack. After two nights in her house, I felt I was saying good-bye to an old friend. And immediately, I met my next new friends. Laura, a Facebook friend I would never have known without writing a book, had referred me to a lovely couple, Bob and Carolyn, family friends of hers.

Bob and Carolyn

After a needed shower (My goodness, I had a lot of showers in Iowa, unusual for long-distance hiking.) they served me barbecued ribs with potato salad, beans, and fresh cornbread. Yum! We got to know each other, and I had a feast. How grand was that? Carolyn was a music director for two churches. Bob was an engineer with his own business in retirement.

The weatherman had dire warnings for the next day: rain and cold and even snow. The polar vortex was going to dip down to hit the northern part of Iowa. It did not sound like good hiking weather, and my hosts were concerned about my determination to stick to my schedule. We compromised.

They graciously agreed to help me out with another night in a warm house, so I could slack-pack through the wet and cold and be assured of a warm place to stay. I was so grateful. I was even more grateful the next night. Not only do I meet gracious and generous people, they save me from my worst decisions.

After a breakfast of oatmeal and Polish bread, I took my pack, loaded only with warm things, first-aid kit, drinks, and gloves, including big, floppy waterproof gloves Bob gave me. I dressed in my rain gear as it was already raining and would continue to do so all day long (or worse).

The first three miles weren't too bad, for a rain hike. I stopped at a Casey's for a restroom and food: a sausage-and-egg croissant for a second breakfast and a sub to take with me for lunch.

It was colder by the time I left the Casey's, and the wind was picking up more force. Crossing a street, I turned to look for cars, and a wind gust twisted the umbrella, breaking one of its stays. Oh, no. It was still usable, but a disaster waiting to happen with one sharp pokey dangling stay which could punch a hole in the umbrella. I held it very carefully.

Another quick three miles, and I reached the first tunnel under a road and found a trailside restroom. The restroom served its intended purpose and was also a shelter in which to eat my sandwich. I put on my down jacket as soon as I stopped, but by the time I was through eating, I was beginning to get chilled.

The wind was strong by then, and I stowed the umbrella, and also my glasses, no use wearing them in driving rain. Another hour of walking, and the rain turned into hail. For a little while, the trail was slightly protected from the wind by a low berm, but that did not last.

The rain and hail turned to snow pellets and then to snow, coming at me sideways from the right at almost a ninety-degree angle driven by wind. My right side and the right side of all my gear turned white with layered ice and snow. It was quite miserable weather.

As long as I kept walking, my core was reasonably warm, even though the howling wind was trying to suck all heat away. The most difficult thing was trying to keep my hands warm. They were stiffening in the cold, not wanting to move at my command in any kind of coordinated way. Peeling back two layers of gloves to look at my GPS or email from Bob was a major challenge which left my hands still colder.

Bob was coming back from his music gig in Des Moines and would pick me up. I was definitely ready to bail. There was no way in the world I would have been able to erect a tent in that gale-force wind and ice. It is probably not too much to say being picked up was a life saver. With that pickup, my life was not in danger. Without it, it might have been. Bob walked toward me on the trail because he was worried for me. He said it looked like I was meandering from side to side, staggering, though I think it was simply wind gusts pushing me.

When I got into his car, the warmth of the heater surely felt good. When we reached their home, Carolyn had chicken and dumplings and a lovely salad, along with freshly baked peach pie all ready for us when we arrived. I hung my wet things on their banister, and Bob tinkered with my umbrella, fixing it so that it worked again.

"Engineers fix things." he said. He'd somehow tied that broken piece together with a spring and it worked like an umbrella should. (I'm still using that umbrella two years later. Good engineering.)

All the time I was with Bob and Carolyn, we visited together as if we had been friends for years. They also added to my store of knowledge of the people in Cedar Rapids.

The first night I had learned about the immigrant

populations in Cedar Rapids and that the *mother mosque* in Iowa was there. The second night we talked about church politics and music, thoroughly enjoying ourselves. We also talked about Star Trek. They were also Trekkies and were going to celebrate their anniversary with a Star Trek theme. I lost some points by not remembering a particular Star Trek episode. Then I gained some points by remembering an episode and also knowing the words to Sky Boat Song. I learned the Sky Boat Song before Captain Picard, at Girl Scout Camp, a half century earlier.

Such fun we had, talking while the rotten weather raged, and meeting them became another treasured memory in the overflowing scrapbook of my mind. So many wonderful people, so much generosity shared, so much friendship with those who once were unknown strangers. Every stop was not guaranteed to work out so wonderfully. But that one joined so many others that brought such pure joy.

Three days of walking without full pack were lovely. But it was time to hoist it up again and hike away. I sang a blessing for Bob and Carolyn. Carolyn went off to play for church, and Bob had a musical gig in the other direction, and he dropped me off on the trail on his way. I hiked away from those friends of a Facebook friend who then became friends of mine.

It was still cold at the beginning of the day, but very little was left of the white blanket of snow that had covered the fields when Bob picked me up. The sun was out, storm gone, and the sun made it seem warmer than it really was. Within a mile, I had shed all my warm layers except my rain jacket.

Arriving at Center Point five minutes before the service was to start at the local Disciples of Christ Church, I stayed. That was my brand before I'd become a Lutheran, so it was fun to sing old familiar hymns not in the Lutheran Hymnody. Of course, a hiker with a backpack stands out in a church service, and I stand out more in a small country service because I sing loud enough to be heard. I lucked out doubly that Sunday, as they were having a potluck following the service, to which I was invited.

Diana introduced me to all and asked me where I would spend the night. I showed her on my map. A little later, she gave me the name, address. and phone number of someone who lived right where I wanted to stop. She said she had talked to them, and they would find a place for me in an outbuilding or a barn. That sounded good to me.

Others at the potluck warned me of a bridge under construction on my trail, but another lady said it was passable by foot. Later that day, I found the bridge indeed passable, and Garnet, the woman from church, was there to meet me again, and we renewed our conversation for a while.

The afternoon turned progressively colder and windier after that first morning sun. I had not expected Iowa to be so windy. My mistake. Iowa's farms were formerly the windswept prairie. I knew from the forecast on my phone that it would rain in the night, and with the wind blowing fiercely, I was looking forward to the shelter found for me by the church ladies. I tried to call the number I had been given but got no answer. I found the correct street number, verified by the last name printed on a parked farm truck. But no one was at home, and no one answered the phone number.

By this time the wind was howling, and I needed shelter. What to do? I called the number again and told the answering machine I would poke around to see if I could find a space under shelter. I hoped that would be all right as this had supposedly been agreed to. Most of the outbuildings seemed filled with farm equipment and the flotsam and jetsam that accompanied farm work.

I finally found a spot in an open shed that also held an old tractor, flatbed trailer, and horse trailer. What looked like a produce market stall had enough space for me under its roof. I found some cardboard to put down as a first layer as farm outbuildings are often not the cleanest of places. I put my two trash bags out over the cardboard and my tent over that, not erected but as sort of a bivy/cowboy camp. It worked. I was out of the wind and under cover.

I phoned the number again to tell them where I was. It was a strange situation, a place where people supposedly knew I was coming and had agreed to my being there, but no sign of the people. Maybe they would come home later. I was tucked in and glad to be under shelter. That was enough.

I had no bon-vivant conversation at that stop. Not every stop is perfect, but a hiker really doesn't need much. No one appeared to come home all night long. Very strange. I hoped my erstwhile hosts were OK, and there had not been an emergency in their lives. I didn't have access to water, so could not make breakfast, most of which I drink. I packed up and headed on, grateful for the shelter of the night, even if the circumstances were strange.

That bike trail did not go by farmhouses very often. It was three miles before I came to an accessible farmhouse that looked like someone was home. Lu graciously gave me water and let me mix up and eat my breakfast. We also talked a lot.

When I reached Brandon, I walked toward the main road looking for food. The T-by-T had an M in towns where meals were supposed to be possible. But that M did not tell me what kind of food, where it was, or how far off trail. I found a little Corner Pub within two blocks. Good enough. I had a double hamburger and used a convenient wall plug to charge my electronics.

Back on the trail in the afternoon, I was really dragging. My left foot had been giving me lots of grief. My back was hurting, and I was just plain tired. Coming to a lake, I stretched out for a while on a picnic table. It was hard to leave that horizontal position on the table, but the countryside did become more interesting as I hiked along. There were more trees alongside the trail, forest instead of farmer's fields. Mud River had large areas of muddy wetlands, living up to its name.

And then the flowers started. Dutchman's breeches bloomed in abundance. Then big patches of Virginia blue bells stole the show. There were spring beauties, and another white flower whose name I should have known but couldn't call to mind. Flowers, sometimes thickly spread, were all around me all the way to McFarlane State Park.

I paid for the privilege of being the only camper in the campground, but I did use the flush toilets, had ample water, and had a pretty campsite with Dutchman's breeches and bluebells out my tent door. The restroom was the first one I had ever seen that said it was a tornado proof room. I hoped I wouldn't need that knowledge.

Though it rained in the night, it stopped when I awoke. Considering myself lucky, I wiped down my tent and packed up. Back on the Cedar Valley Trail, an interpretive sign told me Iowa had eight different kinds of frogs. I hadn't known frogs came in so many kinds, but I had been hearing them sing.

When I reached La Porte City, rain commenced to fall, blown sideways by the wind. The restaurant was closed. In the grocery store, the restroom was on the fritz, and they had no sandwiches to buy. I bought a package of seafood salad to eat for lunch under a park gazebo and used the sport-field restroom.

The locals in the grocery store told me another bridge, which was signed *closed,* was passable for foot traffic. On their direction, I climbed locked gates at both ends, but the bridge itself seemed perfectly sound. Off and on in the afternoon, rain fell, and winds blew, but my raingear and umbrella held up well, keeping me dry.

That last Sunday, one gentleman I had talked to at the church had asked what wildlife I had seen in Iowa. That rainy day I saw lots of little brown snails about as big around as a quarter. I crunched one by accident when I was looking up at the far distance while still moving forward. I felt bad I had destroyed his house and life, but a bicycle path was not a safe place, though snails flocked to its surface.

As I approached Gilbertville, the wind and rain picked up even more. My hike plan said I should get dinner there. It was three-tenths of a mile to the east straight into stiff wind while I crossed the Cedar River. The first place I saw to eat was an old corner bar called the Cornerstone.

I came in dripping rainwater and asked if they served food. At first glance it seemed more bar than pub with food. The men at the bar were enjoying their drinks and conversation with much colorful language. Seated at a table by the wall, I ordered a burger and fried cauliflower from their short menu list and took the time to write my journal.

When I decided to get back to hiking, the bartender wouldn't give me a bill. Asking questions about my hike, he said the tab was on him. Well, that was nice. And hearing the conversation, all the guys at the bar were somewhat astounded to learn I was walking across Iowa. A chance to tell about the trail and to receive kindness can come in any form and place.

Three miles after leaving the Cornerstone, in blowing wind and rain, about an hour from darkness and needing a place to be, I stopped at the first house I saw. It had a flight of stairs to the front door, which I climbed to knock, but no one answered. I carefully climbed down the wet wooden stairs, not wanting to slip and fall, and was walking toward the back door on the lower level and hoping for better luck when Mark and Tina drove into their driveway.

"What are you doing?" Mark called out, wondering what a hiker with backpack and umbrella was doing walking to his back door behind a fence. I explained myself and asked if I could stay under the overhang under the stairs. They were a bit amazed at their random visitor, but the result of our conversation was an offer to stay in their man-cave room on the bottom floor.

The Cedar River had flooded the area in years past, so they had built their house on top of the flood-prone lower story and converted that level to an enclosed room, complete with wood stove, big TV, couch, refrigerator, and other comforts, though it wasn't where they actually lived. Mark fired up the wood stove and, having quickly looked up my book on Amazon to verify I was who I said I was, peppered me with questions about my hikes as I unloaded gear.

Mark and Tina had just come home from the hospital where they had become grandparents for the second time. They had their two-year-old granddaughter for the night. They also had a little dog upstairs and a beautiful black-and-white Husky in the backyard with a doggy door to a fenced off part of the room I was staying in. I was grateful to have found shelter, be warm, and have my wet gear drying. In the morning, Tina asked for my *Trailjournals* information. They had become interested followers.

WATERLOO

Not having far to walk that day, I stopped at a Casey's. They had no tables or chairs, but they were quite accommodating in making me a place to sit by moving cases of pop around. I contacted my old neighbor, Don, who was flying into Waterloo to visit his sister. Then I called his sister, Jean, who was coming to pick up both of us. Pickup details arranged, I had a donut and started off again.

My path continued along the Cedar River. A guy fishing at a bridge caught a big catfish as I walked by. He took it to show his wife sitting in a car on my path, and I was able to admire his catch, too.

Reaching my pickup destination, the personnel at the restaurant on the corner let me sit at their outside tables and chairs to wait for Jean. She picked me up, the first time we had met, and we went to the airport to pick up Don. Then we drove to Dumont, about fifty miles away. I hadn't realized she lived quite so far from Waterloo when planning my hike. Don had said she lived near Waterloo. It seemed a long way to a walker but not that far by car.

Don and Jean

We three hit it off great. Each of us, all aging folks, retired for an afternoon nap, and I had a blessed shower and started my laundry. It surely felt good to be horizontal. Don fixed dinner, liking to take over the kitchen when he visited his sister. We talked of our families and trails and had a lovely evening.

My son follows my inReach, a GPS device that gives him a real-time track of my whereabouts. He sent me a slightly worried text: "Why are you in an airport? Have plans changed?" I explained we had picked up Don, whom he knew growing up. It was nice to know my son was watching.

A rest day followed that short day. I met more of Don's relatives, we played cards, Jean and I became good friends, and a good time was had by all. A radio blog from San Francisco requested an interview on my website, and, since it was a rest day, I responded and had that interview. Being a hiking author, again made this trip different than the others.

The next day, Jean and Don drove me back to Waterloo to my pickup waypoint, and I started on my slackpack for the day. Of course, I needed a restroom as soon as I started, after the hour-long drive to Waterloo. Two blocks walking and half a block from the trail, I spied a fishing-and-bait shop. Yes, I could use the restroom. Afterwards, three or four guys asked many questions about my hike. I had fun talking of trails. And that subject segued into telling them about my book, my second-favorite subject.

I walked onward then, over city streets, followed by a two-mile levee walk beside the Cedar River. I passed Electric Park. There was a reason for that name. The bike trails in the Midwest are generally rails to trails paths. The one I had been on since before Cedar Rapids was once an electric railroad called the Cedar Valley Road. There was excess electricity from the railroad, available for a huge amusement park, built and named Electric Park. The amusement park was long gone when I passed the spot, replaced years ago by a Dairy Cattle Organization and show. But the sign remained to tell me of the history.

The ADT goes north all the way to Waterloo for a chance to walk through George Wyth State Park. It was an enjoyable place to walk, through trees and spring flowers. Eventually, I came to water flowing across the trail right before a picnic area. It flowed smoothly about an inch deep and was no problem crossing in my thick-soled hiking shoes.

After the picnic area, I was again a little confused with trails and roads, and two women stopped to help me out. They were very impressed with my hiking exploits and wanted to shake my hand. That has happened to me several times over the years. It often strikes me as quite funny. I am the same person I was when no one particularly noticed me or wanted to shake my hand. It *was* fun to be recognized for doing something out of the ordinary. But I confess it still feels somewhat incongruous. I am just me.

My pleasant walk through wetland forest was thick with flowers: Spring beauties, Virginia bluebells, yellow and purple violets, even some Dutchman's breeches The most prominent flower was, perhaps, rue anemone, their white masses resembling snowdrifts beside the bike trail.

Austin, a young bicyclist who'd just finished with his classes at the University of Northern Iowa, had a flat tire. We walked and talked together for a while as he pushed, not rode his bike. And when we parted ways, he wanted a selfie with me.

When I once again stopped to check the location on my GPS, a friendly, older biker stopped and offered assistance with directions. That led to conversations about the ADT and all trails everywhere. This section near Waterloo even had the

ADT marked on the detailed trail markers. Wow. Someone knew this trail existed and marked it in a formal way.

I stopped to get an ice-cream cone, and shortly after that I lost the bike trail. It seemed to disappear. I'm not sure where it went. I could see my waypoints. I was practically standing on one, but I'd lost the trail. No real problem there. I could see how to get to the next waypoint on the road. Eventually, I knew I was on the trail again.

I was beginning to get tired and grumpy, though. I called Jean and arranged for a pickup on Nordic Drive. My foot hurt, a lot. I put on a forefoot elastic sleeve that Don had given me to try. He had been carrying it in his kit since his race-walking days. It was very tight and exceedingly uncomfortable, but I kept it on and half-an-hour later, my foot was much improved. The discomfort of the tight elastic dissipated, and the pain for which it had been prescribed was gone, as well.

Jean and Don picked me up half a mile short of my goal, and I was glad to return to Dumont for a shower and Don's good cooking, plus enjoyable conversation among the three of us. I would miss them as I traveled on. Staying with them had been a most enjoyable interlude. As the old Girl Scout song goes: *"Make new friends; but keep the old. One is silver and the other gold."* In Don and Jean, I had both old and new.

Don made bread pudding with blueberries for breakfast, and we put Jean's maple syrup over it.

Great way to start the morning. I was glad I had looked at Jean's Google map before I set out. I did not waste any time freaking out when the trail went north and then *east*. Up to that point, I had traveled more north and south and east miles than west across Iowa.

When I reached the Sergeant Trail, I saw a sign that said six miles to Waterloo, probably to the waypoint I had left sixteen miles before. The trail around Waterloo had included nice woods, river walk, and wildflowers. But really! Sixteen miles to go six seemed nuts. Then again, I had a lovely time with Don and Jean. It was all good.

On to Marshalltown

Sergeant Trail was a very straight shot to Hudson. I took a long rest and had a sub for lunch, leaving with a nice soft-serve ice-cream cone on a beautiful 70-degree afternoon. After Hudson, I finally started getting westward miles.

The scenery changed from river walking and wetlands to rolling hills and broad expanses of cultivated fields. Zanetti Road was just straight road walking, an up-and-down road over hills. As I walked by, a lady walking in her farmyard asked how I was doing. I told her I was getting tired and had just thought about asking if I could put my tent up in her yard.

She called John and put me on the phone to ask. He said it was OK, as long as I was not an ax murderer. I reassured him I was not, didn't even *have* an ax. I was just a little old lady hiker. Putting my tent up in their yard under an evergreen tree, I used their restroom and water, and took my bath with water in a plastic bag in my tent.

My hosts weren't interested in talking. I, having talked overmuch visiting with Don and Jean, appreciated quiet while observing John, the hard-working farmer, hauling manure loads to his fields even after dark, his rig lighting up my tent with bright lights each time he passed.

The next day was a long one. I was concerned about thunderstorms in the weather forecast and woke up very early to get as much walking in as possible before the afternoon thunderstorms hit. I was walking by 6:30. It was a short mile to the corner and a straight shot down to Reinbeck. But my foot started hurting a mile before I reached there, so I stopped to put on Don's foot *strangulator*, my name for that elastic band, as that is what it felt like, putting it on.

Before I reached town, I heard church bells, but there were no churches on my trail. No church for me that Sunday. The gentleman at the farm store let me use the restroom and told me about a small restaurant and a Casey's. I debated what to do for lunch, but walking by a little grocery store, the smell of fried chicken was overpowering. I walked out of the store with fried chicken, an apple, and chocolate cupcakes. It was sort of a balanced meal.

My directions told me to take the Pioneer Trail, but cryptically warned me the trail was incomplete in some places where I would have to take parallel roads.

After only six blocks, the surface changed from bike trail to what looked like mowed trail. Surely, the trail would not be just six blocks. The mowed part led to a bridge with what looked like an old railway levee beyond. Maybe it was still the trail. I crossed the extremely dilapidated bridge very carefully as some pieces were missing. When I got almost to the other side, I saw there was no more mowed path, just high grass and unkempt shrubs. "Oh no," I said out loud.

About that time a guy on an ATV hollered at me from the other side of the bridge, "Do you know you are on private property?" Well, no, I didn't know. I walked back over the dangerous bridge, back to the crossroad and up to the highway.

I walked on the highway to a rest area with picnic tables, where I ate my fried chicken for lunch. I took off the foot *strangulator* there, and my foot behaved the rest of the day. The Pioneer Trail continued from the rest area. Bike trails were much nicer walking than the highway—when they were there.

I was hot and very tired when I reached Morrison, so I took out my foam pad, stretched out on the trail, and closed my eyes for about twenty minutes. That rest made me feel much better. The bridge for the road was closed in Morrison, a major construction project underway to replace the old bridge, but the small bike-trail bridge was not affected by the construction.

In late afternoon, the western sky became increasingly black. Lightning flashed and flashed. When it started to rain, I quickly put on my pack cover and hoisted my umbrella. I should have put on my raingear, too.

It poured rain in typical Iowa fashion, sideways with heavy wind that kept trying to collapse my umbrella. My head and upper body stayed dry, but my shorts and shoes were quickly soaked. There was lightning to the left of me, lightning to the right of me, and lightning overhead, quite a thunderstorm. I was glad I was in a green tunnel with trees lining the trail and not out in the open. I walked along holding the umbrella into the wind and counting from lightning strike to thunder's roll. There were quite loud thunder peals, but, theoretically, none closer than one mile away.

The Pioneer Trail came to an unsigned junction, one-part bicycle aggregate, and one-part mowed surface. The mowed surface seemed to go directly toward my next waypoint; the bicycle aggregate went to the highway. I took the mowed path toward my waypoint, but it just made a big loop back to the bicycle trail near the highway. Signage would have been nice.

In the violent rainstorm, I wasn't interested in setting up my tent. At Grundy Center, I stopped at the Casey's for dinner. They told me a motel was on the road I would take out of town. OK, I took the motel. It was an unplanned, unbudgeted stop. It was not cheap. But I could not resist the temptation on that soggy evening, even if it was pricey.

I slept like a log and did not hurry out of bed. Wandering down to the breakfast bar, I found the best motel breakfast bar I had seen since I had been in Japan for my son's wedding. I had scrambled eggs and sausage, biscuits and gravy, and a blueberry waffle with strawberries on top. I considered filching a hardboiled egg, bagel, and cream cheese for lunch, but I needed to eat the food in my pack, and pastors shouldn't be filching anything. Sigh. There was more good food than I could eat, though I did my best.

The day was mostly very long and straight road walking. After taking me up to Waterloo, the ADT was taking me south in large chunks, at least they seemed large to me on foot. I made three-and-a-half miles westward and more than nine southward. So goes the ADT in Iowa. I was glad to turn down K Street after a blast from a truck almost knocked me over. K had less traffic, though also less shoulder for safe walking.

I stopped at a couple business places for use of the restroom. This old lady can't pass up a good restroom. At one of my stops, the woman who said I could use the restroom looked up my book and web site right then and was following me by the time I left.

Mostly that day, I just pounded out miles. Tiredly walking through the edge of Beeman, I stopped at the offices of Bayer, same symbol as the aspirin. It was the same company, but they'd bought out Monsanto, and that Bayer office was in charge of shipping seed corn and soybean seed.

They kindly let me use the restroom, mix up my dinner, and rest in their company meeting room. A boss sort of man talked to me about the trail, which inevitably led me to mention my book as he warned me they closed at 4:30. I packed up to go, and as I left he hurried to catch me and called me by name as he shook my hand. I smiled. That meant he had looked up the book. He had more questions, but they had to close, and I had to go.

A few steps later, it started to rain. I put on rain gear and pack cover under the post-office awning, and then I put up my umbrella to walk the Comet Trail, a two-mile trail between Beeman and Conrad. The fuzzy white blooms of wild plum flanked the trail, and a gentle rain fell in thin showers, as I paced between shrubbery and trees. The railroad berm to the side invited me to camp. Half a mile before Conrad, I did, out of sight from any human habitation. The spot I found was just big enough for my solo tent, sacrificing a few roots of the wisteria rankly growing everywhere.

I wondered if prairie chickens were in the area. I heard something that reminded me of the chukars in Northern California, but I was in my tent and could not see the source of that sound. I also could hear traffic on a nearby road, but I was completely out of sight in my secluded spot, rain pattering on the walls of my tent.

In the morning, I moved up the trail with heavy mud shoes while several cottontail bunnies scampered away from me. Good black Iowa dirt makes good black Iowa mud. I stomped a while in a mud puddle at the edge of town to wash the majority of black goo off my shoes.

A Casey's was right on my way, with a local revolving breakfast club in session. They wanted to know about my journey, so I joined them. A couple there had hosted hikers before and wondered where I had stayed the night. I reassured them I had camped leaving no trace and was unseen unless someone found the exact spot in the morning before the violets perked up again. Since my campsite was above eye level from the trail, that would be difficult to do.

Having too much fun talking to people, I left the Casey's late and then immediately ran into another guy on a sidewalk who wanted to talk, too. I had been doing an awful lot of talking for an introvert, even if hiking was an absorbing passion of mine that I liked to talk about.

I asked at a farmhouse before B Street if I could have lunch under a tree and so met Richard, a Navy Vietnam Vet on portable oxygen. He came out to talk to me while I finished my lunch. This time I mostly listened. He had tales to tell about his life, his family, and the lives of his elderly friends who were worse off than he was. He still tinkered in his shop, drove his own lawn mower, and could manage his property. It was my privilege to listen.

After using his restroom, I said good-bye and turned south on B Street, going a very long way south, eight miles to Albion.

Soon after I had turned on B Street, a car stopped, and the driver asked if I needed a ride. When I said that would be cheating, since I was on a hike, he drove a little farther, but stopped again and waited for me to catch up. Would I like a little fresh-cut asparagus?

I had seen people cutting wild asparagus at the edges of ditches by the road. Beautiful asparagus. I said I would take a couple stalks and planned to eat them raw with dinner. He stuffed some in the pocket on the back of my pack as I stood there talking.

Running low on water, I knocked on the last farmhouse near to the road, but no one came to the door. Then there were no other farmhouses near the road for six miles. As I walked those miles, a highway patrol cop asked if I was OK, as he had received a call about me, and highway walking was unusual behavior in those parts. There was no hassle from him, just concern, allayed when he saw my gear and heard I was on the ADT.

Besides my lack of water, the next biggest problem was that six-plus miles was way too long to hike without some kind of bathroom break. I was on a pretty busy highway with no cover and no houses. Eventually I came to a crossroad and walked down that road to find a ditch not too steep to get into, so as to be less visible while I watered the grass in relief.

I had not planned to walk farther than thirteen miles, but no likely stopping place presented itself. I had another offer of a ride, which I turned down, as I doggedly walked toward the town ahead. How could I say I walked across Iowa, if I didn't walk across Iowa?

At the turn at 160th, a guy in some sort of business establishment, where I obtained much-needed water, suggested a slightly shorter route to town to connect to my waypoints. My weary feet took the shorter route. What? There was a big picnic shelter on the shorter route. I felt like I surprisingly had struck gold. It was probably a big enough shelter to protect me even from wind driven rain.

I asked at a house across the street if it was OK to camp there. There was even a porta potty near some ball fields. It looked perfect to me. That person referred me to another a few houses on, where I met Lynn. She once had been mayor of the town; she would know. Lynn said she would call into the town council meeting, which was happening at that very moment, and tell them she had given me permission to stay there. That way no one would hassle me.

Having done due diligence in getting permission, I went back and ate a dinner of cheese, Korean pork jerky, and delicious fresh asparagus, topped off with an extra trail bar, and then a Snickers. Lynn had given me water, but it was too late to cold soak my dinner. My collection of miscellaneous items had provided protein, veggie, oats from my trail bar, and Snickers for dessert, a reasonably well-balanced dinner even if not one I had planned.

Since I certainly knew by then that rain falls down sideways with the wind in Iowa, I moved three big trash barrels into the center of the shelter for a wind break and set up my cowboy camp on my trash bags spread on the sheltered side. I laid out my gear being careful to weight light items when

I set them down to keep them from blowing away in the wind. I brushed my teeth, used the porta potty, and was ready for bed, dressed in down pants, down vest and jacket over my long johns, tucked in my down bag, toasty warm.

Just before dark, a lady walked over the field of the park from the south and asked if I wanted a cup of coffee. I thanked her but said I didn't drink coffee. Then she offered popcorn. No again, because I was ready for bed. She pointed out her house across the field and said if I had any trouble, I could knock on their door. I told her many thank yous, but I was all set up. I should have told her more about my travels, but I was too weary even to talk about trails, and she went back home. That she had taken the time and energy to walk over to me left me in a comfortable glow, knowing I had friends nearby, who would help if need be. I might hike solo, but I was not alone.

The storm hit about 2:00 in the morning, driving wind accompanied by rain. Fortunately, my barrel barricade kept me almost dry. The outside of my sleeping bag was slightly damp by morning. Looking at the very wet cement just past the protection of the barrels informed me that setting them up had been a good idea. The rain had reached more than ten feet inside the shelter, but I was mostly dry.

I walked to the Casey's in Albion and was again impressed with Casey helpfulness. They had a back room for their breakfast club. No club was there, so it was mine for breakfast and thoughtful staging for my day. I ate a second breakfast and contemplated my decisions. It was going to be a very wet and windy day. Whatever I wore going out that door, I would have to live with. There would be no clothing adjustments possible in driving rain.

I took off my longies and decided I would be warm enough hiking with rain pants over hiking pants, my two shirts, and my rain jacket. Wool socks (my bed socks, not my usual hiking socks) were the best choice as my feet would inevitably be wet, and wool still holds warmth when wet. I rearranged my gear and wished my motel was closer.

Oh, well. I sucked it up and left with a reasonably good attitude into howling wind and driving rain. I had to use both hands to control my umbrella with my hiking poles dangling by straps from one arm, but all my systems for rain walking worked well. I reminded myself that I didn't like walking when it was hot.

Another policeman stopped to see if I was OK, but he seemed to approve of my rain gear and decided I was probably capable to keep on walking. All went well until I had to turn and walk directly into that thirty-plus-mile-an-hour headwind. I was glad there wasn't much traffic because I had to hold the leading edge of my umbrella with both hands before my face and could only see under the edge of the umbrella about a foot ahead of me as I walked on the edge of the road, hoping any drunks were at home sleeping it off and not on my road swerving into me.

Stopping at a very substantial farm operation on Summit Road, I met a nice young man named Tom. He seemed to be in charge and invited me into a huge heated farm garage with very large farm tractors. After I used the restroom, I sat in the provided chair, ate my trail bars, and talked to Tom.

He was very interested in my hike and where I stayed at night. (Normal questions and interest, no alarm bells in my head.) He said he could find me a place to stay the day I would leave Marshall-town, and he got on the phone to do so. Thanks to Tom, I would be staying with Gene. I was given Gene's phone number, and Tom gave me his, too, and told me to call if I had any trouble within a fifty-mile range. There are wonderful people everywhere. Have I said that before? Well, over and over again, I found it's true. Fortified by trail bars and the promise of trail magic in my future, I went out again to face the headwind.

As I reached the outskirts of Marshalltown, I called Pastor Greg from the ELCA Lutheran church. When I had planned my hike, I had contacted him to ask for a ride to my motel from the trail, which circled the town. But I couldn't reach Greg, only an answering machine. It was not a good day to wait around. Rain came down heavily again, or sideways, driven by ferociously blowing wind.

My bladder was about to burst. It had been too long since the restroom in Tom's farm garage. I was getting a little worried, but kept trudging along, telling my bladder to last a little longer. Four tenths of a mile from my destination, an older gentleman in a truck pulled over and asked if I needed a ride. Close enough. I accepted. I called Greg's number and told his answering machine that I had found a ride to my motel, and he didn't have to come.

Kenny, my chauffeur, had been at a Bible Study at his church the day before and been challenged not to consider his faith a spectator sport, but actually to help someone out. I was the person he helped out, putting his lesson into practice. I was glad to help with his Bible Study by being that person.

The Economy Inn cost half as much as my earlier unplanned motel stop. But it was clean, the water was hot, and the shower felt great. When I asked if they had a washing machine for guests, the answer was *no, but*. I paid $5 to get all my clothes washed. There was Wi-Fi, TV, microwave, and fridge. It was great hiker digs, though the mattress was a bit lopsided. A nice guy checked me in. A nice woman washed my clothes. Many food choices were nearby—one reason I had chosen that motel. It was a good place for a rest day, and I was happy to be resting.

The temperature dropped to the 30s that night. I *can* camp when it is cold, but I appreciated a bed and heat. I had a phone interview with Kate from Outside Magazine, who wrote a story about me. That was fun. I patched my gear. All was ready to go again.

Pastor Greg took me to the trail in the morning. The sun was shining, and the sky was blue. The trail itself was not too exciting that day as I walked on paved bicycle trails next to busy highways. The paved bicycle trail had been put in when the four-lane highway was built. Good planning. I was happy it wasn't raining, and I had no traffic to worry about. Startlingly, the news feed on my phone said a mountain lion had been seen on the outskirts of Des Moines. Really? Never would I have thought a mountain lion would be found in Iowa. It seemed strange to read of mountain lions while cars whizzed by on a busy highway.

Gene, the farmer Tom had recruited for my lodging, picked me up and had many questions for me. By the time we reached his nearby home, the offer of an outbuilding for shelter expanded to a spare bedroom, shower, and dinner, so we could continue talking. How could I not accept?

Gene and Jane were gracious and delightful people. I appreciated the caring way Gene had with his wife when she was having problems. I thoroughly enjoyed myself talking with them, and I think they enjoyed our conversation, too. Gene drove us to Marshalltown for burgers at Culver's, within sight of my motel. I thought it very funny to have driven back to where I had begun the day. That's the difference between feet and wheels.

After dinner, they took me on a driving tour of the tornado-damaged parts of Marshalltown. A tornado had hit the town the previous July. And there were still many houses with tarps on roofs, houses taken out completely, windows boarded over, and splintered trees. The City Hall was incased in plastic and scaffolding.

Marshalltown had been hard hit. Gene said Habitat for Humanity was building homes in the town, but he didn't know exactly where. I would not have seen the tornado damage without that tour by car, as my trail skirted the town, and my motel was in an undamaged section. A tornado has terrifying force capable of deadly destruction but can skip and hop, sparing some, while neighbors half a mile away bear the brunt of its force.

A fear I faced in planning that year's hike on the ADT was simply being in Iowa in tornado season. On foot I was defenseless. Sometimes setting a goal and focusing on the goal takes you past your fears. Annie from Facebook had it right. Our fears don't completely go away, but if we do not focus on them, they do not control our lives. I was focused on walking across Iowa. I was not in charge of the weather. I had experienced unseasonable heat, gale-force winds, snow and ice, buckets of rain, and beautiful days. I did not experience tornados, though I saw their damage. Could I have experienced a tornado in Iowa? Yes. But I did not. Not everything that is possible happens.

When I was a young mother, I used to joke that

my job was to worry about everything. If I worried, nothing bad would happen. Worrying was my full-time job. A silly joke. But that silly joke did point out that so much that could happen, doesn't. To be afraid of everything dire that *could* happen would take all my energy. There would be no time for life or living. Worry once. Recognize the danger and the risk. It does exist. Make a choice, and then move on. I chose to focus on my goal instead of fear.

Gene drove to the edge of his farm field, and we looked for newly sprouted corn. Not up yet. I like the focus farmers have on the future growth of crops. There are always possibilities of disaster in farming: flooding, frosts, no market for your crop, trade and tariffs beyond your control. Someone told me many years ago that farmers must be the most optimistic people in the world because they keep planting and focusing on growth. Sometimes all the strikes are against them, and they lose. Recently, many farms have folded, bankrupt. Bad things can happen. Tornados can strike. Farms can fold. But Gene, a *retired* farmer who still farmed, eagerly looking for new sprouts of corn, was the picture of farmer optimism to me.

As I made my breakfast in the morning, Gene asked me more hiking questions. Gene and Jane were

well into their 80s, maybe more. Age and circumstance did not dim their curiosity when encountering someone doing something they had never
heard of before. Gene drove me out to the trail.
Good-byes were said, as I put on my rain gear and
walked on in a drizzly bit of rain. How lucky I was
that Tom had set up that meeting for me on the
day I fought the wind and rain and sheltered in
his farm garage north of Marshalltown.

I was soon on a real country road, gravel and dirt,
with hardly any traffic. The country road went up
and down the deepening convolutions of rolling
hills. My pace slowed, and I was working harder
but enjoying it more. Bathroom breaks were not
as difficult to manage, and the roar of traffic had
disappeared. I heard birds singing and saw a her-
on at a creek.

Reaching Rhodes at early lunch time, I found a
covered picnic area. Perfect. Well, almost perfect.
The restroom doors were locked. But I knocked
on the door across the street and was granted use
of their restroom before I ate my lunch.

The day was cloudy, cold, and sometimes spit-
ting rain. I wore my down jacket under my rain
jacket, while I stopped for lunch, but removed
my warm layer when on the trail again. It was a
real trail, the Heart of Iowa Nature Trail. I liked
it. Embankments on both sides cut the wind.
There were wildflowers. I was always happy
seeing wildflowers. The trail didn't last all the
way to Collins, but it was lovely for nearly three
miles, a long green tunnel with thick woods on

one side, the bank on the other.

OK, where could I find a place to be for the night? I always wonder if things will work out, but, somehow, they always do. I have learned to trust that something good will happen or that I will be able to make do with whatever circumstance I find. I can't say I *fear* I won't find a place to stay each night on the ADT. Though, except for planned stops for rest days and receiving a re-supply box, I never know what will happen or where I will stay. I *can* say there is always a wonder and a nervousness in the pit of my stomach, when I get near my planned stopping point and wonder what I will find. I no longer consider that a fear, just anticipation and wonder.

I knocked on a farmhouse door and introduced myself, asking if there might be space in an outbuilding as it again was supposed to rain. Sure, was the answer. And in a flash, I had a place to be in a farmer's office, an open-door policy for the restroom, a towel and washcloth for a shower, and then they left me with free rein to their house and whole farming operation while they went out for a couple hours. Incredible! When they returned, Ann and Jack and I chatted about the trail. They claimed it an honor to have helped me, the first time I had heard that phrase since the west side of Annapolis. But this time they knew I had written a book making the context different.

Ann and Jack's farm

A Fall

In the morning, I walked past a pink, brightly blooming crabapple tree and down the road. I didn't even get out of town before I gave myself a very bad Mother's Day present. I fell. When I was younger, I fell frequently on trails, but never came to harm. In Nevada, I had fallen and seriously hurt myself. Each year I was older. As each year passed, a fall had more chance of causing damage. I didn't need a rough mountain trail or a root or rock to catch my step, just Iowa's very different (to me) construction of roadside drains.

A few towns back, I had noted to myself the different construction of storm drains in Iowa. Instead of grated drains in a fairly flat gutter, Iowa drains were cut under the curb. Streets had a slanted scoop leading to the cut under the curb. I had warned myself how easy it would be to twist a foot between the flat surface of the road and the slant heading beneath the curb. In Grundy Center, I had carefully stepped around those drains.

But that morning, with no sidewalks, I was carefully looking at the big truck coming at me as a possible imminent danger and not where I was placing my feet. The step threw me off balance, and I crumpled to the pavement. At least I wasn't going downhill, and I didn't fall on my face like I did in Nevada. But I took all my weight and the weight of my pack on one outstretched hand between thumb and fingers. When I scrambled to stand again from lying in the road, I checked myself for damages. My new replacement knee had a scrape through my pants but was not really hurt. My old replacement knee had a bit of a knock and hurt briefly. My hand hurt—a lot, though I seemed to be able to move it

I walked on, reached the Heart of Iowa Trail again, poles on my pack, and my right hand held up in the air or leaning on my bottle or GPS, which was attached to my chest strap. I didn't try to move my hand, other than to see that I could when I first stood up. I walked with elevated hand up high all the way to Maxwell. It slowly hurt less as time went on, but it didn't want me to move it at all.

At Maxwell I stopped and ate two huge pieces of pizza, holding them with my left hand instead of my dominant right. A donut was easy to manage for dessert. My little finger and thumb were fine. I had a little function. The other digits were not. I did what I could with elevation and compression, putting on my tight glove to slow down swelling and kept my hand up in the air. Besides hurting, it was very unhandy, as I am quite right-handed. Buckles and pack belt were hard to manage.

I figured I didn't walk on my hands, so I might as well walk on. I knew I had sprained it severely but didn't really see the point of stopping. Stopping wouldn't fix it. I could not go back in time and not fall. That was the only thing that would have helped.

The day was good. No rain, not hot, not cold. The

crushed limestone trail was level. I started seeing corn sprouting. Some farmers hadn't planted
yet due to the cold, rainy weather, but some had.
Birds sang to me, and I sang back.

I was not happy about my hand, though. Severe
sprains take time to heal. I already had arthritis in
all my joints, including my hands. Adding trauma
would not help arthritis.

TRAIL MAGIC SLACKPACKING

Reaching Cambridge, I found the Tattered Toad, the only bar or restaurant in town. The bartender was a sweetie. He called some folks to find where I could camp and promised he would call the police to tell them I was a hiker, not a bum.

He loaded up my Big Zip water bladder with ice for my hand and water in the morning, and I started walking back to the trail and my proposed camping spot. I wondered how I could set up my tent using only one hand. While walking with my hand high in the air, I met Rhonda and Kurt. They offered their house or their church across the street for an easier solution than tenting. I accepted.

Rhonda and Kurt were youth ministers and led the praise band. I stayed that night in the Methodist Church. They prayed for me, and I asked them to come back from their house across the street after I got cleaned up and I would sing Holden Evening Prayer for them. (Holden Evening Prayer is a sung service of prayer created by Marty Haugen for Holden Village.)

Holden Village is a Lutheran Retreat Center in the Cascade Mountains in Washington. I carry a couple copies of that service with me, for myself or sharing.) When they returned, we talked about the trail and sang. I was so glad I didn't have to try to put up my tent with just one hand. I was spiritually, physically, and emotionally cared for by Rhonda and Kurt.

I was ready for bed, sleeping on a comfortable couch with my injured hand propped in an elevated position on ice. It was hugely swollen. None of my wrinkles could be seen.

I had a slow start in the morning. It was hard to do things without my dominant hand. But the good news was I could also use my fourth (ring) finger in the morning. My first two fingers were still not available.

It was only three miles or so to Huxley. A few people were walking on the trail that day. One older gentleman asked if I was the Lutheran minister. Kurt and Rhonda had me up on their church Facebook page the night before, so he knew about me. It was fun to be recognized.

Being minorly famous was about to be a very important part of my Iowa hike. While in West Branch I had been contacted on my phone by a fan who had followed my trail journal for years. I had no idea Kathy lived in Iowa and had already passed her town, but we were making plans to meet after Des Moines, near her mother's home.

I had also been contacted by Brian, who had walked across Iowa on the American Discovery Trail and had heard of me from the American Discovery Trail Facebook group. He was a Godsend to me. When he first contacted me offering support, I already had a contact in Des Moines whom I had earlier recruited through a Facebook hiking group.

I could not think how he could help me, though I hated to turn down kind offers. After falling, my situation changed, I *did* need help. These people seemed to fall out of the sky just when I needed them. Some hikers would say, "The trail provides." As a Lutheran pastor I had a different answer. I was so thankful for all that extra help.

Brian

I picked up a sub at Casey's in Huxley and took it with me to eat under a row of trees two miles farther on, juggling it with my good left hand and what was functional on my right one. The remainder of the day was mostly uneventful walking, reaching my goal not long after 5:00. All the way I held my hand in the air, gently moving, stretching my injured fingers to improve circulation and range of motion. Brian picked me up at the end of my day, taking me to his home. I had new friends, a one-handed shower, a bed, and a promise of a slackpack for the next day.

I had to eat awkwardly holding a spoon with my thumb and last two fingers. The night before, I wouldn't have been able to do that much. I *was* worried about my hand. What if my diagnosis was wrong? Brian took me to the Urgent Care Center to get it checked out. Nope. Not broken. The Doc concurred with my diagnosis. My instructions were to keep doing more of the same: elevation, compression, and ice when I could. Everything was overstretched and sprained. Severe sprains take time to heal. Seeing a Doc relieved me, and it would relieve my children, too, to know their mother was not completely nuts and irresponsible.

Rain in the morning made me appreciate Brian's help even more. I couldn't imagine how I would have packed up a tent in the rain with my dominant hand only minorly useful. It would have been a challenge I would not have enjoyed. But I could walk. And, since I was helped by Brian, I could slackpack. I quickly donned raingear, both pants and jacket, put the raincover over my pack that held my lunch, first-aid kit, and water, and hoisted my umbrella.

As I walked down the road under pouring rain to Big Creek Lake Park and Marina, low rumbles of thunder sounded overhead. The park had many amenities. I used the restroom as rain drummed loudly on the roof with great force. Walking through a wooded area on a paved bicycle trail, I admired views of the lake and saw many covered picnic areas.

The rain stopped about 10:30, and the weather changed to pleasant sunshine. The amenities changed to occasional trailside benches as the smooth pavement wound southerly, mostly through woods, followed by a trip over a dam and through a marina. Brian walked in on the trail from the other end to meet me, and we enjoyed hiking together the rest of the way to his car. Company on the trail was a pleasant change from all my solo hiking.

I had walked all day with my hand up in a permanent wave or resting on my water bottle hung on my chest strap, sometimes moving my fingers, trying for a fist, sometimes letting the hand rest. The swelling decreased as the day progressed, and by night in Brian and Annette's house I could hold a pen correctly to sign his copy of my book. I couldn't have done that the night before. That night, when I took my shower, I could gingerly hold the washcloth in my right hand if I was very, very careful.

The next morning, Brian came with me again on the trail for 1.3 miles. One of their big dogs came, too. I was so grateful for Brian. He and Annette had two big dogs and one little one, their adult daughter, and two cute twin granddaughters under two-years-old, all staying with them, and yet they found room for me. Being able to slackpack and have a comfortable place to stay after my walking day was just what I needed, giving healing time for my hand.

The next day's walk followed the Neil Smith Bike Trail beside Saylor Lake, then the Des Moines River south. Interpretive signs informed me I was walking in the largest unbroken section of forest in central Iowa. Though Iowa's forests fell to the plow between the late 1800s and 1950s, there now were efforts being made to reforest farming areas. Iowa's forests, though small, were growing. Rain was only a memory as I walked on that sunny day under the dappled shade of woods.

Wild blue phlox were the most bountiful I had seen in Iowa, banks and banks of pale blue kept my spirits high. I walked all afternoon beside the Des Moines River. Running quite high from all the rain, brown river water swiftly flowed past me, once only half a foot below my path, and it certainly did not have far to rise to cover the trail. A few days later, I heard that the trail there had flooded. As it was, I passed many wetlands flooded beside me as I made a turn and approached Des Moines.

My hand was slowly healing. I could blow my nose with that hand and wipe my bum, though that still caused pain. You learn how much you depend upon your dominant hand when you can no longer use it. I tried to use my trekking poles, very gingerly. But the impact of pole on ground jarred the hand too much.

Brian continued to be my support person that

afternoon, picking me up and delivering me and all my gear to my Airbnb where I would stay three nights. That first night in Des Moines, I also had a new contact and support. Pam was the hiker on Facebook who had volunteered to help me in Des Moines. She would have housed me, but my allergies to cats did not allow for that. She had been the one to find and suggest the place I booked.

Pam and Mary

After my shower, Pam and Lenny picked me up and took me to dinner. Pam brought her copy of my book, which I gladly adorned with my signature. After I devoured salad, steak, and veggies, we went to Snookies, a popular local Beaverdale community ice-cream shop. I had a hot fudge Sunday with a huge amount of hot fudge, my favorite. The ice-cream shop had families standing in line for half a block on that warm evening. Locals know all the best places to go. Pam and Lenny then took me to the grocery store, so I could buy what food I needed for my day off without walking anywhere. And the whole evening we kept up a steady stream of trail talk.

I would see Pam in two more days, but first I would rest. The most strenuous thing I did on my rest day was go up and down a flight of stairs a few times between my bedroom and the kitchen.

I iced my hand, and it continued to slowly improve. Ligaments don't have much circulation, though tendons and bones do. Once you injure yourself, you cannot quickly un-injure yourself. Tincture of time simply takes a lot of time.

I had walked more than 300 miles to get to Des Moines. I still had 200 more to go. The next day would be a wet one, a thunderstorm forecast after my rest day in the sweltering 90s. I would have another day of slackpacking. Pam was at my door promptly before 7:30 to take me to my pickup point of two days earlier, leaving my gear behind. That day my hike began in pouring rain accompanied with a bit of lightning and thunder. But within a half hour, I had peeled off my raingear because I was too hot. Walking under my umbrella was better, even in the rain, as the rain was falling down that day and not sideways.

I walked through neighborhoods on streets. I looked at the variety of landscaping and what was blooming in other people's yards, much as I do at home walking in my own neighborhood. I also observed my garbage can color trivia. In Des Moines, besides recycle and trash, containers colored tan and green, there were charcoal-gray cans for compostable material. For some reason even I don't know, I have thought such trivia interesting ever since I saw bright-pink containers in Delaware and fluorescent yellow in Maryland. Who knew trash containers came in a rainbow of colors across the USA?

Bunnies don't just live in woods. I saw them in neighborhood housing areas, too. Birds with flashes of bright orange darted by, possibly orioles, though I never saw one still enough to be sure. In the afternoon I saw a goose family with toddling goslings. I took their picture, in spite of the hissing of the gosling's protective parents.

I could have bought food numerous times, and there were ample opportunities for potty stops in commercial establishments. I ate my lunch at Hy-Vee using their table and chairs, after buying chocolate milk from the Kum & Go. Urban hiking has its perks. The afternoon was spent walking the Clive Greenbelt Trail, a nice trail with gentle curves pleasing to the eye beside overfull Walnut Creek.

The Creek was a madly rushing river, by my standards—some places flowing only a foot below trail level. Twice it was closed off beneath road-crossing underpasses and filled with chocolate-brown swirling water. The sun came out for the last hour of my walk, and it got very hot, very fast. Pam met me as agreed, and gave me cookies, too, as well as taking me to B-Bop's to get my burger and a shake. She then took me back to the Airbnb for my last night in Des Moines.

I had company the next day. Pam picked me up in the morning, and we drove to 165th Street, where we met Pam 2. I walked with those two younger women, both named Pam.

We headed out, they in their rain gear, and I with my umbrella, slackpacking again. Walking and talking, we enjoyed each other's company. The miles went by enjoyably with people to talk to. I like hiking by myself, but I like hiking with others, too. They are different things, both enjoyable to me. On a long solo hike, it was great to have days to hike with others, too. Pam and Pam thought it was fun to hike with an author. I have hiked with friends before, but this trip introduced me to strangers who wanted to hike with me because I had written a book and then became new friends. Pam 1 and Pam 2 were also bikers and had cycled this way before.

In Iowa, bicycles are king. A famous bike trek across the state happens each year, on slightly different routes. People come from all over the country to bike the RAGBRAI. (Register's Annual Great Bicycle Race Across Iowa) Registered riders and organized support meant hordes of bicyclists trekked across the state each year, descending upon rural towns for nights along the chosen route. Tent cities spring up overnight, and mountains of food are served. I think Iowans were not quite so surprised at my hiking across the state as those I met in other states because they all knew about RAGBRAI. Treks are treks, on foot or on bike, different, but similar in having goals and covering distance over multiple days.

Having the need to find a restroom on a very long open stretch, I stopped at a farmhouse. Day hikers and bikers do not usually stop and ask for a restroom, though Pam and Pam had heard I did. They were also much younger than I and could go for greater distance without the need. They waited, somewhat skeptically, I think, as I walked up the driveway to the door.

I introduced myself and explained what I was doing. Then I asked for what I needed. On that day I met Donna and used the nice restroom in her house. I chatted with Donna for a few minutes more and then went out to the two Pams, who were waiting in the sun, and we went on.

A few minutes later, here came Donna on a little John Deere. She wanted our pictures. Pam 2 took pictures also, of me chatting with Donna, perhaps amazed or impressed that I now knew someone previously unknown to her, though she had ridden past that house on her bicycle before. Then, we all were friends. Perhaps the Pams would stop to see Donna on another day, another hike, or a bike trip.

Both Pams remarked that they saw different things walking than they saw riding bikes. Early in the hike that day, Pam 1's bright eyes caught two turkey vultures perched in an upstairs window of an abandoned house, looking out at the road like two old crones peering at the traffic. They flew off before we could get a picture.

At the Ortonville Road, we read the interpretive sign about the Orton Circus. Yes, a real circus, with elephants and leopards, acrobats, and other performers, used to tour midwestern cities, wintering there with ample pasture to care for circus animals. Circus and town were gone. Interpretive signs remained. Another little town of memory was Kennedy, a town that briefly thrived in conjunction with the railroad, and the railroad was now turned into trail for our feet or other's bicycles.

Pam 1 was a great organizer and take-charge kind of person. Pam 2 had relatives who could help me in Nebraska on my next year's hike. I had wondered if I would go on to Nebraska or stop with Iowa. If I had support, I took going on more seriously.

The trail turned to woods and flowers. White-and-pink honeysuckle were blooming, and we saw star of Bethlehem and Virginia waterleaf, too. Reaching Adel, we stopped at the ice-cream shop. Flowers were good. So was ice cream.

We left Pam 2 waiting for her husband, and Pam 1 and I walked on to the Brickyard, where Brian had told me there was a place to eat: Brickyard Burgers. On the way, Pam 1 pointed out Freedom Rock, a large rock painted with the United States flag and patriotic scenes. She told me Ray "Bub-ba" Sorenson was painting a Freedom Rock in every county in Iowa. Some veterans had requested that their ashes be mixed into the paint. Locals told me things I might not have known just from walking the trail.

The weather was threatening another thunderstorm with high winds and lightning. It seemed a better decision to stop, than to go on. We stopped, though the day was a little short of the miles I had planned. I would need to get up earlier the next day. Brian, yes, Brian again, picked us up and drove us to Pam's parked car. I transferred my gear to Brian's car and said goodbye to Pam. Support from Brian gave me another slackpack. Meeting both Pams was a real treat. Perhaps, I would meet them again, on another day, another year, another trail. Anything is possible.

I stayed with Brian and Annette for one more night. My hand was slowly healing, and my heart was blessed with friends, company, and support. Another friend was just ahead.

Brian took me to the trail behind the Brickyard in the morning. He then went on with all my gear to find the farmhouse of Kathy's mom. Kathy, remember, was the hiker who had followed my trail journal for many years. She had been disappointed that I had passed her before she knew I was walking Iowa this year. Coordination with Brian and Kathy allowed another day of slackpacking and a chance to meet and hike with Kathy.

I started out that day with rain gear, but the gentle mist did not amount to much. I was soon hot enough to take off both my rain gear and long sleeve shirt to stow away in pack. The Raccoon River Valley Trail, lined with trees to break the wind, provided pleasant walking. When there was a break in the trees, the stiff wind let me know it was still there, blowing across the prairie.

The day before, a trail-maintenance guy in a truck had talked to me and the two Pams. Knowing where I was headed, he tracked me down on the Racoon River Valley Trail. He had looked up my book and wanted a selfie with me. Being minorly famous continued to be fun.

Stopping at the Casey's in Redfield, I ate my piece of pizza while sitting on pop cases, a good cure for me if being famous went to my head. Chocolate milk and Pam's cookies finished off my meal on those pop cases, a fine repast for a hiker. An uneventful afternoon of more pleasant walking brought me to Linden at a reasonable 4:15, and I called Kathy for my pickup.

That night I was treated to a feast. Kathy had arranged a get together with Kathy's mother, Kathy's husband, her brother, her sister, and her sister's three teenagers. We had a great evening together and I provided entertainment telling trail stories. We all took pictures to record the event. What a wonderful family. What a wonderful gift for me to meet them all.

Kathy

Kathy had followed my *Trailjournal* for at least five years—maybe more. She too wanted to hike with me. After breakfast, Kathy's husband, Rick, insisted on giving me much better cheese than I usually carried. He had brought it back from Wisconsin. It was much tastier than my standard fare. Rick walked with us at the beginning of the day. Kathy and I chattered nonstop the whole day long.

The trail is an amazing place to meet people. And when someone has followed you on your journal for a long time and left comments for you to read over the years, meeting them in person for the first time was like meeting someone I already knew.

Our trail was lined with trees and bushes,

greenery of all kinds, and one big patch of purple phlox. We enjoyed the scenery, but even more, we enjoyed learning more about each other. We ate our trail snacks at a Subway and bought sandwiches there to eat later. For lunch, we perched on the sheltered side of the cement ring base of a silo, while the wind continued blowing. My, the wind surely did blow in Iowa.

Rick met us at the agreed-upon road at 2:30. We had already hiked thirteen miles. Wow. That was extremely good time for me. It felt like Camino walking, with plenty of time for a shower and relaxing before dinner. I washed my clothes, too. I, Kathy, and Kathy's mom, Nancy, had another home-cooked dinner provided by Nancy: roast, mashed potatoes, noodles, fresh veggies, orange fruit salad, and more pie from the night before, far more than I needed, but every bite delicious.

And I still wasn't through slackpacking. Ever since Brian had picked me up seven days before, I had been walking with just a daypack and had lodging and company and, more often than not, meals provided for me. No, it is not always like that on the American Discovery Trail. But the people in Iowa outdid themselves, showering me with help and hospitality just when I needed it. My hand had all that time to be healing, and I had all that time to be amazed at the goodness of people.

Saying good-bye to Nancy in the morning, Kathy drove me out to where we had stopped the day before. I then said good-bye to Kathy, too, as I headed north on a very windy, cloudy morning, as she drove away with my gear to give to her sister, Karen. I had a face and a friendship to go with the notes Kathy had left for me on *Trailjournals. com* over the years. I treasured knowing her in real life now, as well as in e-life.

The wind was beating in from the east. The bicycle trail was sometimes lined with trees and bushes that cut the wind, and sometimes not. Without a windbreak, the gusts kept trying to knock me over. The windswept prairie was not just a handy phrase for authors; the wind had real bite and tried to sweep me up, literally.

I stopped at Herndon at a bike trailhead and found a porta potty. Porta potties were called Kybos in Iowa, short for "keep your bowels open." Well, OK, then, a new name. Whatever one called it, I was happy it was a clean one and out of the wind. I put the lid down to sit, used my sanitizer and ate my trail bars, not the first porta potty in my life, or on the trail, in which I had rested and eaten.

When I reached the turn onto 330th, the wind was at my back pushing me along. I liked that part. Unfortunately, soon there was rain to join the wind. First it was just light rain, although pushed by wind. Then it was heavy rain, also pushed by wind. That afternoon, finding a place to pee in a hurricane, or Iowa's equivalent, was problematic. I managed once, sheltered by an old horse trailer.

I could tell I had another tiny hole, or a few of them, in my rain pants as my legs got wet with all that wind-driven rain. My feet were swimming in my shoes. My feet liked their foot bath, though the rest of me wasn't enjoying it much. But I kept walking and ticking off the miles, not speedily, but steadily.

At a farm beside the road, no one was at home at the house, but the barn door was wide open. I ducked inside, out of the wind and rain. Relief. For a brief break, I shared the shelter of the barn with a flock of chickens, including a rooster who kept crowing at me like a watch dog—a watch rooster. I decided I had enough of the weather and called for pickup. I knew it would take Karen, Kathy's sister, at least a half hour to reach me, so I ate some cheese and crackers, and then pounded out another mile and a half in the rain before Kathy and Ian arrived.

I climbed soggily into their car, taken by angels to the land of dry. I was glad to quit early, and glad for a shower, dry clothes, and heat. I think one of my shoes had at least half a cup of water to pour out when I took them off. I bet they wouldn't be completely dry by morning, but, in a house, they would be dryer than if I were tenting.

I liked the opportunity to get to know Karen. I decided she and my daughter had a lot in common. They both home-schooled their children and had military husbands. Karen's husband was Navy, my daughter's husband Army.

While I still couldn't cut my food with a knife, lean on my fisted hand to move in bed, or use it to get up and down from ground or floor, my hand was much better. And I had another night in a bed while the weather raged outside.

ADVENTURES WEST
AND SOUTH

Although I had been spoiled rotten with all this trail support, it was time to get back to being a backpacker. My body and legs would just have to get over the shock of carrying a full pack once again. Karen drove me back to the trail. The rain was gone, but the wind was fierce.

My day was spent fighting the wind. It wasn't exactly a headwind. It came from the southwest this time. Wind can come from any direction in Iowa and can change directions on a dime. While eating with Karen and her family, I discovered that my route had circled a town hit by a tornado, causing damage but no deaths. *Ordinary* wind in Iowa was quite enough. I hadn't been close enough to the tornado to see it. Just as well. I didn't really want to.

Using my poles once again after a week of rest, I braced into the fierce wind and leaned on them. Then, playing push-me, pull-you, the wind would suddenly disappear, leaving me lurching like a drunk. I stopped at a farmhouse to ask if I could use a restroom and eat in their backyard behind the house protected from the wind. Yes, and yes, they answered. And I did.

The wind continued after lunch, making me feel like I was heading up a hill. Heading into Coon Rapids it *was* uphill. No, Iowa is not all flat, and roads, often cut on a straight grid, went up and down those rolling hills.

Iowa's roads aren't always level

Reaching Coon Rapids, the wind was lessened by trees and houses. I stood on a corner near a herd of Shetland ponies. A young family came by to pet the ponies, and I asked if there was any food in town as it was not marked so on my T-by-T. There most certainly was, a grocery store which had been owned 100 years by the same family. There was a small deli in the grocery that served meals, and a table in the back for me to sit and eat. They were very hiker friendly, gave me promotional pens, too, which I stashed in my belt pouch.

After my fried-chicken dinner, I followed my

waypoint flags out of town past 140 on N 46 for 2.7 miles and then knocked on a door and asked for permission to camp. Three large dogs and eight cats were in the yard. I wondered if I should stay, or if the animals would be a problem, but I was tired, and houses were sparse past the town. With permission granted, I put my tent up behind the garage, hoping it would break the wind, though I wondered if the wind direction would change and being behind the garage wouldn't help.

The cats were very curious and wanted to come in. I had to bat them on the nose and swipe them with my extra pole to keep them away. Holes in my tent from the claws of cats playing pounce would be disastrous. The dogs were curious, too, but learned faster to stay away.

Later, the lady of the house asked if I wanted to stay in their camper, but I was all settled in by then, and the weather in the night was supposed to be good. I liked my tent, my portable home on the trail that I had not used for many days. I settled in, and the yard animals were quiet, too.

In the morning, however, I did not leave unscathed. One of the kittens jumped on my tent. I quickly batted her off, but she had poked a hole with one tiny claw. I quickly mended it with duct tape so it would be ready for the next rainstorm. That done, gear packed, I headed south. The ADT in Iowa was again meandering. I would travel mostly south until I came to Red Oak.

That day, the sky was filled with scudding clouds,

but there was no rain. Yay. And the wind was minimal. Double yay. The temperature was perfect for hiking, warm enough for short sleeves and shorts by afternoon. The countryside was hilly, more interesting than all the flat farmland I had seen. Of course, that meant more up and down. No, it was not like climbing mountains. But if you add up several seventy-five-to-a-hundred-foot hills and several twenty-five-to-fifty-foot hills in a day it counts as up and down.

I had lunch in an old road cutout making a flat spot with pleasant views of newly sprouted corn, separated into terraces by ten-to-fifteen-foot grass strips. Karen had told me each road cutout used to go to a farmhouse when the land was filled with small farms. Small farms were bought out by larger farms and combined. I wondered how life had fared for all those small farm families who had sold their land to others.

I dozed, listening to stillness, birds, and an occasional car, getting a bit of sunburn on my face as I rested. There had been so many clouds and so much rain, I had not thought of sunscreen until my face turned warm.

Coming within range of my stopping point, I passed three houses and stopped at another one, recently constructed, near well-kept outbuildings and silos. Two girls and three dogs were playing outside. Their mom, Katie, came to the door, and I asked for space in an outbuilding as another storm was approaching. Katie made a phone call to her husband, and I was offered the sun and the moon and stars, too, or in other words, the spare bedroom, private bath and shower, and food. I accepted.

Katie was a very good cook. Besides Jeremy and the girls, she often cooked for a farm hand or two. I finished off my last trail dinner and ate their dinner, too. Katie and I enjoyed talking and the girls' eyes got very large as I told trail stories. It was a good thing I was inside, as it stormed, poured, and rain fell sideways while I enjoyed cleanliness, food, and conversation with good folks.

I dawdled in the morning, waiting for the last of the storm to stop as my phone forecast said it would. I saw the girls leave for the school bus and spent time chatting with Katie. Later than usual, I headed out for the walk to Audubon, striding over roads that led me up and down.

Reaching Jay (7th) Street, I took it, later turned on South Division, then turned again to the address of my Airbnb, only a block or two south of another waypoint. Gregg and Brian met me with a taco. Nice greeting. It was delicious. They liked to cook and said they would cook for me while I was there. Bonus! I did not need to worry about food, and the meals they served, I considered gourmet quality.

Besides the good fortune of meeting Gregg and Brian, former ADT hikers, Boston and Cubby, contacted me by email. To my surprise, I learned they lived in Nebraska. I had followed their hiking journals on Trailjournals.com and had chosen the northern route on the ADT simply because it was the route they had walked. I guess I hadn't read the part that said they lived in Nebraska. As another bonus for the day, I talked on the phone with Cubby. Knowing they lived in Nebraska was added incentive to continue on into Nebraska for my spring hike another year.

Dinner was steak, baked potato, and asparagus. Brian and Greg were gems, gracious hosts. I even like their news station and their politics. Brian, Greg, and I did not exactly discuss politics, but I observed, in sharing their home, that our politics were in close alignment.

Politics, by the way, was something I rarely discussed while on the trail. I was a hiker needing aid. The people I met on the ADT were gifts to me and taught me graciousness from many different points of the political spectrum. I had my preferences, and do now, too. But connections made with others were more important to me than political views.

I knew many of my angels on the ADT thought as I did about such things, and others did not. I learned to appreciate each person, though I wondered how some had come to their views. In our country, so divided politically, I reminded myself that gracious people met my needs, regardless of their political leanings. Each one was a beloved child of God, though their stands on many issues were, and are, not understandable to me, not ones I espoused then, or agree with now.

I knew each one as a person, not as a foe. I looked for connections, not divisions. I knew our differences sometimes existed. But all those friendships I had found had coalesced around my needs and trail stories, sometimes also in discussions about the need, or not, to fear.

I tried to live my life and take a hike, not controlled by fear, especially fear of those I did not know or those with whom I disagreed. Parker and Debbie and my old neighbor, Don were the only people I had met on this year's hike whom I had known before I stepped my feet to trail. All the other people were new to me, once strangers, who became my friends.

I tried to shelve fear of the future, for instance, what each night would bring in lodging, who the people would be whom I met, until the time came to find my nightly place to be. Truly, all events in our futures are unknown. We make assumptions and plan our best to prepare. But plans are only plans, good to have, but not certainties. I tried to be polite. I tried to live as my faith directed me. I walked. That was enough.

On my rest day, Brian took me to the dollar store so I could pick up tortillas for the trail. Then we went to see the star attraction in Audubon, Albert the Bull.

In days gone yore, Audubon was the rail station for farmers bringing their cattle for shipment to Chicago. It was a big deal. They loaded cattle in as many railroad cars as they could fill, and the farmers and their wives went, too, for a celebration in Chicago where they would sell their cattle. T-bone Days were still celebrated there, and the section of trail I would walk the next day was called the T-bone Trail.

Related to cattle-drive days and celebrations, a guy named Albert had the idea to create a thirty-foot-tall bull. It was made of concrete. Even though the bull was hollow, it was still a lot of concrete.

It took two years to build him, and it was in a Super Bowl commercial in 2018. The locals were somewhat miffed, though, since no locals, only actors were in the commercial. The Bull is named Albert, in honor of the guy who had the idea. Like most everyone who visits Audubon, I had my picture taken with Albert the Bull. He was pretty darn big.

Dinner, cooked by Brian and Gregg, was delicious: extra-large and juicy pork chops, cooked perfectly. That meat was so tender, even I could cut it with my right hand holding the knife correctly. Brian and Gregg asked for an autographed copy of my book in exchange for those delicious meals. What a deal! I sent it to them after I returned home.

The hard thing about starting out after re-supply

is that the pack is heavier than when you arrived. I kept telling myself it was a small re-supply and it couldn't possibly be as heavy as it felt. The day was lovely. The sky was blue. The sun was shining. I was on a nearly level, half-shaded bike trail. There was just enough wind to keep cool.

I walked past Albert the Bull and set out on the T-bone Trail. And there were flowers. Spiderwort lined the trail. Most were the same deep blue of the spiderwort beside my pond at home. A few startled me with a bright-pink shade. I saw one white one and all the shades between deep-blue, pink, and white. I did not know before that spiderwort came in more than blue.

Brian had told me this part of Iowa had been settled by the Danes. They had a replica of the Little Mermaid (the famous statue in Copenhagen) and had a Danish Festival every year. I passed the turn to Hamlin, a town named for Brian's Great-grandfather, who came there in a covered wagon. Becoming friends with locals made my hike the richer as they shared their knowledge and their history.

Though I reached the turn early, Exira was supposed to be my dinner stop. A bicyclist resting at a table at the crossing said the Casey's was only two blocks over. Yeah, sure. Bicyclists aren't walkers. It was half a mile away. But it didn't really matter. That's where I had said I would find my dinner, so I had to go there. I walked to Casey's and ate a pint of ice cream, then I put a sandwich in my pack for dinner, along with donuts for my breakfast.

My umbrella was used for a sunshade all afternoon. When I reached Brayton, I met an older gentleman riding his bicycle. We had matching scars on our knees. He had two knee replacements, just like me, the most recent one acquired only two-and-a-half months earlier. He wanted to ride the RAGBRAI in July. I was not the only crazy older person pushing limits in pursuit of goals on trails. He invited me to stay with him and his wife in Atlantic the next night and told me to cancel my motel. I just kept getting unexpected gifts in Iowa. I accepted his invitation for the next day's night.

First, there was the night in Brayton. My benefactor could ride his bike to Atlantic before nightfall, but I was done for the day. I set up my cowboy camp under a picnic shelter in the Brayton Park. At 3:30 in the morning a thunderstorm hit, with horizontal rain and wind coming from a different direction than it had blown when I laid out my gear. I scrambled to rearrange my position and crawled into my tent like a bivy bag on the ground. A good deal of sleep was lost in booming thunder and attempts to stay mostly dry.

When the rain died down, the wind was still fierce as I dressed and packed up carefully, without losing anything to the wind, which was trying to snatch each item for a ride to the next county. I hadn't had enough sleep. Oh, well. Time to go, though clouds were still dark and threatening.

After three miles, the sky turned brighter, and the sun shone. The wind, however, blew hard and in my face for most of the day. In open areas, it was hard to maneuver while the wind sought to knock me over.

At a highway, I discovered the trail went behind a Days Inn and a gas station. Restroom and snack-break time. I added a hot dog to my snacks since they were selling them in the gas station. At least I gave them business in return for the use of the restroom.

A mile farther along, a guy named John rode his bicycle up behind me, dismounted from his bike, and pushed it while he chatted with me. His bike was an old Huffy, and he was a country good old boy. He called himself the Mayor of Lorah. I think it was a joke, as it didn't look like anyone else lived nearby. But what would I know, just walking by? I didn't know what to make of him at first but having someone to talk to helped me get the next two miles in, even though I was tired. He turned around to go home when we ran out of trail and hit a gravel road. I kept walking and found a woman at a nicely kept-up farm who gave me water.

Finally reaching the shady streets of Atlantic, I called John (John, the cyclist with two knee replacements, not John, the Mayor of Lorah) and he picked me up. He and his wife, Jody, had a lovely home they graciously shared with me. They offered me another slackpack for the next day and another night with them. Accepting help from strangers brought me benefit after benefit. Before walking across Iowa, I would never have believed I could have so many slackpack days without friends I already knew before beginning my hike.

There was a severe thunderstorm watch the next day. That forecast meant I did not start anticipating a dry day, and I had some concern about the possibilities of tornados often spawned by thunderstorms.

John drove me to the spot where he had picked me up, and I set out on a windy day with light rain, rain suit on, and umbrella up. When the rain let up, it was quite a nice hiking day, though the sky remained threatening. Under the shade of clouds, it was cool, and there wasn't much traffic on my routed roads. Shouldering only a slackpack, I moved well and did not mind rolling hills and fields.

I observed farmer geometry in the green rows of emerging corn contouring around hills, parallel lines extending equidistant from each other, straight or contoured. Farmers in Iowa had trouble getting their crops planted in 2019 because of all the rain. But those who had managed to plant their seed, were rewarded with bright-green lines of corn. Precision planting even in the dark was made possible with bright lights on tractors with programable sensors resulting in perfectly planted rows in precise geometric parallel lines.

Approaching White Pole Road, it became evident that my luck with the weather was going to change. Clouds became very dark, and thunder first rumbled and then cracked loudly. Lightning sent brilliant, sharp spears to ground a mile or so ahead of me, and the storm was headed my direction. I decided the better part of valor was to quit a short bit early and stay mostly dry and un-speared by electricity.

I called Jody. Then I walked on the wrong side of the road because I did not want to be a lightning statistic. I wanted the pseudo-comfort of the line of trees on the right side, not the barren, stick out like a sore thumb for lighting to strike me target on the left. There was enough shoulder on the right to make that a faintly reasonable decision.

Jody picked me up on Lewis Road. It was a shame not to go farther, since it was early, and I was slackpacking. Choosing to stay dry and safe had commanded my decision to call her.

I shared a trail meal that night for John and Jody to taste and because I didn't want to carry extra. They served me spicy brats, beans, and salad. I had the better part of that bargain. John and Jody were both retired attorneys who reminded me of the clan of my first husband in Ohio. That clan also had two attorneys.

In the morning, I packed up, and John drove me to my starting point on his way to shop for a new bicycle for his birthday. I hope he found a good one. And I hope he was able to ride RAGBRAI.

It was a misty, moisty morning and cloudy was the weather, as the nursery rhyme goes. I didn't meet an old man clothed all in leather, as the nursery rhyme goes on to say. But I met lots of big loader trucks carrying dirt. Their big muddy tires sprayed fine mist and fine mud at me as they passed. I didn't like that very much. It was to get worse, but first I stopped at the state park to use their restroom. That was the only place I could sit down until I got to Griswold.

A mile before Highway 48, the truck traffic stopped. They had been hauling dirt from somewhere down a connecting road to somewhere else on some other connecting road. On the first mile after their turn onto the road I was traveling, mud dropping thickly from their tires made the road very soupy and slippery to walk. The truck drivers were nice, though. They made multiple trips past me and started waving and slowing down as they passed me. That helped—a little.

I launched into a good rhythm with my steps, both morning and afternoon, and made quite good time on those long sections of road. I distracted myself by letting my mind wander about other things. I wasn't having deep thoughts, just searching my memory for something to occupy my brain while my feet kept moving mindlessly over long straight roads.

Reaching Griswold, I found the Casey's, a newer

one, with tables and chairs. They had all the fixins for subs. I ordered a sub with enough veggies to make me happy and some chocolate milk. I was going to have my usual ice cream, too, but an employee had a big chocolate cake to celebrate their graduation and wanted me to help them eat it. I was too full after the cake for the ice cream. Sigh.

On the long, straight road in the afternoon, I could see four miles of road ahead of me before the road reached a hill. No thought was involved in finding my way, just walking. My attention shifted to farm fields. Some farmers had indeed planted their crops, and they had come up. But more rain had saturated their fields. Low spots resembled rice paddies, green shoots barely seen above lakes of water, where water should not have been.

Another oddity struck me at the edge of a very big unplanted field which stopped at a steep gully over a little creek. Sticking out into the gulley *five feet below* the edge of the field were three big plastic pipes coming out of the ground. Water poured out of those pipes into that little creek. And all that water gushing from the ground appeared to be ground water from under the field. There was no drainage ditch there and no houses closer than a mile away. Just three ten-inch diameter pipes pouring water. Mmm, well, there *had been* a lot of rain.

My planned stopping point for the day yielded no farmhouses, so I had to walk farther. Walking nearly eighteen miles was a very long day for this old lady. Finally reaching a farmhouse, I knocked on a door and asked for a place to pitch my tent or an outbuilding to avoid possible rain.

After the usual introductory conversation, I was shown to an outbuilding where many things were stored, including a table-saw which had left lots of sawdust on the floor. They brought me a cot and a chair and offered me a shower. I accepted. I found the broom to sweep my part of the outbuilding floor, set up my gear on garbage bags, was clean and happy to be inside.

I was even *more glad* to be inside later as it poured rain at 5:00 in the morning, just as the forecast had promised. My benefactors were not early risers, and their yard was beautifully landscaped with no place to dig a hole. A mile down the road, I found a spot for leave-no-trace business and hoped no one was looking as I ducked behind tall grass off the road. I know, that's too much information, but it is part of life.

I made myself sing songs that morning, as I knew that would take my mind off how tired I was. Although the weather was good, I was not at my best after the long day before. I asked to use a restroom at another farmhouse, just because I wanted a place to sit down. My knees complained. My foot was not happy. My back ached. My hand hurt, and I was tired.

The day turned around when I approached a house asking to have lunch under their trees. Joyce offered her kitchen table and a glass of lemonade.

How could I refuse? She was fascinated with my hike, and we chattered away while I fixed and ate my usual trail lunch, just the combination of food, company, and rest I needed.

She also had local knowledge and could tell me where my motel would be found in the next town. She, like many others in Iowa, offered to give me a ride. I explained that a hike was walking, not riding. But since the motel was to the left, a mile off trail, she offered to have me call her from my waypoint, and she would give me a lift from there. Deal.

Her son came home then and also had to hear what I was doing. He too had good local information. He looked at my T-by-T, knew the area, and thought my route was all above water, a serious consideration as I neared the Missouri River. Perhaps, I would be able to cross the Missouri River as I had planned.

A friend from Washington had written me online, astounded at the remarkable luck I had finding trail angels, complete strangers who assisted me and became my friends. Yep. It had been amazing.

I had also received a message from a hiker finishing the AT, who said she would not be able to ask complete strangers if she could camp in their yard, so she couldn't do the ADT. Think of all the wonderful experiences and gracious people

I would have missed, if I had not asked. I think 99% of the land from the Atlantic to the Rockies is private property. This trail is very different from wilderness trails. But its charm to me was meeting the locals as I went along.

I tell the people I meet about this trail, other trails I have hiked, and the book I have written. I am aware that I and my actions will reflect on every hiker they see after me, for good or for ill. I have found the world is filled with wonderful people. Those who are not wonderful are the exceptions, not the rule. But they do exist.

The woman who gave me a ride from motel to trail in Waverly, Ohio was also supposed to mail my re-supply box to my home, a box which I had filled with items I no longer needed. When I got home, the box never came. When I tried to contact her again at the motel, I found out she had been let go, an addict and untrustworthy.

I was very sad for her addiction as she had seemed a friendly soul, amazed and interested that I was hiking. And I was sad for me as I had to replace my favorite black down vest, and my maps of that section of Ohio were lost forever. Addictions are cruel afflictions, damaging to all relationships, not just the one between that woman and myself.

I do try to be aware of my surroundings, whether I hike in wilderness or down a road. I may appear confident and brave, but that is not always the case. There are people in this world who could do me harm. I am not unaware that is true. But

I had met, oh, so many people who had been so good to me. My experiences and stories ran quite opposite to a culture which emphasized whom to fear. Yes, there are people who are not wonderful, though vastly outnumbered by those who are.

On that day, refreshed by rest, food, and company, equipped with local knowledge, I accepted a short lift to the motel where I had a shower, a rest, and washed my clothes. Dinner was next door to the motel at a family-owned-and-operated Mexican restaurant with delicious food. I *liked* walking the ADT. I loved the people I had met. I would rest that night, and my aches and pains would recover, my body just that much stronger for its work, and I would hike again the next day. Life was good and would be good the next day, too.

I added almost a mile of non-trail hiking the next day, half a mile back to the trail plus almost half a mile by missing a waypoint. Oh, well. After that, it was a very long road walk. I was tired of road walks. They had hills and no shade. But there were flowers.

White anemone bloomed in drifts. Blue spiderwort made several appearances and I saw a pink beardtongue. Charlock (an invasive) added yellow. White morning glories (bind weed—an invasive you never want in your garden) looked nice by the side of the road and even came in a shade of pink as well as the more common white. Yellow pea and stands of red-and-white clover also brightened my walk.

The sun shone for a while, but then became obscured by smoke from forest fires drifting down from North and South Dakota. What is in the air in one state doesn't stay there. The earth has connections, too, atmosphere moving faster than I could. With my umbrella up for shade, I kept fairly cool.

In the tiny town of Emerson, I walked by a closed bar and grill. But the window sign said *open*, so I tried the door. The bar and grill had been closed for a couple years. But that day, the building owners were inside. I had a bathroom break, they gave me water, and I told them about hiking while resting in their cool building, closed but not closed, open to me.

The road walk after that was long and hot. I stopped at a little roadside park just to lie horizontal on the picnic table bench for twenty minutes before rousing myself to go on.

Reaching Lambert, I looked for a place to be. I passed farmhouses, but the farmers weren't at home. And I got my first turndown in Iowa from a single mom, who thought she might get in trouble with her landlord. She gave me water, though, and I trudged on. Farmhouses were far apart in this stretch. I saw houses on a crossroad and turned off my route on that road looking for a place to be.

At the first two houses, no one was home. At the last house of the three, workers were building a deck, and they told me to go ahead and knock; the owners were at home. The owners offered me a bed and shower. And I gratefully accepted. Pam and Cliff were my gracious hosts whom I entertained with trail stories that night.

Famous Me, More Famous Cubby

In the morning, the world was newly washed with a light rain. It seemed pleasantly cool, until I had gone a couple miles. Then it seemed hot and muggy. While walking on the road, a truck drove up behind me, and the driver asked if I was the "young lady who had written a book."

"Maybe," I answered. "I wasn't young, but I had written a book." The driver worked with the male half of the biker duo I had met outside Exira. The truck driver drove on to work and told the biker I was coming into Malvern. The biker jumped in *his* truck and drove out to meet me. Then he drove alongside me at my pace while we talked, chatting for a while. His wife had already downloaded my book and was enjoying it. Eventually, he had to drive on, as other cars wanted the road, too. It had been quite fun to talk to him on that road. And, before he left, he said he and his wife might see me again in Silver City.

I had lunch in Malvern. I arrived just too late for breakfast and before lunch was served at the C&M Café. I walked across the street to the more upscale café, which was over-run with a horde of bicyclers. I had a cinnamon roll there for mid-morning snack and then walked back to the other cafe for their lunch special, followed by an ice-cream cone to go.

Thus fortified, I set out again. I was very glad to get off roads and onto bicycle trails again. Bike trails were level and had shade for much more pleasant hiking. I did have trouble maintaining hiking speed. Shade or no, I was hot and sweaty, and my enthusiasm dwindled.

After four miles, really dragging on the last one, I found a covered picnic table behind tall grass and stretched out on the tabletop. The day was better in the shade while in horizontal position listening to the breezes blow in the trees around me. Rest and cooling temperatures gave me what I needed to walk the last stretch of the day into Silver City, a tiny town boasting a church, a cemetery, a bar, a bike shop, and a post office.

A sign said camping in the little trailhead park was not allowed. But Mary Jo, the owner of the bike shop, let me put up my tent behind her shop. I used the trailhead porta potty and the water spigot. It was all I needed. The bar provided dinner. Mary Jo sold snacks, and I bought Cliff Bars for breakfast. She gave me an ice-cream sandwich for free.

I was almost ready to tuck into my bag to sleep when Dan and Carol found me (the bicycler outside of Exira and the guy in the truck I had met earlier in the day). We had a great time talking. I blathered on at length with an eager audience. Dan said he knew the area well. Looking at my T-by-T, he volunteered to scope out my last day, meet me at a trailhead, and tell me what they found regarding passability and flooding. They also gave me a brownie, but I was too tired to eat it then. Dan and Carol had become great fans and friends. After they drove home, pleasant evening breezes and softly singing birds lulled me to sleep, at home in my tent.

Considering all the trail angels that had been mine as I had walked across Iowa, I thought more than my share of surprise encounters of the best kind were quite enough. Amazingly, I had one more day with an extraordinary angel. Cubby, of Boston-and-Cubby fame, had stayed in touch the last few days and had decided to come and walk with me. Boston and Cubby were far stronger and more accomplished hikers than I would ever be.

I had followed their journals and was thrilled I would get to meet Cubby. You might think I would have gotten used to people dropping out of the sky wanting to hike with me after following my journey across Iowa. It still amazed me. Here was one more gift of trail magic. Cubby showed up in the morning, and my gear was transferred into her driver's car, so we could walk a slackpack day.

The trail was no longer roads, but pleasant bicycle trail through corridors of woods, shaded most of the way. My attention was not focused on aged knees, aching joints, or injured hand, nor was it really on the trail. My focus was absorbed in conversation with Cubby.

Cubby

Boston and Cubby were Triple Crowners and Grand Slammers. A Grand Slam is walking all three National Scenic Trails, AT, PCT, and CDT (The Triple Crown) plus the American Discovery Trail. They did them by thru-hiking each one, going end-to-end of each trail in one season of hiking, not section hiking as was my style. Cubby was the author of the journals I had read on Trailjournals.com, gleaning information about the ADT. And now I had the privilege of walking with her.

We talked and talked and talked. I can't exactly say the miles flew by, but they disappeared in very respectable fashion as we told each other trail stories and a bit of our life histories. It was a great way to spend my second to the last day on the American Discovery Trail.

Mary E. Davison

When we reached the Tastee Treet at the trailhead, we stopped for the day and for food. I had
one of the best burgers ever, and Cubby was buying. As we sat there at the Tastee Treet, I decided to call my niece in Omaha. Somehow, for the
last night on the trail, I just was not enthused
about knocking on another door, even though my
record of experiences doing so had been so very
good. Diane and family agreed to take me in one
day early, and Cubby agreed to drive me to their
house.

As we were loading my gear back into my pack
from Cubby's car, Dan and Carol drove up. They
had scouted out my trail for my last day from
their car and said there was only one spot they
saw under water, just before turning north on
24th Street.

So, I showed up a night early at my niece's house
and said good-bye to Cubby. I hoped to see her,
and Boston, too, the next year. Due to family circumstances and great distances between us geo-
graphically throughout our lives, I did not know
my niece well. The ADT gave us a chance to be
better acquainted.

Friends, family, and scouts, too, all in one day.

Last Day Challenges

One day of hiking on the ADT remained for my spring hike. Cubby had warned me I would be in the open in the sun. Nope. No sun. As usual, I had rain and thunderstorms. At least the rain fell down, not sideways, for the first half of the day.

Under an overpass, I rearranged my rain gear and tried something different. I didn't want to wear my rain jacket but wanted to have dry shorts. I tied the rain jacket around me with its sleeves, pulled it down and zipped It up. Voila! A rain-skirt. Now why had it taken me all my many years of hiking to do that? My umbrella took care of the top half of my body and I walked dry even though rain poured down. The day was warm enough, my feet liked sloshing in the rain.

Walking around Lake Manawa it rained harder still. An older gentleman also out walking in the rain asked me if we were both crazy. He *liked* walking in the rain. Long-distance hikers hike in most anything the weather chooses to be. Otherwise, we wouldn't get anywhere.

After Lake Manawa, I walked on a levee between Indian Ditch and a lot of fields in a flood plain covered with water, and I glimpsed the Missouri River beyond. The flood plain was supposed to be planted farmers' fields. Last year's corn stalks tilted forlornly over water, which was the extension of the river.

Approaching the highway underpass, the wind picked up, and the temperature dropped. I stopped, sheltered underneath the highway above me, and I put on my rain suit in the usual way, jacket on top and pants on the bottom. I needed the rain suit for warmth in the wind. I ate left-overs from my food bag, greatly improved by the luscious brownie Dan and Carol had given me, and I finally found the opportunity to eat.

Just before 24th Street, the bike trail was under water. Dan had told me about that part. Since the day was so wet, I did not opt for the parallel road where cars were spraying rooster tails of water. Since my shoes were already squishy, I was less wet walking through the low spot, tadpoles scurrying away at each step, and a few hundred drowned worms on the surface of the bike trail underneath the water. It was like fording a river without a current.

North on 24th, I crossed to go around the ball fields. After a quick stop at a convenient body shop to use their restroom, I went on to the Western Historic Trails Center. Even though the building was closed, the outside interpretive exhibits were nice, although I was rather distracted by lightning and thunder closer than I liked.

Past the Western Historic Trails Center, the trail submerged under water, lake or overflowing river. I could not tell how deep it was or see the trail emerge. Nuts and horse-feathers.

The trail goes where?

I checked the map on my GPS and considered a slight detour to River Road to be the best choice. But that road also disappeared below water, and I could see the current of the Missouri not far from the placid flooding closer by. I could not see road past water.

One last try was the levee behind the closed building of the Center. Nope. It went to a dead end behind a six-foot chain link fence instead of connecting to the highway. I could see my next waypoint on my GPS, only two-tenths of a mile away. But there was no way to reach it without a long walk or a swim. I was not a swimmer.

My GPS map revealed how I could connect by back tracking all the way to 24th Street, going up to 23rd Avenue, walking to Nebraska, then dropping down to the second waypoint past the one for which I was aiming. It took me four-and-a-half miles to go a mile and a half. A hiker does what a hiker has to do.

23rd Ave was a bad road walk, no shoulder at all and two lanes of traffic coming at me, with a curve limiting their visibility of me two-thirds of the way. I didn't mind road walking if there was at least a foot of shoulder. But that road had none, plus puddles and broken pavement at the road's edges lurking to trip me if I had my eyes on cars instead of road. Well, it wasn't supposed to be the trail, but that day, it was mine.

Halfway through the bad-road walk, the weather changed completely, from heavy rain and thunderstorms to completely clear sky and hot sun. I took off my rain gear at a bus stop bench, then used my umbrella for sun instead of rain. At least its shiny surface reflected sun and made me more visible to cars.

Finally reaching my waypoint, I followed the T-by-T. But one more flooded area appeared *under* the Casino. Solving that problem was simple. I just walked through parking lots on the other side of the building.

The ever-changing weather on that day was like a review of Iowa, experiencing all of Iowa's weather in one day. Well, almost, at least I didn't get another ice storm or a tornado.

The Bob Kerry Pedestrian Bridge was an impressive

structure curving over the Big Muddy, otherwise known as the Missouri River, also known as the Mighty Mo. People were taking pictures of a large artwork, a tall, foil-like silver figure. I read information on various interpretive signs. Many people were enjoying the then-sunny day, strolling, jogging, and taking family outings across the bridge from state to state. I joined them and crossed from Iowa into Nebraska.

Bob Kerry Pedestrian Bridge from Iowa to Nebraska

Diane and Jim picked me up in Omaha, on the other side of the bridge, and we went to the airport to pick up one of their daughters, who was coming back from China where she had been in school. That night we had a grand dinner of *build your own* tacos. Another of their daughters, plus one of her friends who wanted to meet me, also came from Lincoln. Diane's mother was there, too, whom I had not seen for several years.

I signed Laura's copy of my book and a blank page that Cindy, Natalie's friend, could glue in the book she was going to buy. We talked trails, my book, and China. Adventures and connections come in many forms. The next day I did not walk. I flew back home.

From the Atlantic to the Missouri, from Delaware to Nebraska, over four springs of hiking I had covered a lot of ground, discovering America. Perhaps, in another year, I would continue on and walk across the rest. In my late 70s, I contemplate only the next year for sure. I already had completed half of Colorado and bits of Utah and Nevada. Trails still lead on. I still can walk. There are more lines of trail to connect. Nebraska first, then I'll skip to Utah. Finishing that, I'll see what's next.

EPILOGUE
CORONAVIRUS

In the winter of 2019, I compiled journal, notes, and thoughts to write this book. I wrote that last paragraph thinking the book was almost finished. I wrote the following chapter, reread, and proofread for a few times, getting ready to send the manuscript to my editor for her help. And as I did so, the tsunami called COVID-19 exploded in the US in the spring of 2020.

Now there are new fears to meet and leave behind, one way or another. For some, the leaving will be dust-to-dust as the words of the worship service on Ash Wednesday says. For others, there will be a new day, different from the ones before, shaped by the ones we're living now. By the time this book is published, who knows which one I will experience? That's a sobering thought.

Hmm. I think I wrote somewhere in these pages we can only live the day we're living. We cannot live more than one day at a time. A corollary to that truth is that I wish to live until I die. Letting our fears rule, we can die early. I'd rather not. I'm still alive though my habits and goals are changing. Remember, fear does have its positive uses.

Even if there are changes to my life, I can learn to jazz-hand wave instead of hug and walk a greater distance away from others. There still are flowers, the grass still grows, and I can connect with others by words in print, electronically or by words spoken by phone or on Zoom. I have had to cancel 2020 hikes, for my benefit and the benefit of others. I have no wish to become Typhoid Mary, or the COVID-19 form of that. Walking across Nebraska asking strangers for water or for a place to put my tent, I could catch or spread the virus, and my age is in the danger age. And I still contemplate fear and faith.

FEAR AND FAITH

Some fears are good and keep us safe. Some fears hinder our living full and abundant lives. Finding the correct balance between those fears is a life-long challenge. We need to find a place between, on the one hand, thinking that there is nothing really to fear in this world, taking no preventative or cautious steps, and on the other hand, being so afraid that we stop engaging with others in the world or taking any risks at all, which leads to the antithesis of living.

Where any one of us find that balance is related to an enormous number of factors, including our own life experiences, what we have been taught or heard, physical ability, personality type, and most definitely, the people we encounter on any trail or, more broadly, on our life's journey. I have shared my thoughts and experiences so that you might now reflect upon your own. Perhaps you wish to leave some fears behind and are working to do so. Perhaps that has been too foreign a concept for you to even consider.

So many people are afraid of so many things, especially of the people they don't know. I met people on the ADT, all types and kinds by ethnic background, espousing differing politics, religious faith, or none. Each person I have met along this trail became a precious jewel to me. They are the America I discovered. I do not fear them. I treasure that I met them. I treasure their kindness extended to meet my human needs.

Walking on the National Scenic Trails, I met people, too. From all over America people come to walk those scenic trails. People from other countries have come to America to walk those trails, also. I have been fortunate to live, visit, and hike in other countries, as well. There is beauty everywhere, in every land and every people.

As I practice the art of leaving fear behind, fear is not high on my list of regular emotions. Oh, I still fear some things. Irrationally, I fear filling out official papers, riding public transit, getting lost in cities. As I age, I am more cautious where I place my feet, and heights which never bothered me before, I am no longer eager to scale. COVID-19 is a concern. If I were not concerned, it would mean I wasn't paying attention. But I intentionally try not to spend much time fearing.

Even with coronavirus and its consequences present in the world, I live. I do try to care for myself, learn new safety procedures, attend church by Zoom. I hope I live past this virus contagion racing through the world. But there is way too much that interests me in life to waste too much time fearing, even now.

Trails always beckon; perhaps I'll get to walk some more. But for now, I can research other trails for my possible future. I watch my grandchildren grow, even if in pictures sent by text or online instead of in person. I plant my garden anticipating growth to see and food to eat and stock my freezer.

I walk in my neighborhood, if not on a trail. There still are strangers I have not yet met. I recently met another author/hiker on my neighborhood walk. I live. I will adventure forth again to see new sights, learn new things, and make new friends, as life allows. I live. And I will work at leaving fear behind.

I am not the only adventurer on trails or roads. There are many far more adventurous than I, who have traveled farther, faster, done more exciting things. My friend, Bag Lady, hikes or rides a re-cumbent trike. She has ridden that trike on roads across America, down the Baja of Mexico, and she has hiked or biked in Morocco, New Zealand, Australia, and many European trails. She simply camps beside a road wherever she ends up. She tells me America is a very safe place. I agree with her, though she travels far beyond me in distance, countries and adventures.

Yet neither she nor I are completely nuts, nor just naïve. We know there are people with bad intentions. Evil does exist. She or I could come to some bad end at the hands of others. That has happened to some adventurers. Such occurrences make the news and stoke our fears. But tragedies are not the usual. In our adventures, the usual is meeting strangers, making friends. Most of the things we fear, though possible, are not likely to happen, though they could.

Errant viruses and aging bodies subject to fail-ures of all kinds are also real. Yet in spite of fears, either related to reality or to our imaginations, whatever our path of life or even death, I believe we do not walk our trails alone. Different hikers are sustained by different things. For me, my faith plays a large part.

"Yea, though I walk through the valley of the shadow of death, I will fear no evil. For thou art with me" (Psalm 23:4 KJV).

I don't think to myself, "Nothing bad could ever happen to me." Bad stuff happens. Bad stuff has happened in my life, but rarely on a trail, even on an urban trail. My life is held by God's promise, not a promise for always pleasant trails, but a promise my solo walk is not alone.

I like to think in scripture bookends: the 23rd Psalm on one end and Romans 8:38 on the other.

"For I am sure that neither death, nor life, nor angels, nor principalities, nor things present, nor things to come, nor powers, nor depth, nor anything else in all creation, will be able to separate us from the love of God in Christ Jesus our Lord" (Romans 8:38 RSV).

I am God's beloved child, held in God's arms no matter what befalls me. It is *possible* I may not return from some adventure. It is *possible* I might not make it home. It is *possible*, anywhere and any day, that I will be injured or will die, at home or on a trail. It is *possible* I will catch COVID-19 with fatal consequences. If not those things, something else eventually will fell me. After all, we do all die sometime, although I would rather not hurry the process. I'd like to hang around a few more years, hike another trail, spend time with my family, maybe even write another book.

In ultimate terms, I trust the God who holds me in life and in death. Just as I wrote in that early ADT journal, "*I will try* to be mindful of that embrace in wilderness, through raindrops on leaves, sunrises, creepy crawly critters, in my relationships with two-legged critters, on roads and through towns and cities." I will try to trust that presence and that love, live or die.

I am bold enough to proclaim to you that you, too, are God's beloved child, held in God's arms, whether you walk in fear or confidence, on a trail or on some vastly different road of life than mine.

My intent in writing this book was twofold: to give you a taste of what the American Discovery Trail is like and to stir your own thoughts about fear and the possibilities of leaving fear behind, especially fear of strangers.

Sharing my faith was not my intent as I started writing, but the nature of my experiences on this trail and in my life demanded to be part of the story, too. It is part of who I am. So—three subjects blended together. If those three subjects touched you in any way, I have reached my goals, regardless of my writing talent or lack of it.

Happy trails wherever you may walk, on trails or other journeys of your life. And through your life and through its close, I pray for *your* peace and trust (and mine), held in the arms of a love greater than any from those whose touch we feel on Earth.

ACKNOWLEDGMENTS

One cannot write a book like this without a lot of help. First and foremost, all the people I met along the way who helped me hike the ADT, friends and friends of friends and fans, support people planned and unplanned, those who answered a knock on their door, who talked to me along the trail or who just popped up out of nowhere to aid me with spontaneous offers or conversation. I'm sure there are even more than that.

When it came to writing the book, a number of people read some or parts of it. I want to especially thank Cubby (trail name) for her attention to detail and for calling me out about unwanted, and unnoticed by me, comments which could have been called racist. Her honesty was not easy to hear. What was most embarrassing, causing me shame and anguish, was that she was right, and I agreed. I should have known better. But after digesting and processing some of my racial bias which was leaking out in words, I thought more deeply about adding more of my history and heritage.

My decision was not to subtract but to add more, to put my words in context for myself and others, while still remaining true to my experience. I also cleaned up some of my language. That would not have happened without being called to account by another person, and I thank her deeply for doing that. I, no doubt, still made mistakes. I live in a country with ingrained biases, no matter how hard I or my family have tried to move past them. I am still trying. This book and my life are the better for her comments.

I want to thank my friends Roland and Kathy and the daughters of Ethel, the sister of my heart, Rojeune and Vyla for simply talking to me or reading parts of the book I was concerned about. My African American friends and extended relatives gave me calm advice or just grounded me in myself by being there for me.

My friend and buddy, Kathy (a different Kathy than Roland's wife) gave me much encouragement and helped me think more of better word choices in general, as well as hiking with me even in the time of Covid as we learned to take masks with us.

Teresa Crumpton of AuthorSpark.org was again my editor and deserves my thanks both for her work on this book and for hanging in with me when we had difficulties communicating. If my readers find errors and mistakes, please know I was the last reader of this manuscript and the responsibility for those is mine.

Lindsay Heider Diamond was my cover artist again providing her wonderful gifts: Graphic Design – Illustration – and Fine Art, www.lindsayheider. com. A hiker in the Smokies, Rachel Goetze Black, provided the photo for the cover. It was just the feeling I wanted of a road to travel around a bend to the promise of unseen things about to be revealed, both exciting and perhaps fearful.

Many thanks to my children who support and put up with their mother, sometimes helping with technology. And thanks too, go to my grandchildren who went on walks with me.

Chuck Norris and Tigger (trail names) were long distance hikers I met on the Appalachian Trail and again on the Pacific Crest Trail. They read the manuscript and contributed a blurb for the back of the book. They are also well-known trail angels, now on the AT, helping hikers wherever they can.

Laurel Foot, ADT thru biker/hiker on the ADT as well as a member of the ADTS board of Directors and the editor of the ADT Newsletter also contributed a blurb. Laurel has contributed much in years and time to the American Discovery Trail, and I appreciate her time and review given for me.

For all those who encouraged me to write another book, I give my thanks. And for all my readers without whom the effort would be fruitless, my special thanks.

ABOUT THE AUTHOR

Mary has been a lot of places and done a lot of things. After all, she is 79 years old. Besides turning her hand to writing of her hiking adventures, she has been in the Peace Corps, a physical therapist with a specialty in pediatrics, an Army wife, a pastor of a church for sixteen years, a gardener, and retired. She is the mother of two and grandmother of ten. (Outdoor Grandma) In her spare time, she preaches and plays the cornet.

Trailjournals.com (Medicare Pastor)

Facebook.com/MaryDavison

Website: maryedavison.com

ALSO BY
MARY E. DAVISON

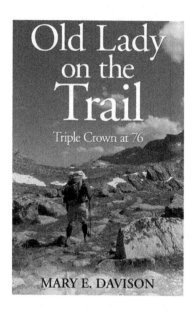

Beginning long distance hiking at age 60, Mary takes you with her on her trail journeys. With her, you can experience encounters with the wilderness from the Eastern ranges of the Appalachian Trail, the challenges of desert, snow, granite, thick forests of the Pacific Crest Trail, and the rugged and remote grandeur of the Continental Divide Trail. Mary completed the Triple Crown at age 76.

Available on Amazon.com.

THANK YOU FOR READING

If you enjoyed Aren't You Afraid?, please leave a positive review on Amazon and/or Goodreads to help other readers decide on this book. Telling your friends would also be wonderful.

Made in the USA
Las Vegas, NV
22 October 2020

10233404R00272